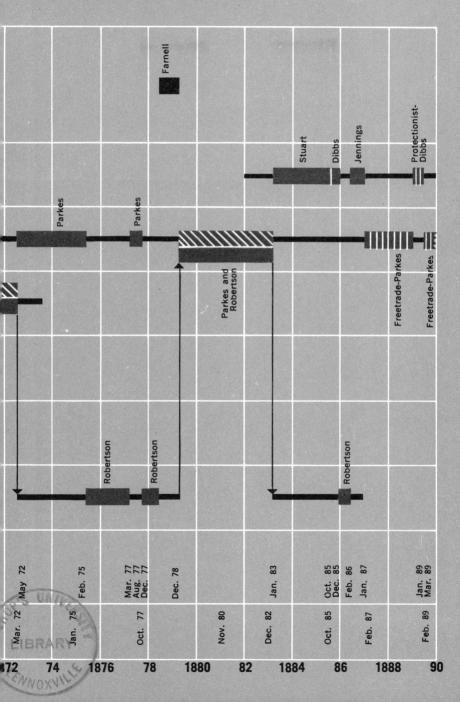

PARLIAMENT,
FACTIONS AND PARTIES

PARLIAMENT
FACTIONS AND PARTIES

*The First Thirty Years of Responsible
Government in New South Wales, 1856–1889*

P. LOVEDAY
*Senior Lecturer in Government
University of Sydney*

A. W. MARTIN
*Reader in History
University of Adelaide*

MELBOURNE UNIVERSITY PRESS
LONDON AND NEW YORK: CAMBRIDGE UNIVERSITY PRESS

First published 1966

Printed and bound in Australia
at the Griffin Press, Adelaide, S.A.
for Melbourne University Press, Carlton N.3, Victoria

Registered in Australia for transmission
by post as a book

Dewey Decimal Classification Number 320.9944
Library of Congress Catalog Card Number 66–13036

Text set in 10 point Garamond type

If you aspire to the formation of a durable government, there is only one course open to you, that is to mature a policy founded on principles sound in themselves and applicable to the present position of the country so that the wisdom of your measures and the vigour of your administration may convince the public mind that you are 'the man for the hour'. Having your work cut out thus in earnest you may rest assured you will not need support in steadily pursuing it, for the majority both inside and outside of the house will always in the long run support that which is right. I do not think any reliance can be placed on the abiding temper of public men or of the public itself. To carry their sympathies with you, you must impress them with the decisiveness of your own progressive action. They must feel that you are the first man or they will never acknowledge you as the first.

Henry Parkes to Charles Cowper
4 August 1857

Foreword

BY ROBERT A. DAHL
Stirling Professor of Political Science
Yale University

Political parties are such visible and vital fixtures of modern democracies that it takes a strenuous effort of imagination to conceive of how a party-less democracy might function. The virtues of political parties are pretty well taken for granted these days—at least in the English-speaking world. I have the impression that the critical stance Ostrogorski took toward political parties at the beginning of this century is generally regarded (by the few who continue to read what he has to say) as old-fashioned, atomistic individualism; I am inclined to agree.

Yet there is also, I think, a fairly widespread concern about the functioning of modern parties, particularly in countries like France and Italy where the virtues of their party systems are not always as visible as their vices. In the Fifth Republic, General de Gaulle has capitalized on the discontent with the party system of the Third and Fourth Republics; in Italy it is common, in certain quarters, to speak harshly of the consequences of what many Italians have come to call *partitocrazia*.

One problem in appraising the contributions of parties to democracy is, as I have already implied, the difficulty of conceiving how democracies might function without them. One of the values of this study is that it provides us with a detailed portrait of a representative system without organized political parties. It serves, too, to remind us how recent an invention is the political party as we now know it. To be sure, some historians find what they choose to call parties in Republican Rome; but these were loosely organized factions of notables, rather like the ones described in this volume. The longest lasting republic in history, that of Venice, endured for the better part of a millenium without political parties; but Venice, though very much a constitutional republic, was also very much an aristocratic one;

vii

the nobles, who managed to avoid sharing their constitutional sup-remacy with the middle classes from the beginning to the end, never counted more than a few thousand adult males.

It is approximately true, I think, that the political party as we now know it, highly organized, professionally led, permanent, regularly competing in elections, held together by a durable core of members and officers, and supported by a substantial mass of loyal voters—this kind of a party is a phenomenon mainly of this century. The United States, it is true, is an anomaly. But it is an anomaly simply because the conditions that later led to mass-parties elsewhere existed there almost from the time of the Constitutional Convention in 1787; recent historical research establishes that the prototypic modern party, with the characteristics I have just enumerated, came into existence between 1796–1808 under the leadership of James Madison and Thomas Jefferson—a party, incidentally, that has remained in existence con-tinuously since that time. But elsewhere an essential condition for this kind of development was lacking: widespread suffrage. In Britain, the Second Reform Act led directly to the Birmingham Caucus, a milestone on the way to modern parties. But one often forgets that in most of Europe the widening of the suffrage came in a burst from the 1890s to the end of the First World War.

As Max Weber pointed out a half century ago, what preceded the modern parties were, typically, parties of notables. And one might profitably think of the factions described in this volume as an Austra-lian and on the whole democratic equivalent to parties of notables. In a number of countries parties of notables have provided an ex-tremely important transitional stage to modern democracy; in some countries, as in Britain and Sweden, the stage has been a long one, in others, such as the United States, rather short. In many places, including, I feel sure, New South Wales, the system helped to develop the habits and skills required for democratic institutions; in a few— Italy in the age of Giolitti and *trasformismo* furnishes an unhappy example—the practice of factional politics for narrow ends served mainly to discredit parliamentary government.

Why did the system work as well as it did in New South Wales? One is tempted to fall back on the mysteries of the political culture of English-speaking peoples (although an American is obliged to remind the rest of the English-speaking world that the white stock in Missis-sippi is about as 'pure' in 'Anglo-Saxon blood' as any place in the world, including Britain). But beyond these mysteries two other factors were, I suspect, critical: the homogeneity of the notables and the population, combined with an even more critical factor, the small electorate. An impetus to the growth of parties and the displacement of government by notables and factions was generally furnished by two kinds of needs, one coming from inside the notability itself, the other from outside; these were the need to mobilize votes in the parliament, and the need to mobilize voters outside parliament. Both of these needs increase with numbers: and this is one reason, surely, why the system of factions came to be increasingly less capable of surviving as the number of voters in New South Wales grew from 42 thousand in 1856 to 290 thousand in 1890. Both of these needs also increase with the severity of conflict, and as the authors show, the intensification of cleavages gave rise in New South Wales to organizations such as the Free Selectors Associations that foreshadowed the development of political parties in the modern style.

The system of factions was bound, of course, to disappear. As the years wore on, as the electorate expanded, and as conflicts intensified, the system became more and more anachronistic. Yet while it lasted (so these pages suggest to me) it worked well. One need not lament its demise—as Ostrogorski might have—but perhaps Australians, and all friends of Australian democracy, have good reason to be pleased that this stage in political development, which most countries in the modern world have not had the good luck to pass through, was, on balance, relatively benign and constructive in New South Wales.

Acknowledgments

Many of the ideas which form the basis of this book were developed in the course of research we conducted separately as postgraduate students, one of us at the University of Sydney, and the other at the Australian National University. We wish therefore to thank General Motors-Holden's Pty Ltd and the Australian National University, which provided the scholarships that enabled this early work to be done, and also our supervisors, Professor J. M. Ward and Mr L. F. Fitzhardinge, whose interest and advice stimulated us in innumerable ways.

Professor R. N. Spann, of the Department of Government in the University of Sydney, was the gadfly who stung us into the idea of working together: we also owe him thanks for stirring us when enthusiasm flagged and for criticism of the manuscript we eventually produced. Dr F. B. Smith, of Melbourne, and Mr B. E. Mansfield, of Sydney, read our final draft and made a number of valuable suggestions for improving it. We were assisted in the later stages of our work by travel and typing grants from the research funds of the Universities of Sydney and Melbourne. Mrs H. M. Nelson, of Sydney, gave us most efficient help in the task of collating and checking material.

We owe to the officers of the Mitchell Library, the Dixson Library and the Archives Office of New South Wales a debt which others who have benefited from their courtesy and erudition will understand to the full, and we appreciate the generosity with which the Trustees of these repositories permit scholars to quote from their riches. We are also grateful for having been able to use the resources of the National Library, Canberra, the Library of the Australian National University, the Fisher and Baillieu Libraries, and the State Library of Victoria.

We also wish to express our appreciation of the painstaking work of the editorial department of Melbourne University Press in final preparation of the manuscript for publication.

P.L., Sydney
A.W.M., Melbourne

October 1964

Contents

Introduction

RESPONSIBLE GOVERNMENT was inaugurated in New South Wales in 1856. For more than thirty years no political parties emerged in the legislature, and government was carried on through majorities organized around parliamentary factions. So much has long been generally known, though the nature and operation of these factions have never been examined closely, and it has remained an open question whether responsible government was a markedly different system then from what it has become in the context of formal party structures. That it probably was different is implied by modern writers on the party system. Louise Overacker's summary may be taken as typical: the pre-party system, she says, was one in which 'alignments were fluid, personalities were often more important than policies, and governments were maintained in power by shifting, often heterogeneous, combinations of groups'. The result was 'political instability, reflected in the bewildering number of Cabinet changes, and the changing procession of premiers'.[1] And H. V. Evatt's opinion—with its additional pejorative note—exemplifies a view held by many writers on the origins of the Labor Party: in the twenty-five years after 1890, he tells us, the 'Labour Party gave significance and some coherence to the political life of a country which before 1891 had been controlled in the main by opportunists and demagogues'.[2]

A closer study of the faction system shows that these judgments are misleading. The factions were capable of yielding stable government, even if they did not always do so; and some of the instability of politics at the time resulted in fact from attempts to form governments *without* faction support. Overacker's picture rests on the observation that no less than twenty-seven ministries were formed in New South Wales between 1856 and 1891. In the years between 1856 and 1887, when the faction system prevailed, twenty-three ministries were formed, making the average life of each of them a little over sixteen months. But if the four non-faction ministries[3] and the five clearly unstable ministries[4] are excluded from the total, the remaining ministries had an average life of nearly twenty-seven months; this figure rises to thirty-one months if the four formally distinct ministries of Cowper and Robertson in March 1860 to October 1863, and again in October 1868 to December 1870, are counted as the two ministries which they in fact were.[5] This was not strikingly less than the average life, thirty-four months, of the twelve stable ministries of the next thirty-four years.[6]

Once we identified the factions and the members of parliament clustering around them, it became apparent to us that they and they alone provided a focus for the politicians' loyalties, which were often of surprising duration. What is more, our analysis showed that the 'independent' members (that is, the members not attached to faction leaders and approved of for this reason by contemporary commentators) were the people who produced most of the uncertainties of parliamentary life. These uncertainties were of course increased by the difficulties faced by leaders able to exercise only a covert and fluctuating influence in the electorates, and by the likelihood that even when firmly committed members were elected a proportion of them would be forced to give up their seats after short terms by the lack of parliamentary salaries or by occupational commitments. But the facts, which S. Encel has noted, that 'a stable core of politicians held office for long periods' despite the frequent changes of ministry and that this core included not only the leading figures but also a 'second tier' of men,[7] can be attributed to the stability of the factions in the parliamentary flux.

In this book we offer a brief account of the development and character of these factions. The story begins with the expectations of the fifties that clear-cut liberal and conservative parties would develop in the new legislature. These expectations soon proved illusory, and factions, not parties, emerged as the bases of division in parliament. To examine the effect of the factions on responsible government we have discussed some of the manoeuvres and intrigues that lay behind the formation and defeat of ministries, the work of faction leaders in the electorates and the attitudes of cabinet ministers to the joint responsibility the system imposed on them. We observe the faction system under increasing stress in the late eighties as two parties appeared, claiming free trade and protection as their articles of faith. What we describe therefore is the history of a political system —how power was won and lost—rather than a history of politics in the period.[8] Although we have woven into the story some account of legislation, we have not attempted to construct a connected narra-

tive of the policies of governments or of the broader political movements behind them, except in our treatment of the 1880s.

What happened in that decade can best be explained on the assumption that the political development of the previous twenty-five years
took place in an atmosphere of social stability and against a background of sustained economic growth. Since no systematic studies
of a sociological kind exist from which a precise picture of the changing
life and character of New South Wales may be drawn, we can only
record the general impression we have gained from contemporary
comment that this was a period of considerable social calm. As the
Sydney Morning Herald saw it at one point late in the sixties,[9] life in the
colony seemed usually to flow on undisturbed by political crises:
it was, after all, a life of buying and selling, of cultivating farms and
tending flocks, rarely affected in visible ways by the struggle of
politicians for power. But there is much evidence to suggest a new
sense of social disturbance in the mid-eighties, matching and largely
stemming from better-known economic difficulties as the pace of
growth faltered. N. G. Butlin, for example, sketches out this picture
of the recession:

> annual additions to population had reached their peak in 1883;
> assisted migration had largely been suspended by 1885; the rate
> of industrial expansion was tapering off rapidly; the pastoral
> industry was encountering increasing difficulties including the
> short-term effects of drought and fall in wool prices; and public
> investment was recovering its peak level. Building activity in
> N.S.W. responded quickly to the preliminary recession of 1884–86,
> as both rents and wage-rates declined.[10]

A situation such as this was well calculated to lay bare incipient
social tensions and interest-group conflicts, and provided the essential
background against which the struggle for political power assumed a
wider significance.

Recent historians have looked at the factions through the eyes of
contemporary commentators,[11] who indulged the expectations of the
time by a grand manner of denunciation when they spoke of politics.
But mistaken modern impressions of the faction system do not arise
simply because the exaggerations of the day have been accepted at
face value. Contemporaries took their attitudes to factions from
Burke who put into the hands of the nineteenth century a definition
of party by which almost any group of members, even in the House

of Commons,[12] might be damned with the epithet FACTION. Burke's prestige has tempted modern writers to accept the old judgments of faction when they come down to us in the familiar and respectable language he employed. Few if any nineteenth century parliamentary groups could be stamped approvingly with the label PARTY by being described simply as a 'body of men united for promoting by their joint endeavours the national interest upon some particular principle on which they are all agreed'.[13] Not seeing the weaknesses of Burke's idealized definition, contemporaries looked for a 'generous contention for power' between members combined by their belief in 'manly and honourable maxims'. They found little evidence of these things, and decided that they were looking at a 'mean and interested struggle for place and emoluments'.[14] The survival of the term faction with its pejorative overtones has meant that when modern parties are contrasted with factions they automatically gain from Burke an image that is idealistic and one-sided. This image is not only inappropriate to the mass organizations of modern democracies, but it is one in which the 'mean and interested struggle' for material things that takes place in any party is cast into the shade. In fact, no one would now dispute in any other context that parties have such a side to their activities. What is more, Burke himself can be convicted of oversimplifying and whitewashing eighteenth century parties by his definition.[15]

These objections apart, contemporaries might well have paused to consider whether Burke's opinion of faction was applicable in a colony so different from late eighteenth-century Britain. Four relevant differences may be specified at once: the absence of a well defined class structure, the relatively egalitarian instinct of the population, the far more democratic electoral system and the development of of cabinet government. These, to say nothing of the economic differences between the two countries, make it extremely hazardous to transfer Burke's ideas uncritically to the politics of New South Wales in the nineteenth century. Those writers who did consider these differences at the time[16] went on using Burke's definition as if the differences explained why parties had not developed, when the relevant question was whether the factions conformed in fact to Burke's description.

There is no disputing that the factions were without coherent and distinct bodies of doctrine, principle or belief and that they lacked the organized structure and extra-parliamentary basis of modern democratic parties. At the same time, it is important to observe that faction members had strong political opinions and that the factions and the two short-lived parties after them did grope towards some of the instruments of political action—the caucus is an example[17]—which have been taken to be inventions of the Labor Party.[18] Admittedly, the factions were interested in place and emolument, but again their interest in these things was moderated by other competing interests, especially by their leaders' firm sense of executive responsibility and their determination to imitate the spirit of nineteenth-century British administration.

If the factions had exhibited only those characteristics attributed to them by contemporaries, it is inconceivable that parliamentary government should have survived for so long in New South Wales without falling into crises and chaos or, alternatively, becoming a façade for personal rule.[19] But neither of these things happened. Parliamentary government in the colony when compared with the original in Britain was distorted, but it was a copy none the less and the faction system must be credited with helping to make it so. Crisp argues that 'parliamentary government cannot be at once stable and progressive without some degree of party cohesion and discipline'.[20] He presents the Labor Party as drawing the constitution back to the ancient and natural—at least the proper and British—party way of government, even though others have regarded it as a party with methods and ideas foreign to the established norms of the British system.[21] But the truth is that the factions—though having certainly failed to enforce formal discipline—had in fact long provided a considerable degree of cohesion and stability as judged by the practice of the time. Furthermore, the changes made by the Labor Party in the character of parliamentary government drew in New South Wales on a heritage which already included an established cabinet system[22] and the rule that ministries held office only with the support of majorities.

The character of the majorities in parliament is, of course, more important to this argument than anything else. The majorities of the years before party, and the factions around which they were constructed, have always been presented as so personal and fluid that, besides being incapable of providing stable government, they defy understanding and description as groups. We have gone behind the hyperbole of contemporary public comment on politics to discover what the faction leaders themselves knew about the majorities on which they depended for power, and we have come to the conclusion that there is no impenetrable or bewildering mystery about them. The facts, though more prosaic than the legends, are not less interesting.

CHAPTER ONE

1856

A COLOURFUL CEREMONY took place on 22 May 1856 in Sydney's still unfinished Houses of Parliament. Loyal colonists had crowded Macquarie Street to watch 'the most distinguished among the elite of Sydney'—civil, military and ecclesiastical—enter the building. Inside, the Usher of the Black Rod, 'in full costume of black velvet lined with crimson satin', bustled around, directing visitors and raw members to their places in the Legislative Council chamber. The men stood. Benches were occupied by the ladies: conspicuous among them, Lady Denison, the wife of the Governor-General, sat with some of her numerous children. In hushed silence, the President of the Council read Sir William Denison's commission appointing members to open parliament. The members of the Lower House—the Legislative Assembly—withdrew to elect their speaker.

The ceremony had been brief, but, as the press commented next day, 'notwithstanding the imperfect state of the new building, the effect on the whole was imposing'.[1] With those 'proper forms which conduce to good order', parliament had begun its deliberations. A new era had opened in the government of New South Wales. Perhaps the newly sworn legislators might have winced had they known that the grave viceregal lady who sat watching them that day had recently written this ironical, but apt enough, prediction:

It is amusing to see these young countries starting with their new constitutions ... This is, fortunately, an older community than that of Victoria, but, even here, I suspect that we shall have some odd scenes before people and things in general settle down into a quiet state of working under the new regime.[2]

The contrast between the uncompleted building and the ceremony was a symbol of many things in the colony, not least of them the new constitution itself. It had been drawn up locally in 1853 and embodied in an Act of the Imperial Parliament to give it binding force before being brought into operation in 1856.[3] To discourage those who thought of amending it, the *Sydney Morning Herald* claimed that the

6

constitution was 'superior to any on either side of the Atlantic'.[4] But the bitter debate which accompanied its formulation had not been stilled by its adoption, and powerful political groups in the colony stood dedicated to its early modification. In particular, the provisions which set up a nominated Upper House and which preserved an electoral system devised in 1851 by the old colonial legislature to represent 'interests' rather than population remained as focal points of dispute.

The constitution was also 'incomplete' in a more profound sense. It dealt mainly with the future legislative institutions of the colony and left undefined almost all the details of the relations between them and the executive. The men who drafted the constitution intended that the new system of government should be modelled on that of England as closely as circumstances would permit, and they had provided legislative institutions accordingly. But outward forms could suggest only in broad terms the life that still remained to be breathed into the new constitutional creation. That could not simply be prescribed: as British experience abundantly taught, it had to emerge through the interplay of actual political forces, and in the young colony these forces were bound to be vastly different from those which had given the British constitution its contemporary form.

Before 1856 the legislature in the colony had consisted of a single House, the old partly elective Legislative Council; the executive heads of the government were chosen and appointed to seats in the chamber by the Governor. These officials had been subject only to criticism in the Council, not to the loss of their offices by an adverse vote. Now the legislature was divided into two Houses, of which the Lower was wholly elective. Executive officers were to be chosen from both Houses by the Governor, acting on the advice of a leader in the Lower commissioned by him to form a government, and they were to hold office in charge of the administrative departments only while they could command the support of the Assembly. Although the Governor still had important powers under the constitution—to dissolve parliament and call elections, to nominate the members who were to constitute the Upper House and to give the royal assent to bills passed by the legislature—it was generally believed that they would be exercised on the advice of the executive chosen from the Assembly.

However, it remained to be seen how far the Governor would in practice be reduced to a mere 'cipher'; his responsibilities were Imperial as well as local, and Denison liked to remind his early advisers that the analogy between his relations to them and the Queen's to her ministers 'is incomplete and will only serve to lead us astray'.[5]

There was ambiguity here, just as there was obscurity about the part the Upper House would play in the legislative process. Its powers, although undefined in some important respects, were considerable. The men who framed the constitution had intended it to act as a conservative check upon ill-considered legislation which they expected the nascent democracy of the colony to father in the Assembly. Clashes between the two Houses were expected and the Council was given almost co-ordinate powers in legislation, though alterations to the Constitution Bill before it became law weakened the Council's power to preserve its own structure against pressure from the Assembly.[6]

But it was obvious to all who looked for the power of the state behind its pomp and ceremony that the Lower House, not the Council, would be the centre of colonial politics. Here ministers were to be chosen; here would be marshalled those majorities upon which ministries must rest. Such was the clear implication of the term responsible government, the prize of the new system, as it had been understood in the colony at least since 1853. Such too was the obvious conclusion to be drawn from the analogy of the House of Commons, on which the Assembly had been modelled. If this seemed clear enough, it remained to be seen how potential ministers would be identified, and how their support would be organized in the House. Some colonists versed in English precedents fretted lest the Governor might attempt, like George III, to explore his influence in the legislature and construct majorities with the aid of placemen and other dependents.[7] They postulated, by contrast, the ideal of a ministry relying on 'the free and unbought support of the independent representatives of the Country', though, beyond suggesting that members should support measures rather than men, they offered no prescription for translating the ideal into action.

In its practical implications, this was an ideal not far removed from the conviction, voiced strongly by some conservatives in the constitution debates of 1853, that 'no government will be able to stand which does not call into its ranks the active business talent of both houses'.[8] Orderly and stable government, they thought, could be secured only through men properly 'trained to the public business', but these would necessarily be limited in number in the initial stages of the new parliamentary system. For an unforeseeable period, in fact, it would be 'absurd' to imagine that government could function on a 'party' basis: time and experience would be needed to produce a sufficient reserve of talent for that. Pressed to its logical conclusion, this argument involved—as Macarthur saw plainly—at least a temporary rejection of the principle of collective ministerial responsibility, for no government of the talents could long survive unless ministers were answerable only for their own departments.

As T. H. Irving demonstrates,[9] some of the mist surrounding these issues was dispelled by discussion in the colony between 1853 and 1856. The belief that ministers had to be collectively responsible to the Assembly for their administration displaced the idea that they might be held individually responsible by both the Governor and the Assembly. Placemen were in effect eliminated by the terms of the clauses finally adopted in the draft constitution to confer pensions on officers retiring from the Assembly on political grounds. This change at least opened the way for cabinet and party government, as some participants in the Council debate on these clauses in December 1853 realized clearly. During 1854 and 1855 the press repeatedly gave attention to this question, and the conviction gained ground that—as the *Sydney Morning Herald* put it—'parties will be requisite to give stability to Government, and respectability to the Opposition'.[10] Beneath the discussion simmered a fear—potent among conservatives and liberals alike—that without collective ministerial responsibility the superior experience of the old officials would give them 'peculiar advantages' over others in the competition for office, perhaps enhancing the Governor's influence in the legislature, and certainly threatening to curtail to some extent the power of majorities in the Assembly.

In fact, the political atmosphere of the colony in the mid-fifties offered firm ground for believing that 'parties', in the respectable sense derived from Burke, might emerge more quickly than some cared to predict. It was all very well for conservatives apprehensive of social change (like Macarthur) or professional administrators anxious to preserve governmental order and regularity (like Deas Thomson and Denison) to point dolefully to the apparent lack of prudence and talent among popular politicians, and to declare that party government could not be. The fact remained that two broad political movements, conservative and liberal, existed in the colony, reflecting significant differences in approach to its government and to its social and economic development, and providing therefore a potential ideological basis for party action. By 1856, 'conservative' and 'liberal' were not merely *ad hoc* labels applied loosely by contemporaries anxious to find a way of describing trends apparent at elections. They were, rather, appropriate and accepted names for particular attitudes of mind—perhaps traditions—which reached back into the forties and which had crystallized most sharply around the constitutional matters under debate in the early fifties.

So, however sceptical his view of 'party', Governor Denison inevitably found himself counting heads in March and April 1856 to judge whether the temper of the new parliament would be predominantly conservative or liberal. By that time liberal leaders like Cowper and Parkes, who had long since glimpsed the potential of organization in electorate and legislature, were likewise engaged in calculating the party composition of the Assembly, and looking hopefully to the future. As the last electoral returns came in and the parliament prepared to meet, it in fact seemed highly probable that parties might provide the clue to working a system of responsible government in New South Wales.

The leading conservatives of the colony looked to the coming of responsible government with apprehension. As Roger Therry wrote pettishly later,

> When responsible government came, there came with it the necessity of a mingling of classes. The sudden upraising of persons of subordinate rank to a level with the best society of the place created a collision that was at first a little violent and ungenial [*sic*] to both parties. Some thought it was not pleasant to hear a person greet you in the public assembly as 'my honourable friend' who, a short time before, took off his hat and in 'whispering humbleness' besought you as a magistrate 'to put in a good word on licensing day for the renewal of his licence' . . .[11]

The apprehension seems trifling, but this seemingly minor exhibition of snobbery contained the essence of a larger view of social relations. It had its roots in the central assumption of conservative thought: the assumption that a society could only be ordered and stable if its social classes were clearly defined and hierarchically ranked. Wealth and property, political power and social prestige were the primary marks of rank, and the respect of subordinates for those above them in society was the outward sign of inward social balance.

The conservatives' conception of a stratified society gave plausibility to their plan to establish an hereditary aristocracy in the colony when they drafted the constitution in 1853.[12] Even then this scheme seemed inappropriate from any other point of view, and the assertion that an Upper House had to be constructed like the House of Lords seemed to conceal, as the radical and liberal critics of the day argued, some more selfish motive for the scheme. But Wentworth and Macarthur and their friends were not simply aspiring to colonial titles and increased social prestige. Status and rank were to them part of the essential fabric of a stable society fit to enter upon a career of virtual independence and self-government. The argument was usually put in the form of an attack on democracy. G. W. Rusden wrote to Macarthur that

> many persons who wish you well, generally, say 'I like Went-worth's scheme [for a constitution] well enough barring titles—if he would dispense with that I would go with him'—why, this is the essence of the whole thing: this it is which if anything can at all, interpose a check between rabid democratic notions and abuse of power:—without this the mere nominee element [in the Upper House] has its days numbered when it begins to exist . . . Without this element *ingrain* in the people, democracy must ascend and rule the roost.[13]

In Rusden's opinion, constitutional devices, such as the two-thirds majorities required for amending the clauses relating to the Upper House, were insufficient guarantee that conservative institutions could be maintained against democratic movements. Conservative institutions would be safe only if society itself had the elements of rank and respect ingrained in it.

As was most patently revealed in their pleas for a colonial aristocracy, the conservatives' model of society was English. J. N. Dickinson, a supreme court judge, wrote in 1852[14] that 'the existence of social distinctions and the transmission of hereditary honours are congenial to inclinations of Englishmen . . . who do not change their dispositions by emigrating to Australia'. To establish an aristocracy of birth, he thought, would be 'peculiarly grateful to their feelings, by reviving and perpetuating in a distant country the same form of society in which they rejoiced at home'. It was convenient for Dickinson to forget that many of those who had come to the colony had *not* rejoiced in English society: and he went on to speculate about the social groups to whom the boon of ennoblement might be extended. A baronetcy, he thought, should be conferred on an immigrant who not only bought land in the colony but also settled 'a number of married couples as tenant farmers'; or, if it were mineral land he had bought, 'he should . . . lay out gardens and build cottages in which the miners might be lodged; and so, in each case, the village system of England might be fully established'. Dickinson thought that this plan would attract 'moderately wealthy individuals of the middle order' from England and in the colony itself, rather than the established English aristocracy.

Dickinson's ideas were not altogether implausible, since by the middle fifties some 'moderately wealthy individuals' in the colony had established a tenantry on their lands, and some of them formed, in fact, the hard core of the conservative movement. The Macarthurs, with their estate at Camden, were among the better known examples; J. N. Oxley leased forty farms to farmers on his property at Camden a decade later.[15] G. Macleay stated in 1856 that he had an established tenantry engaged in agriculture on his property in the Murrumbidgee electorate.[16] G. H. Cox, a pastoralist (like Macleay, Macarthur and Oxley), had thirty farmers as tenants in the Wellington electorate.[17] W. Lee, another squatter in the west, also had tenants on his land,[18] and in the south, the Campbells' patriarchal estate at 'Duntroon' was now well established. A. Berry, a large landholder on the Shoalhaven, was increasing the number of his 'already numerous tenants' in 1855.[19]

Each of these men was a conservative in the mid-fifties and each had a strong interest in the politics of the day. They resided normally in the country and many were local magistrates. The views of country gentlemen of this class are suggested by the letters of two friends of James Macarthur. J. M. Antill, a large landowner at Picton, wrote in 1857 that although he had

> a very [limited?] opinion of 'His Majesty' *the People* I pity them because they are ignorant and humour them because I think their dispositions are really good and because by management I think a great deal can be done with them.[20]

J. K. Chisholm, another pastoralist in the Camden district, wrote in 1861 deploring universal suffrage and the vote by ballot; they had put power, he said,

> in the hands of the ignorant and unthinking multitude, who merely value their privileges in proportion as they subserve their own aggrandisement and in levelling all superior influences. The recent elections for this county illustrated . . . the pernicious operation of the ballot, the effect of which was to transfer the labouring classes from all respectable and property influence, and place them under the direction of a clique who were actuated by the worst possible motives.[21]

Pastoralists with tenantry were not the only conservatives at this time. Four self-announced conservatives in the 1856 elections offer examples of the diverse social origins and careers of some of the men who formed the movement. J. R. Brenan, a solicitor, had emigrated to the colony in 1834 from Ireland where he had been a large land-owner. In New South Wales he had been variously employed as a superintendent of convicts, a police magistrate and a coroner. He had also practised his profession and, in 1856, owned large estates in the South Cumberland or West Camden electorate.[22] Thomas Barker, who had arrived in the colony in 1813, was a flour miller, tweed manufacturer and director of the Sydney Railway Company. In addition he had interests in banking. He had been a magistrate and nominated member of the Legislative Council (1853–6). He was a political friend of James Macarthur.[23] W. M. Manning arrived in the colony in 1837 as a barrister. He became in turn Chairman of Quarter Sessions, Solicitor-General (1844–56) and Acting Judge in the Supreme Court. From 1851 to 1856 he was an official member in the Council. In 1856 he too was a political friend of James Macarthur.[24] John Hay stood in 1856 with G. Macleay as a conservative in the electorate of Murrum-bidgee. He had arrived from Scotland in 1838 after studying law in Edinburgh, but became a pastoralist in the colony.[25]

Manning exemplifies two groups whose members provided the colonial conservative movement with much of its strength, at least in prestige and experience if not in numbers—the officials of the administration and the upper ranks of the legal profession. Dickinson, Supreme Court Judge, and Sir Alfred Stephen, the Chief Justice, were seldom able to make their views known with propriety, but men like Plunkett, the Attorney-General, or Deas Thomson, the Colonial Secretary, stood alongside the leading pastoralists in support of conservative principles on occasions such as the debate on the constitution.

There was of course a crude sense in which conservative principles were invoked in almost naked defence of material interests. When Robert Lowe asserted in the Commons that the Constitution Bill of 1853, erected on these principles, was little more than a conspiracy aimed by the squatters of New South Wales against the people of the colony, he expressed a half-truth that has been endorsed by most historians.[26] But few of the officials and legal officers who provided much of the theorizing to support colonial conservatism were men of property. They drew inspiration from the deeper wells of tradition: in them a kind of professional pride in public service was linked with a passionate respect for England. We are told that *Coelum non animum mutant, qui trans mare currunt* was a favourite quotation often on the lips of Sir Alfred Stephen; he once rendered it warmly in 'verse':

> Here, from the Parent Land divided far,
> For us, her children, shines no brighter star.
> Changed are the skies, not so the British name,
> Or mind and heart, which still remain the same.[27]

In a crude colonial environment, men of this kind felt themselves to be guardians of a cultural heritage. They were patrons of what arts the colony could boast, and supporters of the Established Church and the infant university. And in their social circle, centred on Government House, they valued and cultivated those polite accomplishments which experience and tradition taught them to associate with upper-class British civilization. Such men naturally had a deep reverence for the British constitution, 'that most excellent of human institutions', as Plunkett described it:

> It is no matter of theory or speculation, it is not the work of yesterday, . . . It is not enough that any change should be good in design, but it should be clearly shown that it is safe by its agreement with all the other parts. I approach that venerable fabric with the same reverential awe that I would the Sepulchres of the illustrious dead in Westminster Abbey.[28]

This thought was echoed by almost all those who spoke in favour of the new constitution. They believed it had been made as close a copy of the English constitution as circumstances would permit. They hoped that, like its great English model, it would preserve order and foster a hallowed cultural tradition. They were loath to see the sacrilegious hands of 'democrats' tear it to pieces. 'Why should we rashly try an experiment fraught with peril, while we have the experience of centuries to guide us . . . ?' asked Macarthur, quoting Burke.[29] The question, at least among conservatives, required no answer.

It was not enough, however, to rest a defence of the constitution simply on the ground that it was modelled on one whose antiquity and contrivance made it venerable. Logic and interest pushed the conservatives to find a more tangible link between constitution and society than a hypothetical social hierarchy crowned with the dreamed-of aristocracy. The colony afforded them no traditions of status and respect to invoke. They argued, therefore, that in any society the elements—interests or classes—ought to be 'balanced' because they were mutually dependent. These interests in New South Wales were commonly described in terms of economic activities—pastoral, mining, agricultural, mercantile, labouring—but whatever the list and the definition, 'in the order of Providence, all these classes, in their several positions, are equally necessary for building up the great fabric. of society',[30] and, as the phrase 'in their several positions' implied, rank in the social hierarchy somehow corresponded to economic activity.

This balance had to be preserved in the constitutional arrangements, and already its necessity had received statutory recognition in the Electoral Act of 1851.[31] In the constitution debate, conservative speakers frequently argued that the elements to be balanced were the three estates, but they made no attempt to justify this by demonstrating any correspondence between the interests and the estates, or between the interests and the institutions. It was simply assumed that the Assembly would represent 'the people' or democracy and that 'members of the higher classes, competent by education and position, can look forward to the honours of a seat in an Upper House'.[32] This would happen even if the Upper House were nominated. It was expected to represent the natural aristocracies that Dickinson had spoken of, shorn merely of their titular distinctions. Wentworth's remark that 'our Shepherd kings . . . are . . . the body most fitted of all in the colonies . . . to receive hereditary distinctions'[33] left little doubt in the minds of their adversaries that the pastoralists had seen themselves as the second estate. With the assistance of the nominees and officials they had designed the Upper House to enable them to balance and oppose the other interests and estates.

The need for a balance, written into the constitution, was further justified by the conservatives' conviction that human nature was basically greedy, selfish, unthinking, ambitious, passionate and given to corruption. Macarthur observed that

> Notwithstanding the greater diffusion of education and general intelligence, human nature is still the same, and human beings will always be subject to the same influences, the same passions, the same impulses, which history records.[34]

Manning added,

> We should look to this immutable element with which we have to deal, and endeavour to make the most we can of the virtues of mankind, and even to turn its vices to purposes of utility.[35]

He mentioned the American constitution as an admirable example of balance established by exploiting human weakness. But Rusden thought that in America democracy had thwarted the provisions of the constitution and 'ruled the roost' unchecked and unbalanced. Wentworth quoted Tocqueville and Calhoun to show the evil effects of unchecked passion, to express his conviction that the classical transition to tyranny and finally to anarchy and dissolution, lately seen in France, was not far off in America.[36] The moral was: America had shown that constitutional contrivance alone would not do and therefore a balanced society of three estates had to be established in New South Wales if it was to avoid a like fate. Once established, that balance should not be lightly altered, and the conservatives usually discredited proposed reforms by arguing that they were either theoretical, speculative and experimental, or originated in the passionate impulses of the third estate.[37] Prudence alone was sufficient reason why constitutional experiments should be resisted. The third estate was likely to be roused whenever constitutional changes were under discussion. Nicholson thought nothing could 'be worse for the political and social condition of any community', and even carried this attitude to the length of regarding 'four or five months of political ferment' before an election as 'a most undesirable thing.'[38]

Men with such an ideology were bound to be apprehensive of responsible government, especially after the Imperial Parliament had granted the new legislature a power of amending the constitution by simple majorities. This seemed to them to clear the way for the destruction of constitutional barriers to unduly rapid and democratic social change. Conservatives were forced to descend to the arena of electoral politics in the hope that they could yet make good their loss of institutional power by winning leadership, prestige and numerical strength in the Lower House. But this was a very hazardous course for them. Their attitudes were a distinct liability in many electorates and in parliament their critics never tired of exposing their class and sectional interests. Within a few years they had withdrawn from politics, either in disgust or after defeat,[39] or had stayed on and won influence only by compromises that dissipated the ideological solidarity and distinctness of their movement.[40]

The first years of responsible government did not prove to them that their fears had been groundless. The removal of the two-thirds clauses, which had been intended to entrench the Upper House and the electoral system of 1851, was the first and one of the most important attacks on the constitutional structure they had designed.[41] The Electoral Act of 1858 was the second. They were soon convinced, in the words of Nicholson, that under this Act the colony was 'doomed' to the 'fullest democratic development'.

There is scarcely a man of mark in [the Legislative Assembly of those who formerly played the most conspicuous part in

public life. Publicans—expiree convicts—journeymen mechanics—
Wesleyan lay preachers—form a not inconsiderable proportion
of the present members.[42]

Frequent ministerial changes, the wrangling over a bill to make the
Upper House elective, the swamping of the first Legislative Council
a few days before its life ended, and the passing of the Robertson
Land Acts all served to confirm the conservatives' worst fears of the
excesses to be expected in a democracy. But by then they were powerless to resist.

They were powerless because they had increasingly lost touch
with reality. In a colony where a vigorous professional and commercial
life and steady extension of settlement had accustomed their opponents
to the existence of a high degree of social mobility, their oligarchical
pretensions had a hollow ring. They could find no allies except the
old official and nominee groups, who brought with them their own
unpopularity. To that was added the aura of odium associated with the
'exclusive' tradition that still clung to the names of families like the
Macarthurs. This unpopularity had been stimulated in earlier political
struggles by men like Wentworth who had now become conservative,
and it survived as a tradition in the liberal movement to be exploited
against them.

Most unreal of all was their conception of the opposition they
faced in the colony. It was as if they paid here, in self-defeating
blindness, the price of confusing barely-confessed economic motives
and an almost wayward veneration for social and constitutional
ideals only half-applicable to New South Wales. Their belief that
democracy must develop on the American or the French pattern
and that it could be checked only by a social and constitutional balance
led them into an undiscriminating denunciation of all opponents
as being little better than Jacobins, anarchists or republican democrats. The falsity of this exaggeration at once sealed their unpopularity
and deprived them of the political insight to exploit, or at least to
second, the eagerness of other powerful groups in the colony to
secure the same order and stability for which they themselves claimed
to stand.

In fact, the most formidable rejection of conservative ideas came
not from the 'anarchists' conjured up by Wentworth's rhetorical
imagination, nor even from the 'radicals' who in truth existed, though
in less frightening form than conservative propaganda proclaimed.
An emerging mercantile liberal movement, crystallizing in the late

forties, stirring decisively to meet the challenge of constitution-making, had come by the mid-fifties to occupy the wings of the political stage. Its members were convinced that responsible government would offer the opportunity for moulding the colony's new institutions to their heart's desire. The movement was moderate, respectable, bourgeois. To associate the word 'anarchy'—even 'democracy'—with it was laughable.

There had been isolated stirrings of liberal sentiment in the forties but the liberals of the colony took no large and organized part in politics until the end of that decade. Then, between 1849 and 1851, the British proposal to renew transportation of convicts to the colony raised an issue which brought many sections of the population briefly together under the leadership of the mercantile and professional classes of Sydney. The Anti-Transportation Association, born at a public meeting in 1849, represented the liberals' first serious essay in political organization. We have the names of eighty-four of those taking part in it, and the occupations of sixty-four have been identified. Forty-six were engaged in mercantile and professional activities, twelve were artisans and retail traders, and six were pastoralists or landowners.[43] This pattern of leadership was repeated in the Constitution Committee, set up in August 1853 to focus dissatisfaction with the Constitution Bill being debated at the time in the Legislative Council. Of eighty-one men taking part in the work of the Committee, fifty-five were in mercantile-professional activities, twenty were artisans and retail traders, and six were pastoralists. Continuity between the two phases of liberal activity is demonstrated by the fact that nineteen of the leading members of the Committee had been members of the Anti-Transportation Association.[44]

These organizations put the men who led them in the forefront of the movement. But the liberal movement did not draw its strength wholly from Sydney: both the Anti-Transportation Association and Constitution Committee gained widespread support from country districts. In 1853 'petitions from country areas against the Constitution Bill . . . added approximately 4,000 signatures to the 2,500 which the Constitution Committee had obtained' in Sydney. These were mostly from country towns, especially those in agricultural as opposed to pastoral areas, and in many of them the commercial, agricultural and professional men expressed their resentment against the pastoral interest.[45] They felt that they were being deprived of political power by the Constitution Bill and the Electoral Act and that the pastoral class would use this power to 'aggrandize itself at the expense of all other classes'.

Liberals could look back over these years with some satisfaction. Transportation had been discontinued.[46] They had managed to kill a proposal in the Constitution Bill to establish an hereditary aristocracy as the basis for the upper chamber. They had had other minor successes. At an 1849 by-election in the County of Cumberland the anti-transportationists had advanced a candidate to test feeling against those prepared to accept more convicts. Their candidate was defeated, but popular opposition helped force his opponent, James Macarthur, to pledge himself to oppose the resumption of transportation, although he was reluctant to admit the reason for his changed opinion.[47] Wentworth had paid for his contempt of popular views on this and similar questions by being placed third on the poll for Sydney in 1851, with the radical Lang, and the merchant, Lamb, preceding him. The merchant liberals subsequently managed to replace Lang with one of their own number, R. Campbell, whose views were 'a happy mixture of popular appeal and liberal principles'.[48]

The liberals' successes, though limited, were sufficient to stir them into greater activity in the Legislative Council after 1853. Three frustrating years of endeavour there taught them the need for firm leadership and led them to conclude—as Cowper's letters to Parkes testify[49]—that, once the new legislature came into operation, they might make themselves a powerful force in it, both in numbers and in discipline, through the methods of arousing popular support tested in their earlier agitation. Given such advantages, they hoped to be able to work to remould the new system from within: to remove the two-thirds clauses, and to reconstruct the electoral system and the Upper House. Opportunities would then follow to write new legislation on such subjects as the disposal of Crown lands and the organization of the administration.

The liberals' optimism, grasp of reality, and moderate successes were highlighted by the decline of the radical movement which had intermittently acted during the forties as the spearhead of attack against conservatism and privilege in the colony.[50] Radicals survived into the early fifties and still spoke in the old phrases, but their attempts to win public support met with little success. They founded three political associations during these years: the Constitutional Association of 1848, the Political Association and the Australian League of 1851. Each soon languished.

The Constitutional Association was set up to agitate for an extension of the franchise, for a fairer electoral distribution, and for radical land reform.[51] It faded away in 1849 in the face of the much more popular anti-transportation agitation. The Political Association

of 1851, its lineal descendant, was formed to fight against the 1851
Electoral Act; it attacked the squatters in very bitter terms,[52] and it
was clearly anxious to bend to its own purposes the anti-transportation
enthusiasm of the time. It had fleeting success when it first caught
the interest of some of the prominent merchants of Sydney, but they
were soon repelled by the flamboyant style of the Association's
propaganda, and abandoned it. A rapid decline followed. The Australian League was launched in April 1850 by that erratic Scottish
radical divine, J. D. Lang. In two inaugural lectures, Lang argued
in favour of independence from Britain, demanded universal suffrage,
vote by ballot and equal electoral districts, and declared that a colony
freed from the yoke of its Governor might abolish the customs
house and federate with the other colonies. He thought a league
formed on the model of the Anti-Corn Law League could work
successfully for these objects, prevent transportation, and promote
British emigration.[53] A few progressive hearts were stirred: Deniehy
enthusiastically supported Lang, and Parkes wrote denouncing
'the dung-hill aristocracy of Botany Bay' and pledging his support
for the League.[54] But Lang won only a small and temporary following
in Sydney, failed completely to arouse the interest of country people
(especially gold diggers), and his League soon fizzled out. 'You are
too early and too violent', wrote a radical friend. '. . . True, it is bad,
but pismires, as we are, cannot eat elephants'.[55] There was, in fact,
no class prepared to follow Lang into battle against Britain, and he
himself was left merely as a demagogic lecturer.

These radical organizations had drawn their most active membership
from petty traders and artisans[56]—a lower social stratum than that
which sustained the liberal movement—and had aimed at educating
the 'operative classes' in politics and winning support from them.
But they proved unable to compete, even among these people, against
the ideology and prestige of the liberals. By 1853 some radical notables
like Hawksley and Deniehy were taking part in the liberal Constitution
Committee; others, like Parkes, had openly joined forces with the
merchants and their friends in the city.[57] Thus the liberal movement
absorbed, or at least won the allegiance of, radical activist elements,
at once broadening the base of its own support, and assisting in the
decline of radicalism. The process was nicely symbolized in 1854,
when radicals accepted Parkes—by now a firmly committed liberal—
in place of Lang as their candidate for the Sydney by-election.[58]

Radical ineffectiveness can be explained in part by the immaturity
of the colonial lower orders, who were accustomed to look to the
business and professional classes for political guidance, and perhaps

too by the 'flunkeyism' which Deniehy assailed as being the pervading spirit of social life in New South Wales.[59] More important, however, was the ideological naïveté of the radical leaders themselves, and the unsophisticated view of political agitation to which it led. Their central tenet was faith in the 'people'. As the *People's Advocate* put it when attacking conservatives during the constitutional debate of 1853: 'Democracy is synonymous with the people—their intelligence, their principles, their enterprise'.[60] Each of the radical organizations shared this faith, believed in the natural rationality of the people, and acted on the assumption that the people had only to be awakened to a sense of their rights to demand them and to demand them with success. The Constitutional Association thought that its activity was best directed to promoting 'free discussion' and the petitions that were expected automatically to follow. The Political Association took steps to set up a reading room and library, and Lang proposed that his League should devote itself to lectures, pamphleteering and public meetings to 'indoctrinate' the colonists with a knowledge of their political rights. Chartist and Anti-Corn Law League organizations were vaguely taken as models, and radicals showed no awareness that some follow-up might be necessary to make political agitation effective. So their organizational efforts, such as they were, lamely followed the traditional pattern of getting up petitions and giving candidates some support in elections. When the expected spontaneous mass movement showed no sign of developing, the radicals tended to explain their failure by charging the 'people' with apathy.

The liberals had come to think quite differently about organization. The phrase 'the people' was often on their lips, but never with the assumption that the people would act spontaneously. Apathy was something to be overcome by organization, not something the people had to be educated out of. Their experience in the campaigns against transportation and the Constitution Bill taught them the value of sustained and carefully planned agitation in winning popular support, which was desirable to offset the political weakness of the liberals in the Legislative Council.[61] In the Constitution Committee they had tested organizational techniques never conceived of by the radical movement, and leaders like Parkes had seen clearly that 'an inchoate mass, "the people", was not a political entity at all, and contributed nothing to the political power of a leader unless it was organized'.[62] In 1853 Parkes drew upon his experience in the Constitution Committee to adumbrate a plan for establishing a permanent liberal central committee, with an agreed and publicized policy, working through a network of local committees. No definite moves

followed to put into action either this or a more precise scheme
sketched out by Deniehy the following year: but both plans were
significant pointers to the way in which liberals were reaching out
towards a new grasp of political reality.[63]

The same tendency was apparent in the coherence of their creed.
The liberal faith was a web of hopes and demands woven around a
number of fixed points: 'the people', the importance of stable government, the need to develop the colony and the virtues of free trade.
As these points could be related and developed in a variety of ways
when the occasion required, they offered the essential groundwork
for a flexible ideology to serve a continuing political movement.
Liberals argued, for example, that stable government, so necessary
for the development of the colony, had to be popular government,
otherwise energy would be constantly sidetracked into disputes about
the constitution and the rights of classes under it. The colonists
would never rest content under a constitution which lacked their
confidence because 'one interest was made supreme': justice and
expediency both demanded that all should be given a 'just share'
in representation and in distribution of the franchise.[64] The general
antipathy to nomineeism, which the liberals had long shared with
many people in the colony, fitted into this attitude quite naturally
and was readily transferred to the provisions in the constitution for a
nominated Upper House. Liberals did not attack these provisions
in the name of 'democracy'—almost all were in fact agreed that an
Upper House had to be conservative—but on the ground that there
was no ancient structure of rank and privilege to be allowed for in
devising a system of government in New South Wales. An elected
Upper House would be a proper reflection of social reality; it would
be conservative, independent of the government of the day, responsible to the people and secure in their confidence.[65] Parkes' *Empire*
managed in 1856 to capture much of the essence of liberal thinking
by observing how, paradoxically, liberals in New South Wales were
the only true conservatives:

> The strongest tendencies of society in Australia are to the develop-
> ment of a nationality pervaded by the spirit of a true and rational
> democracy. In the peaceful process of this development . . . is our
> real conservatism . . . To limit the power of the people; to get up
> an aristocracy of wealth and territorialism; to base the political
> institutions of the colony upon a systematic *distrust of the people,*
> may be the dream of some narrow-minded men amongst us who
> have studied English politics . . . But it is not conservatism in Austra-
> lia, however much its outward semblance may be like the toryism
> of the old land.[66]

The liberals' emphasis on the need for a conservative Upper House, stable government and the development of the colony distinguished their thought clearly from that of the earlier radicals. In its mixture of hard-headedness and idealism, their creed reflected well enough the aspirations of the rising business and professional interests from which their leadership was drawn. Yet their constitutional aims guaranteed popular support, and in their elaboration of the argument that the colony needed to be developed (with its implied corollary that the liberals were best fitted for the task of directing development)[67] they came to put forward programmes whose appeal cut across the obvious boundaries of class or interest. Thus by 1856 they were demanding not merely a new Electoral Act and a bill to make the Upper House elective; they were also stressing the need for land legislation, for a new educational system, for new internal and external communications, for municipal institutions, for an extended system of courts, for reorganization of the whole administrative structure and for reforms in the police, survey and immigration departments.

The 'liberalism' and 'conservatism' of the mid-fifties are best described as two broad movements of thought which were an essential part of the atmosphere in which the new parliament began its deliberations. Though real enough as general touchstones for classifying candidates in the election of 1856, they were too ill-defined to offer a basis for party action in the campaign. No organization existed to claim either of them as its own. Though in Sydney liberal leaders had some success in co-ordinating the conduct of the metropolitan campaign, elsewhere distance, the desiccating influence of localism and sectarianism, and the country electorates' suspicion of leadership from the metropolis blocked all chance of colony-wide organization. Any candidate could piece together the slogans that he thought would be most to his electoral advantage, most consistent with his beliefs, past reputation and possible future action in parliament, and most likely to justify the 'party' label he claimed. The widely used term 'liberal-conservative' was at once evidence that candidates recognized two distinct bodies of thought and that they felt free, within the limits imposed by their electorate and their own attitudes, to choose slogans and policies from both.

The election of 1856 thus did not decide who was to form the first ministry under responsible government. No member was returned as the recognized leader of a majority of members in the Assembly, and the few members who had first-hand experience of executive affairs in the colony had no recognized followers. The resulting uncertainty put the Governor in an advantageous position when it came to choosing his first ministry: no one could criticize him on the ground that he had blundered into choosing a ministry without majority support, whatever its composition. At the same time, the split between liberal and conservative opinion, though blurred and equivocal in its immediate implications, was also a help to him, for as the returns came in, it gave him some basis on which to assess the likely acceptability to parliament of his chosen ministers.

Denison used these advantages with finesse, picked his way adroitly through a series of technical difficulties surrounding the installation of the first ministry, and had the satisfaction of receiving parliament's endorsement of his choice. He had hoped at first that Deas Thomson— the Colonial Secretary under the old system—would be able to form a government. Denison was anxious that the transition to responsible government should be made without endangering administrative stability and efficiency, and having the conscientious administrator's impatience with politicians (as well, indeed, as a near-contempt for popular parliamentary government, at least in its colonial forms) he felt he needed advisers experienced in the administration of the colony.[68] Thomson twice failed to secure colleagues, and the commission fell to Stuart Donaldson, who ultimately won the co-operation of Macarthur, Manning, Nicholls and Darvall. Denison had the consolation of seeing at least one ex-official, Manning, among the ministers, and the conservative bias of the government as a whole undoubtedly suited his taste. Convinced, like many others, that the elections had returned about thirty-four conservatives and twenty 'Liberals or Republicans' to the Assembly, he accepted the ministry and preserved what he was pleased to call his 'indifferent position' as Governor.[69]

The first ministry had thus been formed and took office with the co-operation and support of leading conservatives who included some of the old government officials and many of the pastoralists in the House. The liberals in the Assembly, led by Cowper, were disappointed and angry; they felt they had been cheated of power, and immediately met to consider the course they should adopt in opposition to the ministry.[70] The differences between liberals and conservatives, differences whose implications had been slurred over in the elections, were therefore sharpened by events in the first weeks of the life of the new parliament and the simulacrum of a two-party division appeared in the House at once.[71]

In fact, no parties existed, either in the Burkean or in the modern sense, nor did they develop in the later parliaments. Tension between liberals and conservatives nevertheless set the broad limits within which groupings in the Assembly were at first formed. By the time Donaldson fell in August 1856, there was no problem in identifying his successor, Cowper, who had emerged clearly as the leader of what looked very like a liberal 'party'. Already the principle was being established that ministries would be chosen from distinct and competing groups in the legislature rather than constructed and reconstructed out of the most talented administrators.

In the first parliament, these groups were roughly differentiated not only by the general tendency of the opinions of members on either side of the House, but by the interests with which members were connected.[72] The pastoralists, for example, more hopeful of favourable land legislation from the Donaldson and Parker ministries than from the liberal leaders, were divided unevenly. Sixteen of them supported Donaldson and Parker, nine supported Cowper. The merchants and traders with one exception took the opposition side, while the professional men divided equally between both sides in the House. A similar division of members took place according to the type of electorate they represented: members from urban electorates mostly supported Cowper, and most of those from pastoral electorates supported Donaldson and Parker. Members from agricultural electorates were almost equally divided. But the vital point is that neither side of the House was homogeneous. Besides that, the interests of many members fell into more than one field of activity—by occupation, for instance, one-third of the pastoralists had either agricultural, mining or commercial interests as sidelines to their main employment. The result was that the division between liberal and conservative rapidly lost significance as the disputes about the form of the political system itself died down or were settled and parliament turned to legislation that affected more directly the economic and social interests members represented.

Liberal efforts to alter the constitutional arrangements, which had sustained the division since the early fifties, were crowned by the Electoral Act of 1858. Deaths, defections and electoral defeats were by then decimating the old conservatives: their political hopes were finally ended by the passage of Robertson's Land Acts in 1861. Soon all politicians would claim to be liberals, for the period of bourgeois ascendency in the politics of New South Wales was dawning. But by this time responsible government was a going concern, operating on the basis of group conflict within parliament. In the late fifties observers seeking a rationale for this conflict had stressed the liberal-conservative split, and some of them had imagined that they saw in it the seeds of a genuine two-party system. But factions, not parties, had developed to give order and meaning to the wrangle for political power. And when the liberal-conservative debate died away, it was the survival of these factions which underlay the continued and successful operation of responsible government in conditions differing markedly from those in England at mid-century.

CHAPTER TWO

The Faction System

THE FIRST FACTION in the Assembly took shape around Cowper and Robertson, the liberal leaders elected to parliament in 1856. The followers of these men, as well as the supporters of the Donaldson ministry, were for a time referred to as parties, in imitation of British practice and in the belief that responsible government must automatically entail the formation of parties. But some conservatives, employing the definition of party taken over from Burke, were anxious to label their opponents 'factious' to discredit them publicly. They doubted whether parties could be formed with the speed and deliberate purpose which the liberals had shown when they first met in May 1856.[1] For their part, the liberals indignantly rejected the idea that they constituted a 'faction'.[2] The name implied that they had no social roots, no stable extra-parliamentary backing and that they were simply an ephemeral combination of members hoping to seize power for the sake of its immediate advantages.

A faction, it was commonly held, lacked any well defined body of principles or belief, and all its other deficiences followed from this central defect. A faction ministry would be incapable of governing steadily in the public interest according to a comprehensive and matured policy, because its policy and legislation would inevitably reflect, in an *ad hoc* and shifting manner, the demands of the members supporting it and the interests, by definition sectional and selfish, of the constituencies or social groupings which they represented. The public or national interest would therefore be neglected and sacrificed to immediate expediency. The corrupting effect of faction would be felt elsewhere. Faction ministries were expected to use the patronage within the public service to their immediate political advantage, with demoralizing effects upon the administration. They would exploit the revenue of the colony to assist in building their parliamentary support. Finance would not be allocated according to some rational scheme of priorities, but spent on roads, bridges and harbour works, in such a way as to win votes in the House and to ensure the return of supporters to parliament. Another common belief was that faction ministries would of necessity be weak and unstable, subject to frequent reconstructions and open to defeat after only brief periods in office. Or, if they survived, it would be by coalitions and reconstructions in which all consideration for fixed and distinct political principles would be cast to the winds.

By 1860 no one doubted that the group which Cowper and Robertson had led for four years was indeed a faction.[3] Despite its broad liberal views and the obvious weight of its popular support, it had failed in other respects—as its members themselves had to admit—to merit the dignity of the Burkean epithet 'party'. But if experience had made this clear enough, it had also shown that a 'faction' could serve as an effective basis for ministries and parliamentary majorities. And the pessimists' fears that a lack of genuine parties would result in corrupt and chaotic politics had certainly not been fully borne out.

From the first meeting of parliament in 1856, the liberals under Cowper maintained an obstructive and determined opposition to the Donaldson ministry and to its successor, the Parker ministry. They managed to elect their candidate to the speakership, and the ministry soon found itself almost powerless, with a slim and unsteady majority drawn from conservatives and 'moderates', many of them professed independents. Donaldson resigned in exasperation after only three months in power.[4] Cowper took office but, unable to secure a majority, fell within a month. Parker, leading what was essentially a reconstruction of the Donaldson ministry, succeeded Cowper. In the House he faced the same obstructive opposition that had frustrated Donaldson, and his support was equally unsteady. His attempts to legislate on the two subjects most in dispute at the time—the land and electoral laws—provoked unrest, abstention and opposition among his followers,[5] and in less than a year he was forced to resign.

Cowper thus returned to the premiership, in September 1857, and this time he was more successful. His ministry, a reconstruction of his first, endured and held its support. This came from two groups of members: Cowper's immediate followers, who were mostly experienced politicians and moderate in their liberalism, and a 'decidedly liberal' wing,[6] most of whom were new members from agricultural and Hunter River electorates. The latent tension between these two wings was revealed late in 1857 when, under Robertson's leadership, the more liberal group attacked the ministry's Land and Stock Assessment Bills and helped defeat them. Cowper relied upon votes of independents and sympathetic but unsteady members for majorities in divisions in a full House, and considered resigning. But then, with the encouragement of Robertson and his friends,[7] he asked instead, and with success, for an election.

The election, held early in 1858, left the liberals still in a minority in the new Assembly, even though their opponents had suffered heavy losses. Twenty-three liberals who had sat in the first parliament stood for election to the second, and only one was defeated. By contrast, of the fifteen conservatives from the first parliament who attempted to regain their seats, only eight were successful. But there were seventeen new members whose allegiances were uncertain, and with six independents who survived from the old parliament, these men put the liberals in an insecure position.[8] By this time Cowper had also lost the steady support of two influential followers, Parkes[9] and Forster, each of whom—moved by a combination of personal ambition and growing distrust of their leader—had ostentatiously declared his independence before the end of 1857. Cowper strengthened his position by taking Robertson into his ministry as Secretary for Lands. But late in 1858 he suffered another serious loss when he was obliged to request James Martin to resign the office of Attorney-General. Martin had disagreed with other ministers about a stock assessment bill and the extent of his responsibility to the cabinet as a whole.[10] The desertion of Parkes, Forster and Martin marked the incipient development of new centres of opposition from within the old liberal group.

Through his close association with Robertson, Cowper had secured the firm allegiance of the 'decidedly liberal' wing of the faction, and he won further support by promising two crucial liberal measures: a bill to revise the electoral arrangements of 1851, and, after a subsequent election, reformist land legislation. By the end of 1858 he had pushed the Electoral Bill through both Houses, despite strong opposition in the Council. The new Act registered a first decisive liberal victory. It established adult male suffrage, the ballot vote, and representation primarily by population in new and more equal electoral districts. The promised election was held as soon as the Act came into force in 1859. Although the supporters of the ministry were returned with smaller losses than their opponents, they were once more in a minority in a House which had been enlarged from fifty-four to seventy-two members,[11] almost sixty per cent of whom were new to the House.

There had, as well, been a change in the character of the opposition. Cowper was now challenged not only by conservatives but also by liberals who had deserted him in the preceding parliament and had waited until the Electoral Bill was passed before attacking him. And indeed, the ministry suffered two early defeats which left little doubt that it no longer had control of the House.[12] Cowper nevertheless brought in an education bill, a bill to abolish state aid to religion, and the promised land bills. His supporters disliked the Education Bill and it was overwhelmingly defeated. The ministry resigned and Forster took office.

Forster's ministry lasted only four months. His support was unstable for it came chiefly from the late opposition, and included not only the surviving conservatives but also defecting liberals and independents. Among these men were at least four would-be leaders: John Hay, who had been Parker's Secretary for Lands, Martin and Murray who had held office under Cowper, and Parkes. They had already refused to co-operate with one another in a ministry under Forster's or Murray's leadership.[13] Forster also relied upon the forbearance of liberals led by Robertson. Seven of these men gave him a 'fair trial' for a while.[14] Forster tried to enhance his strength by frankly altering his proposed legislation and adding new bills to it, even to the extent of introducing a land bill under pressure from Robertson's supporters.[15] But this manoeuvre failed and he fell in March 1860. Robertson now took office at the head of his and Cowper's supporters. The new ministry was essentially a reconstruction of the Cowper administration, with Robertson as Premier in place of Cowper, who temporarily retired from politics. Cowper returned to the premiership twelve months later and the ministry continued in office until late in 1863 without any changes in its personnel until shortly before its fall.

The Cowper-Robertson combination was the most long-lived and stable of the early ministries. If the brief interlude of the Forster ministry is discounted, it can be said to have held office for over six years. By the end of that time, it had an enviable legislative record behind it. Besides the Electoral Act, it had to its credit legislation in 1858 to establish municipal institutions, district courts, and a regular system of postal communication with England. It carried through an extended programme of public works, especially the building of railways and telegraph lines. In 1861, after two unproductive years, Robertson's Land Bills were passed: one to provide for sale and the other for occupation of Crown lands. Legislation followed in 1861–2 to control Chinese immigration, to regulate the goldfields, and to abolish the grant of public money in aid of religion. The House sanctioned negotiations with Victoria for an arrangement to remove duties on intercolonial trade across the Murray River. To promote

lementary education, the ministry proposed amalgamation of the
xisting denominational and national school systems. A large majority
n the Assembly carried a bill embodying this principle in 1863, but
t was subsequently lost when the ministry was defeated on another
natter.

In 1861–2 a bill to make the Upper House elective went through
he Assembly but was eventually stifled by opposition in the Council
tself. Cowper and Robertson had nevertheless managed to break the
esistance of conservatives in the Council to their Land Bills in 1861.
And when, in the same year, the original five-year appointments
o this House lapsed as provided in the Constitution Act, they had
eized the opportunity to reconstruct it on a less conservative basis.
Thus, although the Upper House was still a nominated and an in-
lependent body, it no longer had the power to overawe the Assembly
or the ministry and all but liberal extremists were contented with it.
n all, the ministry's various measures embodied the achievement of a
igh proportion of the changes which for years had been demanded
n the name of liberalism, progress and development.

The ministry's strength is well illustrated by the crisis that developed
n 1860–1 when it undertook to have its Land Bills passed. On Fors-
er's resignation early in 1860 the Governor had asked both D. Cooper
nd R. Jones to form ministries before turning to Robertson. Denison
ad at first hoped for a ministry which would bring 'together men
vhose talents and abilities are acknowledged by all, and whose
lifferences have in reality reference more to the detail of measures
han to principles', but both Cooper and Jones failed.[16] On taking
office, Robertson announced that he would give his Land Bills priority
over all other legislation. Since alternative leaders from the opposition
ad been unable to execute the Governor's commission, he could be
onfident that if his measures were defeated in the Assembly he
vould be able to secure a dissolution. The growing popularity of
is land policy had been made evident in the election of 1859; success
t a new election fought on this issue seemed likely, and would
noreover give him an incomparable weapon for forcing land reform
hrough the Upper House.

In October 1860, the Crown Lands Occupation Bill was amended
n the Assembly to remove from it the right of free selection before
urvey over all unimproved Crown land. This, with conditional
purchase (in effect, purchase on terms), was the central reform in
Robertson's scheme. It was intended to destroy some of the advantages
vhich the pastoralists had possessed under the existing land laws.[17]
These advantages, complex and manifold, had aroused a widespread

and heterogeneous movement of protest. Landowners like Cowper
and Robertson themselves had much to lose if the pastoralists man
aged to turn permissive occupation under lease or license, secured
for a nominal investment, into *de facto* ownership. Middle class mer
chants, lawyers, business and professional men—even if they were
not among the favoured few with capital to invest in land—resented
the pastoralists' claim to be the economic backbone of the colony
and found it incompatible with their own vision of New South
Wales as a complex and expanding commercial society. Urban labour
ers and artisans and tenant farmers in the country dreamed that land
reform might make it possible for them to secure farms of their own.
Beyond that, the pastoralists' privileged social position and the
memory of the conservative ideals they had supported early in the
fifties affronted many men who, while having no direct interest in
the land themselves, felt that no class should be favoured over others.
When Robertson's Bill was amended in 1860 in the Assembly, he
sought and obtained a dissolution, and at the subsequent elections
won an overwhelming victory.

Twenty-three of those who had supported Robertson in the third
parliament were returned to the fourth for the loss of seven, while
the late opposition lost twenty-five members and retained only
eleven. Forty per cent of the members returned were new to parliament. In almost all electorates candidates had raised the land question
and had taken a stand for or against 'free selection before survey'.
No other subject was so widely, so precisely or so hotly debated.
The result was as unambiguous as possible in the electoral system of
the day: of the late members only nine were returned who opposed
free selection and at least forty-five were returned who supported it.[18]

The new House swiftly passed the Bills rejected in 1860 and sent
them to the Upper House. There they were amended extensively,
chiefly to limit the effectiveness of the 'free selection' principle. The
Council stood by its amendments when the Assembly insisted that the
Bills be restored to their original shape. Defeat in a quarrel with the
Assembly in 1860[19] had done nothing to abate the Council's in-
transigence: besides holding up the Land Bills, it now rejected a
ministerial customs duties bill and a coalfields and collieries regulation
bill, and balked firmly at an elective Upper House bill. In these circumstances, the ministry advised a 'swamping', to outnumber the
recalcitrant councillors with new appointees, and the Governor
agreed, seeing no alternative in the light of the verdict of the late
election.[20] The appointment of an additional twenty-one councillors
failed technically when the old members of the chamber deprived

it of a quorum by a walk-out which prevented new members being sworn in. But the five-year appointments of existing councillors expired a few days later, and a new Upper House, reconstituted with ministerial advice, passed the Land Bills in the form desired by the Assembly.

Despite its firm handling of this crisis, the ministry went through a period of insecurity in the Assembly late in 1861. Success on the land question did not remove the dissatisfaction of some supporters with certain features of its legislative programme,[21] and the reconstitution of the Council failed to meet the wishes of others.[22] Cowper complained in September of 'the strong indications of restlessness' evident among his supporters, and thought briefly of resigning.[23] But the malcontents were too disorganized and 'too much opposed in principle' to possible allies in the opposition to mount effective censure proceedings, and the ministry was out of danger by the beginning of 1862. In securing himself from this and earlier challenges, Cowper had adroitly employed a variety of the techniques by now well-known to faction leaders anxious to consolidate a majority or to thwart the hostile intentions of defectors and opposition leaders.

Cowper and Robertson had been concerned as early as January 1861 about their position in the House. Their greatest danger then had seemed to come from Parkes, who was clearly becoming an ambitious and capable opponent. In a first effort to weaken Parkes, they tempted Windeyer, one of his closest followers, with an offer of the Solicitor-Generalship, and a warm invitation to join the Victoria Club, over which Robertson presided.[24] The move failed, and Parkes soon added to the conspirators' concern by showing great interest in a plan to attack the ministry on the allegedly unsatisfactory state of the colony's finances.[25] But poverty at this time made Parkes vulnerable, and he accepted the government's offer of a post for a year as lecturer in Britain, at £1,000 p.a., to promote immigration. When he sailed in May, Cowper and Robertson could congratulate themselves on having temporarily removed from political life their most dangerous rival, even though the loyal Windeyer remained to try to hold his supporters together in his absence.[26] The same technique was used again to remove Hoskins, a Cowper supporter who voted for the Land Bills but who broke away from the ministry later in 1861 and sought some public appointment.[27]

The ministry's bill to restrict Chinese immigration and its bill to make the Upper House elective were passed partly in response to the pressure of dissatisfied followers who had threatened to withhold supply if these measures were not brought in.[28] An amendment to the law regarding insolvency was put through the House to meet the dissatisfaction of a number of merchants who had formed a Trade Protection Society to assist creditors recover debts under the old law.[29] A group of members met and demanded that work on the railways west to Bathurst and north to Armidale be pushed ahead at the same speed as the Southern line. In response, the ministry soon found a 'surplus' of £400,000 in the revenue of past years, and proposed an additional estimate of half a million for the railways north and west.[30] Protectionist feeling, which Parkes had attempted to exploit in 1860 and which stirred again in 1861, was temporarily allayed by the appointment of a Select Committee into the State of Manufactures and Agriculture. This Committee took more than a year to report.[31]

Contemporaries who criticized the Cowper-Robertson ministry for its factional character failed to observe that of all the ministries between 1856 and 1863 it alone had provided stable government and a measure of legislative achievement, and that its success had largely rested on the strength of the faction its leaders had established in the Assembly. Neither Donaldson's, Parker's nor Forster's ministry had been based on faction support, deliberately built and carefully maintained. Instead, they had tried to rely on what Donaldson called the 'free and unbought support of the independent representatives',[32] and their ministries were in consequence weaker and far more at the mercy of the Assembly, or of special groups in it, than that of Cowper and Robertson.

None of these other leaders had won a clear following before they took office. They saw their ministries primarily as executive groups obliged to appeal to the House for support; they did not come to office with support largely secured as Cowper and Robertson could. Leadership was given to them on being commissioned to form ministries and much of it was taken from them when they were defeated, as Donaldson recognized by refusing to be considered as the leader of the opposition after his defeat in 1857.[33] Once they had been defeated, their supporters fell apart: by contrast, Cowper and Robertson's following, despite its heterogeneous character and internal tension, remained intact in opposition and was even able to keep its solidarity when Cowper handed over the leadership to Robertson in 1859. The question of importance in 1860 was therefore not whether parties would develop, but whether any other factions would emerge alongside the liberal faction in parliament to compete with it for power.

As early as 1857 some of the independent supporters of Donaldson and Parker had been prompted by the example of a fairly united and efficient opposition to question the value of independence. One of them had explained that he was waiving his independence because of the difficulty of governing by 'party' when members voted on measures without considering the effect of their votes on the fate of the ministry.[34] He was one of the only two steady supporters Donaldson and Parker could claim. A little earlier, James Macarthur had observed that 'only by acting in association with the party whose principles are most conformable with our own' could he and his friends be of political 'weight' and service. The unpredictability of members claiming independence destroyed their 'weight' and made them 'isolated political atoms'.[35] But in fact these reflections made no difference to his, or other independents', voting in the House.

At the end of 1860, the formation of a body called the New South Wales Constitutional Association suggested that other leaders in the Assembly were at last admitting the need of organization of some kind if they were to be an effective force against Cowper and Robertson's faction. After the opposition had amended Robertson's Land Bill, eighteen of its members had met and agreed on further tactics to embarrass the ministry in parliament.[36] The Constitutional Association was formed a fortnight later. Its committee included men who had held office under Donaldson, Parker and Forster, defecting liberals (James Martin being one of them) and members from each section of the opposition, except that headed by Parkes. Its immediate intention was to appeal to gentlemen of 'standing and education' to stand nomination in the forthcoming election and to assist in securing their return to parliament. It professed not to 'prescribe any particular political views' to candidates it assisted,[37] but one of its committee admitted privately that it did demand that they be 'favourable to two Houses of Parliament',[38] while the *Empire* commented dryly that it no doubt selected only those men for support whom it knew were opposed to Robertson's Land Bills.[39]

Little was heard of the Association in the election and it subsequently faded out of existence, destroyed at birth by the tide of 'free selection' sentiment. But the experiment also taught a lesson that was to become increasingly evident: that the electorate would regard with suspicion organizations openly formed to influence elections in the interests of parliamentary leaders. In other words, the constituencies offered no royal road to power. A potential leader had first to win a seat and then build his following in the House by degrees, using the methods Cowper and Robertson had used, and exerting his influence in the electorates only covertly. He had to await the opportunity to overthrow a ministry, if necessary by a stratagem, and once in office to use all the advantages his post gave him to enlarge his nucleus of steady followers and to attract enough additional support to give him a majority.

The Cowper-Robertson ministry fell in 1863 when the Assembly, already dissatisfied with its measures for putting down an outbreak of bushranging, rejected its finance proposals. James Martin now constructed a new ministry, and in doing so, displayed himself as the first leader to succeed in building a new faction in parliament. The political struggles of preceding years provided much of the material from which this faction was constructed. Martin's ministry included a member from each wing of the opposition that had faced Cowper and Robertson in 1861 (Forster and J. B. Wilson), and another member of Forster's old ministry. As he himself favoured tariff reform, Martin won the support of a small group of protectionists who had rebelled against Cowper and Robertson in 1861, and who at that time had probably been followers of Parkes. He obtained further support from members who represented Riverina electorates and were sympathetic to an organization agitating for separation of the area—virtually the western half of New South Wales—as a new colony. Pastoralists were particularly influential in this movement. Cowper had refused to take any steps towards separation when he was in office, so that even while Martin was forming his ministry the separationist leaders turned to him in the hope that he would be less obdurate.[40] Another group of members who supported Martin believed that he might make some provision for state assistance to the clergy,[41] notwithstanding the repeal of State aid a short time before. They hoped that the sale of church and school lands[42] would provide the necessary funds.

Martin failed to satisfy his expectant followers, partly because of his own ineptitude, partly because the ministry was internally divided on some matters of policy, and partly because he did not have enough support in the House. The mercantile community and its friends in parliament were freetraders to a man. Although dissatisfied with Cowper and Robertson's muddled financial administration and disturbed by allegations of a large concealed deficit, they were much more antagonized when Martin and Eagar made financial proposals which were mildly protectionist in character. Their opposition was so strong that within a few weeks of meeting parliament for the first time, the ministry was forced to modify drastically its scheme of duties.[43] Martin failed to win additional temporary support during his first months in office. He could not proceed to satisfy any of the expectant groups supporting him and it was merely a matter of time before his ministry fell. It received the final blow at the elections to the fifth parliament. Martin himself and two of his colleagues were defeated in Sydney by opposition candidates and he suffered further losses elsewhere. Cowper returned to office at the head of the ministry he had led sixteen months before.

Cowper's ministry in 1865 lasted a little under twelve months and its experience showed that as new factions were formed in the House, it was no longer possible to take office and win a majority with the support of one faction alone. Cowper was not unaware of this. Parkes had returned from his lecturing tour of England early in 1863, and was back in parliament in 1864. He opposed both the Martin and the Cowper ministries and was at work building a faction partly by winning old adherents and friends back to his side from other factions,[44] and partly by seeing that political friends were nominated in elections. In a first effort to block this threat, Cowper offered Parkes the post of Inspector-General of Prisons, hoping to tempt him away from politics again. When that move failed, Cowper tried to win Parkes' alliance by offering him the new post, with cabinet rank, of Postmaster-General. Parkes turned that down too.[45] Cowper was beset by ministerial misfortunes during the year. He lost three of his colleagues for private reasons, and then his Treasurer resigned after the House had attacked and rejected his financial proposals. Parkes, after private negotiations with Martin early in 1866, administered the final blow to the ministry and together they took office in its place.

The coalition of Martin and Parkes in 1866 may be taken as the stage in the political history of New South Wales when the faction system was clearly consolidated. No more non-factional ministries were formed until 1877, and then the experiment was brief and unfruitful. This is therefore a suitable point at which to break off our detailed account of the rise and fall of ministries; subsequent developments can conveniently be considered in detail in later chapters and within a different context. Before advancing the story further, it is essential to try to reconstruct what was constantly before the parliamentary leaders themselves: intimate knowledge, seldom committed to paper, of the fluctuating numerical strength of the factions. Without recapturing such knowledge, it is impossible to give depth to an account of the politics of the period. For the story of the sequence of legislation and of governments depends not merely on the inter-

play of interest and attitude; it expresses above all the results of variations in the disposition of factions, and of the leaders' consequent
calculations and manoeuvres.

Accordingly, in what now follows, an attempt is made to analyse
the size and sequence of factions, and to discuss broadly the sources
of cohesion within factions, as well as the general nature of the political
milieu which their operation created. In attempting this analysis, it
is most convenient to consider the period from 1863 to 1887 as a
whole, since the characteristics of faction politics during these years
appear to have remained unchanged, and there is point in noting at
once the complete sequence of factions. To illuminate the analysis,
a brief preliminary résumé of governments after 1866 must be given,
though, as noted above, detailed discussion of this later period is
incorporated in subsequent chapters.

Competition for office between the Cowper-Robertson and the
Martin factions was the main theme of politics in the sixties, though
variations on the theme resulted from the changing alliances linking
these major factions with the minor groups led by Forster and Parkes.
The Martin-Parkes coalition, achieved in 1866, came to an end in
1870, when Martin and Robertson engineered a combination. This
change brought an upheaval in the faction system, from which two
clear factions, led by Parkes and Robertson respectively, emerged
to form the bases for the alternating ministries of the seventies. A
deadlock in the system in 1876 heralded J. S. Farnell's brief attempt
to govern through a non-factional ministry, which in turn paved the
way for a powerful Parkes-Robertson coalition between 1878 and
1883. From a negligible, non-factional opposition, there emerged
towards the end of this period a new combination under Stuart,
Dibbs and Jennings, which restored the multifactionalism of the
House and vied with the remnants of the Parkes and Robertson
groups for power during the mid-eighties. The faction balance over
the whole period provided majorities which in various ways put the
following   ministries in office:

Martin-Parkes ministry, January 1866 to October 1868
Robertson-Cowper ministry, October 1868 to January 1870
Cowper ministry, January 1870 to December 1870
Martin-Robertson ministry, December 1870 to May 1872
Parkes ministry, May 1872 to February 1875
Robertson ministry, February 1875 to March 1877
Parkes ministry, March to August 1877
Robertson ministry, August to December 1877
Farnell ministry, December 1877 to December 1878

Parkes-Robertson ministry, December 1878 to January 1883
Stuart ministry, January 1883 to October 1885
Dibbs ministry, October to December 1885
Robertson ministry, December 1885 to February 1886
Jennings ministry, February 1886 to January 1887
Parkes ministry, January 1887 to January 1889.

For analysis of the factions it is possible to draw on two types of evidence: the reports of members' allegiances and relations with one another, to be found in the press of the day, and in letters, memoirs and debates; and the voting of members during divisions in the House. Evidence of the former type, though scattered and incomplete, is *ipso facto* the more dependable and direct. From such material there is no difficulty in determining that factions existed, and even in tracing occasionally the duration and changes of individual attachments. The problem remains of identifying all members of the factions, and for this degree of completeness it is necessary to turn to an analysis of voting patterns.

The conclusions presented in the tables below rest on a combination of both these types of evidence. Numerous examples of direct statements of politicians' allegiances have been collated: such evidence has been secured, for example, for thirty-six of those who sat in the Assembly between 1863 and 1869, and for sixty-four between 1870 and 1879. Besides throwing important light on the working of the faction system, material of this kind provides us with a valuable check on conclusions drawn from the division analysis. In fact, that analysis permitted the unambiguous classification of a member's allegiance in the great majority of cases, and where independent evidence was available, we found that it always confirmed this classification.

The divisions selected for determining voting patterns encompassed all those on motions which, on the evidence of debates, were thought of by contemporaries as being 'party' questions. Censure motions were obviously of this kind; so too on many occasions were second reading divisions on important bills, especially ministerial bills, divisions on the address-in-reply and on the motions for election of chairmen of committees. Occasionally divisions on procedural questions, or on motions put by leaders in opposition, were contested on strictly party lines, since tactical manoeuvres of this sort constituted a recognized way of testing whether a ministry still had the support of the majority. The selected divisions were recorded in full, and the voting patterns of the faction leaders were observed. The voting on censure and 'party' motions shows that the votes of leaders in office and in opposition were always opposed and that the ministers of the day always voted with the Premier in any matter of importance to the ministry as a whole. The principle of collective responsibility was so well established from 1856 onwards that any division in which ministers disagreed—a very rare occurrence—could be safely excluded at this point from the list of selected divisions as unimportant. Other members whose patterns were the same as the leaders' were taken to belong to one or other of the factions on the appropriate side of the House. The erratic voting of a member, so that he gave as many decisions to one side as to the other, was taken to indicate independence, unless all his votes were at first one way and then the other, in which case he was considered to be in process of changing his allegiance. Members whose votes diverged from one or other of the leaders' patterns by more than one vote in ten or more divisions were regarded as unsteady supporters.

This procedure reveals only the patterns of ministerial and opposition voting if the selected divisions fall within a brief period and during the life of one ministry. But as soon as the list of divisions is extended over a period long enough to encompass several ministries composed of different coalitions of factions, it becomes possible to distinguish the voting patterns of individual faction leaders and their followers. For example: Forster voted steadily with Martin while he was in Martin's ministry in 1863–4, and went into opposition steadily against Cowper when the latter took office in 1865. When Martin assumed power in conjunction with Parkes in 1866, Forster stayed in opposition, voting now with Robertson and Cowper. Parkes' voting pattern shows the same distinct features, *mutatis mutandis*. The fact that over these years Cowper and Martin each had other steady followers whose voting pattern was the same as their leaders' and distinct from one another, permits us to conclude that the members whose voting patterns were the same as those of Forster and Parkes were members of their factions. The voting patterns of those whose allegiances are directly attested by independent evidence establish this inference beyond question, besides providing a check upon the accuracy of the method of analysing the voting.

Once the patterns for faction leaders are established, it is possible to turn back to any parliament or session to determine the allegiances of most of the members at any given time, taking more divisions if necessary. From the analysis of voting over long periods, supplemented by detailed analysis of the House at times of major upheaval, it is possible to construct tables of ministerial, opposition and independent strength (Table 1) and to indicate with some confidence the

Ministerial and opposition strength, as a percentage of the total membership of the Assembly in each parliament between 1863 and 1887, when stable ministries were in power[46]

C-R – indicates Cowper-Robertson faction
M&F – indicates Martin and Forster coalition
P&M – indicates Parkes and Martin coalition
P&R – indicates Parkes and Robertson coalition
D-J – indicates Dibbs-Jennings faction

Parliament	4		5			6		7	8	9	10	11	12
Year	1863–4	1864	1865–6	1866–9	1869	1870–1	1871–2	1872–4	1875–7	1879–80	1880–2	1883–5	1885–7
Session	4	5	1–2	3–5	6	1–2	3	1–4	1–3	3	1–3	1–6	1–2
Faction(s) in office	C-R	M&F	C-R	P&M	C-R&F	C-R&F	M&R	P	R	P&R	P&R	D-J	D-J
Ministerial %	34	27	40	41	38½	38	28	44	31–29	28½	51½	33½	32
Opposition %	27	35	40	39	41½	36½	32	14½	31–33	6	15½	19	23
Opposing factions	M,F	C-R	P,M,F	C-R,F	P,M	P,M	P,F	R	P	'Third Party'	'Third Party' (later D-J)	P&R	P
Independents and unsteady %	30	28	18	17½	17	18	26	27	28	31 (independ.) 22 (unsteady)	23	34	15
Changers %	–	–	–	–	–	–	1	6	2½	–	–	6	25
Unknown %	9	10	2	2½	3	7½	13	8½	7	12½	10	7½	5

Note: Independents include 'unsteady' supporters of ministerial and opposition leaders, unsteady in voting in two or more divisions when compared with their leaders but conforming generally to one or other of the leaders' voting patterns. In parliaments 4, 5, 6, approximately 50 per cent were independents, and 50 per cent 'unsteady' divided equally between both sides of the House. In parliaments 7, 8, 10, only 5 per cent were 'unsteady'; in parliaments 11, 12, about 10 per cent. Members who did not serve the full term of a parliament are counted as having in fact done so: small inaccuracies are thus imported into the table, but these are well within the limits of accuracy of the method of analysis as a whole. Note that when a particular balance of faction strengths is referred to in the text it has been taken from the original analysis for the time in question, and therefore represents the real situation at that point.

faction composition of the majorities and minorities (Table 2). The method is not entirely free of shortcomings, the chief being that the distinction between 'steady' and 'unsteady' supporter is to some extent arbitrary. However, the estimates of faction strengths obtained on the definition assumed above agree well with occasional surviving estimates made contemporaneously by leaders. Again, a number of members in each parliament held seats for only brief periods or were absent from many of the divisions selected, and their voting patterns cannot be determined with confidence, though the importance of such men was undoubtedly reduced by the small part they played in the voting. Further, by determining members' allegiances in terms of support for or opposition to a ministry, the 'opposition' is given an appearance of solidarity which it seldom had. But this defect in the voting analysis can be readily corrected by judicious use of the independent evidence. Such evidence also justifies the assumption built into the method of analysis: that support for a ministry and the internal cohesion of a faction were based partly on the desire for office and the benefits that could be obtained from holding it.

No faction, and only one coalition of factions, Parkes' and Robertson's in 1880–2, constituted a majority of the House between 1863 and 1887. The opposing factions were almost as strong numerically as the combination in office which, to stay in power, had always to win some support from independents and unsteady members. The relative strengths of the faction combinations are indicated in Table 1.

The relative strength of the opposition, as shown in this table, is misleading in one respect. Two or more factions in opposition were not necessarily in alliance, as the factions supporting a coalition ministry always were. The numerical strength of individual factions must therefore be shown in a separate table. The strength of individual factions cannot be estimated with the same confidence as can that of combined factions supporting or opposing a ministry. The possible inaccuracies of the division analysis method are magnified when dealing with smaller numbers of men. Further, it is sometimes impossible to determine which of two leaders a member supported steadily when they were in coalition or in opposition together, or whether his support was given them only because they were in coalition and balancing one another. It was, for example, the destruction of such a balance, between two 'great chiefs' each backed by two 'great political parties', which led several members to withdraw their steady support from the Martin-Parkes ministry in 1868 when Parkes resigned from it. With these qualifications the size of individual factions may be indicated as in Table 2.

Once the legislature had become multifactional, the leaders had to compete with one another not only for the support of new members and independents, but for each other's followers as well. This struggle to win supporters from opponents and from among hitherto uncommitted members made the boundaries of factions vague and uncertain. A leader in office could never count on all his erstwhile supporters following him into opposition after a defeat. There were always a few members prepared to support any government steadily as long as it did not offend them and others whose adherence could be secured, at least temporarily, by a leader who could grant local favours to their electorates or give them other advantages. A member who had been a strong adherent of one ministry might therefore be found giving equally steady support to its successor even though the new ministry drew its main strength from the opponents of the old. Over a period of several ministries, these members could be and were considered as independents, but during the time they gave steady support to a particular leader they were commonly considered as members of his faction, at least for immediate practical purposes. There was always the possibility that they might become permanently attached to him, and in any case, they differed quite markedly from the other type of member, also described as independent, who voted in what was from a ministry's point of view a random fashion. In between lay the members who gave a ministry unsteady support, and the boundary of the faction must be set at the point where steady, if possibly detachable, support passes over into unsteady support and beyond that into independence. The calculation of faction strength is therefore bound to be marginally inaccurate and open to dispute, but the distinctions drawn so far have the merit of being distinctions made contemporaneously by faction leaders and informed commentators, and of showing not only the dimensions but also the character of ministerial strength at any given time. A ministry's majority was normally composed, once the Assembly had become multifactional, of an alliance of two such factions which together gave it most of its support, and a much smaller number of unsteady supporters and independents whose votes changed unpredictably. The actions of such men were not concerted and a ministry could therefore count on always receiving shifting support from their ranks, although it knew that if it did something to antagonize them all it might well be in jeopardy. Opposition manoeuvres and stratagems were commonly directed at discrediting a ministry with these and other more steady members.

At the other extreme there were members whose loyalty to a leader

TABLE 2

The numerical strength of factions 1863 to 1886
(a) 1863–1870

Parliament	4		5		6	
Year	1863-4	1865	1866	1867-8	1869	1870
Ministry	Martin & Forster	Cowper-Robertson	Martin & Parkes	Martin & Parkes	C-R & Forster	C-R & Forster
Steady supporters of						
Cowper & Robertson[a]	25	29	25	23	24	28
Martin	16	11	15	17	17	16[b]
Parkes	1	13	14	12	12	9[b]
Forster	4	4	4	4	3	2
Other members						
unsteady C-R	5	2	1	2	1	5
unsteady M	5	2	3	5	6	2
independent	12	8	8	6	5	7
undetermined	6	1	1	1	2	6

[a] Including in each case the leader(s) of the factions.

[b] Four additional members were in effect steady supporters of Martin and Parkes in opposition, but the data will not permit clear distinction of any of them as either Parkes or Martin men. Here the total number of Martin-Parkes followers was in reality 29.

TABLE 2 (continued)

(b) 1870–1886

Parliament	6	6	7	8	9 (sess. 3)	10	11	12
Year	1870	1871	1872–5	1875–7	1879–80	1880–2	1883–5	1885–7
Ministry	C-R & Forster	Martin & Robertson	Parkes	Robertson	Parkes & Robertson	Parkes & Robertson	Stuart	Dibbs Jennings
Steady supporters of								
Parkes	9[a]	12	35[b]	26	–	–	10	10
Robertson	–	4[c]	9	26	–	–	2	1
Parkes & Robertson	–	–	–	–	24	63	12	18
Cowper-Robertson	28	–	–	–	–	–	–	–
Martin	16	11	–	–	–	–	–	–
Stuart-Dibbs Jennings	–	–	–	–	–	–	42	40
Steady opponents of[d]								
Martin & Robertson	–	12	–	–	–	–	–	–
Parkes	–	–	1	–	–	–	–	–
Parkes & Robertson	–	–	–	–	5	19	–	–
Unsteady opponents of ministry	–	–	–	–	10	–	–	–
Unsteady supporters	C-R5 / M2	M1	P2 / R2	P2 / R1	PR9	PR7	PR2 / DJ10	PR2 / DJ9[e]
Independents	7	10	17	20	26	21	31	8
Undetermined	6	10	7	6	10	12	9	6
Changing allegiance[f]	–	–	5	2	–	–	8	32[g]

[a] Plus 1 or more up to 4 who were steady supporters of either Parkes, or Martin or both.

[b] Probably includes some who had been and would again become independents.

[c] Plus 1 or more up to 6 who were steady supporters of either Robertson or Martin or both.

[d] These being members who did not align themselves with a faction leader in opposition.

[e] Includes 4 who voted to a distinct pattern the same as Reid's and 3 who voted to a distinct pattern the same as See's, both of whom were unsteady in support of D.-J.

[f] Those who having voted steadily by one pattern changed suddenly to vote steadily by another pattern, e.g. 3 from Parkes to Robertson in 1872-5.

[g] Of whom 15 were independents joining either Dibbs-Jennings or Parkes, while 11 left either Parkes or Robertson for Dibbs-Jennings.

was unswerving over long periods, in good times and bad, and these men made up the cores or nuclei of the factions. The type can be best appreciated by noting as an instance the case of William Walker, a solicitor of Windsor. Walker had been sympathetic to Cowper in the fifties, but Cowper's continued association with Robertson in 1858–9 antagonized him, especially when it became clear that Cowper's ministry would be forced to accept Robertson's views on land legislation. Walker came into parliament in 1860 as a supporter of James Martin. He had known Martin as a young man and had 'watched and admired his career as a lawyer and legislator',[47] before joining him in parliament. In the next ten years Walker gave Martin his steady support, while Martin was in and out of office twice, first in coalition with Forster and then with Parkes. Walker's allegiance to Martin had a complex basis. There were cases where personal devotion at the faction core expressed chiefly a selfish hope of riding to power through consistent support of a leader, but this was one ambition Walker did not have. Like other members who believed in the political sagacity of their leader, he had a genuine conviction that the good of the colony would be best served if Martin were in office. To help put him there Walker was prepared to offer steady support. He believed Martin 'to be the ablest and most upright man in the House' and to hold 'political principles more in accordance with my own than were those of his opponents'.[48] Martin's political principles were 'Liberal-Conservative', that is,

> he would uphold all that was good and valuable in the state as it existed, whilst he would grant reasonable reforms, and allow the utmost liberty compatible with order and good government.[49]

In practice this meant, for example, that Walker and Martin agreed on land legislation in 1867 to improve the position of the pastoralists, while requiring of them increased rentals in return. Though at the cost of some local support, Walker was firm in his approval of Martin's Bill:

> he proposed to make the squatters pay more for their runs, giving them in return, greater fixity of tenure and other advantages. Through my voting for it, however, it lost me the support of a number of my influential squatting friends at Richmond.[50]

Walker and Martin also had a common local origin, mutual friends and a similar status in local society. Walker by his own admission[51] was of the 'élite' of Windsor, while Martin had been for many years an intimate and protégé of Robert Fitzgerald, one of the most influential pastoralists in the electorate. Professional ties and respect reinforced Walker's personal admiration for Martin, and a shared political life in the House undoubtedly strengthened it further as the years went on. The two most important local boons which Walker secured from his parliamentary service were the Windsor-Richmond branch railway, provision for which was made by the Cowper-Robertson ministry in 1861[52] at a time when Martin's political power was not yet established, and a bridge over the Hawkesbury river at Windsor. The bridge was promised in 1864 during Martin's first administration and was put on the estimates in 1866 in his second and defeated in the House, before being secured in 1871 when Martin was a third time in office.[53]

Respect such as that felt by Walker for Martin must be judged as one of the most important ties holding steady supporters of a faction together. Humbler followers were sometimes prepared to vindicate their respect by even giving up their own seats to a leader should political misfortune overtake him in his home constituency. Parkes and Robertson, each defeated in the election of 1877, received many such offers, the spirit prompting their authors being well reflected in an ingenuous letter Parkes received from one admirer in Maitland:

> It is reported hear [*sic*] and many people believe it that Mr. Dalley will beat you in East Sydney this I do not believe but if so I will make way by resigning at once the representing of East Maitland for the country wants you and your best services.[54]

Closer to the heart of the faction, time and the experience of working together often mellowed such respect into affection. Robertson was well loved by a little circle of intimates,[55] and surviving letters in the Parkes Correspondence abound in spontaneous expressions of attachment. G. A. Lloyd, for instance, shattered in 1877 at the news that his leader had been defeated in East Sydney, wrote: 'Poor miserable deluded Sydney, to prefer Macintosh to Parkes. All the gas is taken out of me . . . I was congratulating myself on the prospect of success here [Newcastle], but I do not care a fig to go in now'.[56] For many years J. G. L. Innes, who first served Parkes as a minister in 1872, invariably addressed him as 'my Dear old Chief'. In 1881, on the eve of a ministerial dinner, he heard that Parkes was ill, and wrote in alarm:

> Without you, a ministerial Anniversary dinner with me for host would be a fiasco. For are you not my one chief? I am the only one of the present team who was with you in '72 when you for the first time took your proper place as Prime Minister—first and foremost—*facile princeps*—and unless you sit on my right hand on Monday I shall be miserable.[57]

Respect had sometimes to withstand severe testing when the exigencies of the faction struggle tempted leaders into its blatant exploitation. On such occasions other elements of attachment—expectation of favours to come, ideological incompatibility with alternative leaders, the desire to preserve one's own political image—could come into play to help the allegiance survive a damaged personal relationship.

Parkes' dealings with Windeyer between 1866 and 1868 offer an apt example. The two had a close personal friendship stretching back into the fifties and Windeyer had given Parkes political support at least from 1860 onwards. But in 1866 their association was strained when Parkes used what Windeyer regarded as a shabby trick to increase his parliamentary strength. At the time, Parkes was deep in negotiations with Martin about the formation of their coalition ministry. A ministerial reshuffle in the Cowper cabinet forced Robertson to stand for re-election in West Sydney, and the by-election offered Parkes the opportunity of defeating Robertson if a good man could be found to contest the seat. Success in this enterprise would at once weaken Parkes' opponents, add to his own strength in the House, and improve his bargaining position with Martin.

From Parkes' point of view, Windeyer could not be bettered as the man to oppose Robertson. He had been out of parliament for three years, and his reputation as a liberal had been untarnished by any open traffic with political leaders during that time. He belonged to an established family of high repute in the Hunter Valley, where Parkes' political influence was considerable, and he had taken a prominent part in the public life of Sydney as well. He had built up a sound reputation as a barrister since 1857, so that Parkes could contemplate the possibility of his appointment as Solicitor-General in the projected coalition ministry. Parkes thus advanced Windeyer as his candidate against Robertson, informed him that he would be nominated, and arranged for the friends of the faction in the electorate to carry out the campaign. Though Windeyer refused to stand, and even sent a telegram to the *Sydney Morning Herald* stating that 'if elected for West Sydney he would not take his seat', Parkes' agents persisted with the candidacy and he was elected. Windeyer complained bluntly to Parkes that 'no man can make or keep a public character who lets his name be used by others', but by this time the new ministry had been formed and Parkes relentlessly manoeuvred him into a position where he could not refuse to take the seat.[58] Throughout 1866 Windeyer supported Parkes faithfully, although he did not take office.

When Parkes resigned from the ministry in 1868, Windeyer joined

Robertson, the opposition leader, in attacking it, even though it still included two Parkes men, Tighe and Byrnes. Windeyer's assault was made on the ground that Martin could no longer expect the support of members who desired 'practical legislation' and who believed that this could best be secured from a ministry in which the liberal and conservative tendencies of two 'great chiefs' and their supporters counterbalanced one another.[59] In effect, Windeyer made it clear that some of the ministry's steady supporters had sought material benefits and were not primarily interested in liberal or conservative principles except when conflict of beliefs might prevent them getting what they wanted.

Windeyer's public criticism of the ministry was frank enough. In private he was far more outspoken. He wrote to Parkes attacking him and his ministerial colleagues for having neglected his wishes. He reminded Parkes that he had unwillingly taken his seat in 1866 and that he had suffered 'pecuniary loss and professional disadvantage' from holding it. He had consistently offered the ministry 'a warm and generous support, in doubtful cases always giving them the benefit of the doubt'. The coalition, 'then regarded somewhat doubtfully', had benefited from the support of a man whose 'adherence to liberal politics' was unquestioned. He told Parkes that he had 'no relation or intimate private friends to serve' and 'no . . . constituency constantly pressing local demands' as other members had. Yet

> when I did wish to help any one of whose claims I was convinced, I never had those wishes gratified . . . I would not submit myself to the indignity and humiliation of further neglect at the hands of yourself and your colleagues. Mr. Redgate whom you may remember as a warm supporter of us both in past elections for the City,[60] is one to whom I have felt compelled with pain to say this. There are others . . .[61]

Windeyer went on to point out that Parkes had 'served' others, even at Windeyer's expense, and acidly implied that although Parkes could make 'the unique boast that [he] had never served a friend' to put his vaunted patriotism above public suspicion, this was not to say that he had never served anybody.[62]

The complex features of Walker's attachment to Martin, and of Windeyer's to Parkes, were characteristic of allegiances throughout the factions, though at the outer limits the direct bonds between the leader and his followers tended to be fewer in number and weakened by obligations and antipathies to other groups or leaders in the House. The knot of consistent followers at the core of the faction could usually be relied on as a nucleus from which, when the occasion presented itself, a government could be constructed and around which a parliamentary majority could be organized. Some idea of the size and function of such a faction core, and of its importance as a point of stability in the parliamentary flux can be gained by considering one example: the Cowper-Robertson faction as it stood in 1870, shortly before the Cowper ministry resigned.

After his defeat in the House in November Cowper called a meeting of the faction by circular. He announced to his assembled supporters his acceptance of the office of Agent-General in London, and placed before them two questions for discussion: the remoter issue of the succession to the leadership, and the immediate problem of determining the course which the government should take. The meeting possibly left the subject of a new leader undetermined, but it decided that the ministry should resign after securing a month's supply and the temporary continuation of the Stamp Duties Act.[63] This course was subsequently followed. Thirty-one members attended the meeting, and two others sent apologies. It is instructive to note the composition of this group of politicians.

Twenty-two of the thirty-one at the meeting had been regular supporters of Cowper and Robertson in the sixth parliament, but six other steady supporters during the year were absent or no longer in the House. These twenty-eight men may be identified as the members of the faction. The remaining members at the meeting consisted of the three men in parliament who had given the ministry unsteady support during the session;[64] a follower of Parkes from 1865 to 1869 who was in the process of changing his allegiance in 1870;[65] the leader of the old fourth faction, Forster, who had recently resigned from the ministry, and his remaining follower, Macleay; the independents, Osborne and J. T. Ryan; and P. A. Jennings whose position cannot be determined because he voted so seldom in the session. Two other independents[66] who had given more support than opposition to the ministry did not attend the meeting. The combined strength of Martin and Parkes and their followers in opposition during the session was thirty-one, and Cowper and Robertson therefore had to secure support from some of these eleven men whose political backgrounds were diverse and who did not belong to their faction. The ministry's recent loss of three steady supporters made this non-factional support even more important to them than it had been.

The members of the faction itself fell into two distinct groups: a core, numbering sixteen[67] (with the two leaders themselves), and the remaining twelve,[68] a less closely integrated group of men who had not yet served a year in parliament. Those in the core of the faction had been steady supporters of Cowper and Robertson for periods of between six and eleven years, during which time the leaders had been out of office twice, and subject to the inroads Parkes had made on the faction when building his own strength in 1865–6. All the ministers in the Lower House—Cowper, Robertson, Egan, Samuel and Sutherland—were drawn from this core. Some of the less experienced members could possibly have been at the core of the faction, though this seems extremely unlikely, since none of them were either ministers or politically prominent at the time.

The strength of a faction at any given time most obviously depended on its size and on the degree of its cohesion, primarily at the core, and thence throughout the more extended membership. But effective factions were not only close-knit; they tended also to be

TABLE 3

Heterogeneity and representativeness of four factions in the sixties and seventies, as determined by the occupations of their members in comparison with the composition of the whole House

	Pastoral %	Mercantile %	Professional %	Miscellaneous and unknown %
Fourth parliament				
All members	31	20	31	18
C-R faction	28	31	30	11
Martin faction	20	20	44	16
Fifth parliament				
All members	34	25	18	23
C-R faction	30	30	25	15
Martin faction	25	30	33	12
Sixth parliament				
All members	28	26	25	21
C-R faction	21	34	31	14
Martin faction	10	30	35	25
Eighth parliament				
All members	26	27	23	24
Robertson faction	44	24	12	20
Parkes faction	12	34	31	23
Other members	25	22	25	28

heterogeneous in their composition, at least if one can judge by members' occupations. On this test, the Martin and Cowper factions in the sixties and the Parkes and Robertson factions in the seventies were all heterogeneous: the Martin and Cowper-Robertson factions were also heterogeneous when judged by the character of the electorates which their members represented.[69] Drawing members from each of the main occupational classes in the House, these established factions could in fact usually be said to have been roughly representative of the House as a whole.

TABLE 4

Percentage of seats held in each type of electorate by members of the Martin and Cowper-Robertson factions in parliaments of the sixties

	Parliaments		
	4	5	6
Agricultural electorates	%	%	%
Of all members	50	–	52·7
C-R faction	55	40·5	50
Martin faction	40	64	52
Pastoral electorates			
Of all members	12·5	–	8·3
C-R faction	10	8	16·5
Martin faction	10	12	4
Urban electorates			
Of all members	27·7	–	27·7
C-R faction	29	40·5	16·5
Martin faction	30	12	30·5
Other electorates (mixed agric., pastoral & goldfields)			
Of all members	9·7	–	11·1
C-R faction	6·5	11	16·5
Martin faction	20	12	13

It is perhaps not surprising that factions showed these characteristics. For one thing, the chief methods employed by faction leaders to win and hold power in the Assembly—manoeuvre and intrigue—were directed towards the construction of *personal* followings, and not groups narrowly based on common occupational, economic, or other material interests. In the shifting milieu of faction politics, no leader could neglect the hope of securing support in any possible quarter. Besides that, experience soon demonstrated that a group of members seeking to advance a single interest could never hope to win a majority in the Assembly. Pressure groups of this sort indeed came and went, but faction loyalties cut across them, and their only hope of securing favourable treatment was to come to terms with the factions, not to oppose them by operating as outright contenders for power.

In these circumstances, heterogeneity and representativeness were positive sources of strength to the factions themselves. They constituted, in effect, an assurance to members that individual leaders were experienced in the art of meeting requests. For the steady supporter this meant that continued allegiance would probably not be futile. For the uncommitted member it gave some indication of where he might place his support with the most hope of satisfaction. And since independent and unclassified members represented electorates of all types and were to be found among each of the occupation groups in the House, no clear divisions of occupation or interest in practice separated them from those members who had joined the factions. In the absence of such barriers, these men were constantly open to the wooing—even if only for temporary purposes—of the faction leaders.

Given their heterogeneity and the variable range of loyalty evident from their nuclei to their outer perimeters, it is not surprising that factions sought further strength through consultation and the use of rudimentary forms of organization to promote joint action. For while the members at the core of the faction were probably in close personal touch, more deliberate arrangements were often indispensable if the larger group with its fringe of unsteady supporters and sympathetic members was to operate with most effect in the House. Cowper, when in opposition while the Assembly was closely divided in 1856–7, had recognized the advantages to be gained from consultation with his followers, but he and Robertson seem to have been more reluctant to adopt this course once they came into office, at least until the crisis of 1860.[70] By the sixties, however, groups supporting ministries as well as groups in opposition commonly held meetings. Between 1856 and 1887 at least forty such gatherings of members took place. They were referred to as caucus meetings as early as 1877.[71]

Most of these meetings were held at times of ministerial crisis, and by 1870 it had become so much a matter of course that a leader should consult his followers on such occasions that a failure to do so gave rise to bitter reproaches and even to charges of betraying the 'faith' his 'party' had given him.[72] The composition of a projected ministry was occasionally considered at such meetings, though there is no evidence that these discussions tied the hands of a leader about to take the premiership. The members—whether on the government or opposition benches—most commonly met during a crisis to consider the parliamentary tactics they would pursue. Direct attacks upon a ministry were rarely unplanned or carried out simply on the initiative of the leader. Opposition members normally met to draft the motion of censure and to appoint one of their number to move it in the House. More permanent arrangements, particularly for leadership, could also be made in this way.

Early in 1877, for example, after Parkes had resigned leadership of the opposition, its members elected Piddington in his place and promised him steady support.[73] Formal election at a meeting outside the chamber was necessary to convert the most obvious opposition spokesman into a 'properly constituted leader', though only when the opposition was non-factional and disunited. An elected leader in fact stood little chance of survival against the manoeuvres of an ambitious faction leader in the opposition. In order to forestall Parkes, Forster was elected leader of the opposition in 1872 and appointed to move the motion of censure on which the Martin-Robertson ministry was defeated.[74] But within a few months Parkes had prevented Forster forming a ministry and had succeeded in doing so himself. Again, in 1877, Parkes managed in less than a year to displace Piddington, the leader whom the opposition had elected, and within a few months to form a ministry which included him.[75]

The leadership was seldom discussed at meetings of the opposition when its dominant component was a faction. The consideration of parliamentary tactics at a meeting of this type was primarily designed to let the leader test the solidarity of his following and their opinions, and to inform them how they should vote in what might be a devious manoeuvre. At one such meeting in 1872,[76] Parkes had his followers appoint a subcommittee nominally to draft a censure motion, and they then formally adopted it and appointed him to move it. But he himself had drawn up the motion in subcommittee.

Ministerial meetings at which tactics were discussed had essentially the same characteristics.[77] They were chiefly occasions on which the the leaders sought approval of and support for a course of action that had been framed in cabinet. But it seems likely that occasionally in the face of a crisis, a ministry waited to find out whether supporters were prepared to follow them steadily before deciding whether to resign, advise a dissolution or try to continue in office.[78] And at other meetings held in less threatening circumstances followers did undoubtedly make their views known on matters of policy, exercising what was in effect a negative influence in the formulation of government proposals. A meeting of dissident followers of Cowper and Robertson in 1861 demanded specified legislation from the ministry which then attempted to meet their wishes in the next two years.[79] In 1868, after Parkes had resigned from the Martin ministry, some of Martin's supporters had planned to insist that the ministry be reconstructed to effect removal of Parkes' followers, Byrnes and Wilson, but Martin's resignation forestalled the proposal.[80] In 1871 Martin met some of his supporters who felt that they should be consulted about the composition of his projected ministry.[81] In 1884, some '48 or 50' supporters of the Stuart ministry met and forced the Treasurer, Dibbs, to give up his plan for imposing direct taxation by threatening to withdraw their support. Although one member at the meeting said that no minister was present and that no message had been sent to the ministry, another announced that a 'clear indication' had been given to the government that they would not 'carry a solitary proposal in their scheme of taxation until it had been considerably modified'.[82]

But discussion of policy and of the composition of ministries was exceptional. The meetings were primarily tactical instruments intended to give the parliamentary groups greater efficiency and solidarity in their manoeuvres. Their timing and composition were determined by the changing position in parliament, and their organization was so rudimentary that it gave the leaders no disciplinary powers over those who attended. The commitment of members to the decisions of a meeting was moral; direct coercion of those who deviated was out of the question. Like the dinners and picnics at which leaders entertained supporters, the meetings were occasions of mild persuasion, probably the more important because leaders had no organizational powers of discipline over their followers.

The emergence of clear cut factions was accompanied by—and in one sense expressed—the final breakdown of the 'liberalism' of the early fifties as a coherent political creed. As long as the character of the political system itself was the main subject of debate both liberals and conservatives could draw to some extent on English political thought. The result was that the liberal-conservative debate gave, as we have seen, some ideological content to divisions in the first parliament though even then men mattered more than principles and the liberals had often been divided over the precise implications of the faith to which they all paid lip service.

However, the very achievement by 1861 of their first major objectives, in the face of ineffective conservative opposition, left the liberals facing the responsibilities of power in an environment to which English liberal thought was inappropriate. A set of demands and of vague attitudes of enthusiasm for progress and development in the context of free trade survived among them. But these demands and attitudes could only be transformed into a distinct ideology by painful rethinking under the spur of successful and principled opposition, neither of which was forthcoming. For a brief span a few idealists thought that a refurbished liberalism might yet survive in changed circumstances: Parkes, for instance, dreamed of using the *Empire* as a lever to create a great new liberal party, 'an independent power to revivify, elevate and direct the political life of the country'.[83] But his bankruptcy in 1858 took the *Empire* out of Parkes' hands, and, abandoning the search for a new liberalism, he soon gave himself up to the internecine struggle for power that was producing the first factional offshoots from the uneasy ranks of the Cowper-Robertson faction.

Though doomed as a crisp political philosophy, 'liberalism' nevertheless survived in an attenuated form to provide a broad ethos which set the tone for politics in New South Wales until the late eighties. The name 'liberal' as used in the Assembly after 1860 did not denote a man committed to a closely defined set of policies or identifiable as a member of a single parliamentary group. The label referred rather to an attitude of mind that sought the welfare of the *whole* community and not of a section of it, and that rested its faith in the capacity of men of good will, uncommitted to the advancement of special interests, to find objectively beneficial solutions to all legislative problems through the untrammelled interplay of opinion. The ideal was vague, and commitment to it was personal or individual. It was common, indeed, for members to speak of a 'liberal party' that transcended the normal faction divisions which underlay the struggle for power, and, in seeking to explain what they meant, to demonstrate their 'liberalism' by approval of what 'liberals' had done in the past. In 1882, for instance, from the floor of the House and amid murmurs of general approval, a leading politician expressed the ideal when speaking of the opposing leaders of the time, Parkes and Robertson:

The two honourable gentlemen, though personally opposed, have voted for almost all the great measures which have been passed in this country. They have voted for a Lands Act, a Public Instruction Act, an Influx of Chinese Restriction Act and all the great measures which have distinguished the Liberal Party. They have voted together, although they have sat on opposite sides of the House.[84].

The appeal to the past was not without its point. For however vague, the new liberal ethos was—at least in the practical corollaries deduced from it—an extension of the central assumption of the liberal creed of the fifties. Behind the more precise liberal policies of that era had lain a basic determination that responsible government had to be made to work efficiently and promote the general prosperity. Translated into terms appropriate to the shifting politics of faction, this determination now emerged in two corollaries which were taken as essential to true liberalism: that the overriding objective of all politicians must be to secure 'good government', and that both 'good government' and just legislation required of the individual member a degree of independence which would permit him to judge ministries and measures on their intrinsic merits.

'Good government' was itself a phrase often equated with liberalism. It had a legislative aspect ('good government', for instance, could be appealed to as a sanction against measures allegedly designed to assist sectional interests), but it was most relevant to administration. The state had many-sided business and service functions, and it was theoretically essential that these should be carried out with efficiency, economy and freedom from corruption. 'Good government,' in this sense was a natural political ideal in a colony where a large measure of governmental activity in the economic life of the community was accepted as proper, and where politicians represented pre-eminently those groups with a 'stake in the country'. It was a principle which could in practice be used by a member either to justify steady support of a faction leader likely to guarantee 'good government' or to justify independence of faction when the latter, by importing 'irrelevant' complications into politics, threatened to disrupt smoothness and continuity in administration.[85]

Though usually taken as an essential part of liberalism, 'independence' was also a principle deeply ingrained in the colony's political tradition. It had been appealed to, for example, in 1856 by conservatives who refused even to canvass in elections, and who felt that 'party' action by liberals was threatening to introduce ways foreign to the colony. Then and subsequently liberals had resented this charge: they claimed to be second to none in their adulation of independence. The member, it was claimed, should judge all measures on their merits, his standard being the public interest. If he allowed his vote to be influenced by his constituents, by the solicitations of interest groups or by pressure from a ministry anxious about its fate, it was to be presumed that the public interest and good government of the colony had been sacrificed to special and selfish interests until he had proved otherwise. A member should therefore always be independent in his relations with other members, the ministry, his constituents and groups or organizations external to parliament.

Such extreme ideal independence might have resulted in a chaotically unstructured Assembly, but in the classical theory it was, supposedly, asserted only within limits defined by competing bodies of party principles. The member, believing in one or another set of principles, would therefore find that his own independent judgment led him to act in combination with other members, without the need for any mechanical or organizational inducements to do so. Any administration formed on the basis of such support would mature comprehensive and long-term policies for the promotion of the public interest. It would withstand the importunings of the needy and the pressures of special and local interests, each of which, if unchecked, would tend to destroy the integrity and consistency of any policy and reduce ministries to subservience to the the legislature. It was not supposed that special and local interests had no place in the scheme of parliamentary government or that parties were animated by their principles alone. Interests secured representation through parties and it was even assumed on occasion that parties were themselves based in the class divisions of the society.[86] Party was certainly of vital importance. Particular interests were related to the general welfare and both were brought into a harmonious synthesis with fundamental principles by its alchemy. The result, it was assumed, would be two parties distinguished by two stable bodies of thought and policy, the one conservative and the other liberal or progressive.

The unreality of the assumption that such parties would develop in New South Wales had been amply demonstrated by 1861, with the disintegration of political conservatism and the fading away of liberalism as a coherent basis for party action in parliament. But contemporaries seldom wondered on these grounds whether the ideal of independence was inappropriate to the colony. Rather, observing the development of factions as the alternative form of political grouping, they simply condemned these factions out of hand. And forgetful even of Burke's observation that he could not understand how men could proceed in politics without any 'connection' at all,[87] they gave 'independence' a special theoretical significance as the antidote to the evils of factionalism. Martineau, writing from Australia to the *Spectator* in 1867, summed up the general attitude:

> Factious opposition . . . based . . . on no sort of political principle . . . cohering merely with the selfish and almost avowed object of seizing an opportunity for ousting Ministers . . . is a serious impediment to good and honest Government. It is always on the watch to catch any passing breeze of popular clamour as a means of tripping up the Government, and the Government is in self-defence obliged to be equally amenable and subservient. When the administration appears strong and seems likely to remain in [office], the Members of the House crowd their ranks for the sake of the loaves and fishes; and the opposition is left scarcely strong enough to exercise legitimate control over the expenditure. But when the loaves and fishes are nearly all gone, and especially if there is any suspicion of ministerial insecurity, there comes a serious defection from their supporters.[88]

The *Sydney Morning Herald,* always contemptuous of faction politics, argued that in the absence of parties, independence was the only honest and public spirited stand a member could take:

> Ours is a system of government by majorities, but not a system of government by parties, in the sense of party being based on definite political principles . . . As party divisions here do not represent, as they have done in England, distinctly marked differences of political principle and tendency, it is utterly impossible that honest, and independent men can be expected to give to any government more than steady support which may, when occasion requires it, be withdrawn without violation of party fidelity.[89]

This was the attitude succinctly expressed in the slogan 'Measures, not men'.

Members never wearied of pointing out that no man trammelled by obligations to others could hope to exercise that objective judgment conventionally demanded of the wise legislator. The ideal meant that they must ostentatiously declare their independence of their constituents, of outside organizations and even of the ministries they supported. The words of G. E. Cass, representative for the Bogan, when he deserted the Stuart government in 1883 because he disagreed with its Land Bill, were typical of the independent's argument:

> I am perfectly free to act as my conscience dictates; no one can be less influenced than I am by personal considerations in dealing with this question. Since I have been in the House I have identified myself

with no particular party. I have given the present Government that consistent support which I gave to their predecessors. When I first went before my constituents I stated most emphatically that I would not accept a seat . . . if I were to be bound by party ties. My motto was 'Measures, not men'. I said that so long as the Government of the day brought down measures conducive to the welfare of the country I would give them my cordial support, but that if they introduced measures which were inimical to the best interests of the community I should be as uncompromising in my opposition as I had been cordial in my support.[90]

Levien, the member for Tamworth, invoked the doctrine of independence in justification of his refusal to vote as his constituents had asked:

I sit here as the representative, not the delegate, of my constituents . . . I have a duty to discharge to my country.[91]

And at the same time he declared his independence of the ministry:

Firm supporter of the Government though I am, I would not hesitate if they introduced a measure of which I did not approve to vote against them even though my vote should have the effect of putting them out of office.

But as factions plainly existed, many members had to face a discrepancy between precept and practice. This most commonly came to light in comments on the political behaviour of individual members. Few of those who professed to be independents were in fact innocent of connection with one or another faction. They were the more vulnerable because in practice the ideal of independence, like the ideal of 'good government', had its uses for both faction leaders and supporters. It could be invoked by a member to justify a change of his allegiance; it could also be used to discredit the 'thick and thin' supporters of a ministry. On one occasion—similar to many others— a member denounced an opponent who had entered the chamber when a division was called for and had voted with the ministry after enquiring 'where is the Government?'. This, the critic declared, 'was not a credit to the House'. The accused member regarded the charge so seriously that he identified himself and not only defended his conduct but tried to show that he had asserted a form of independence.[92] 'Independence' was of importance in the constituencies too. Electors expected a candidate to make a declaration of independence in his campaign, for they suspected that a member committed to a parliamentary leader would be bound to neglect their interests in a conflict between his commitments to them and to a ministry.

Lip-service to the ideal of independence could only thinly veil the facts of political practice. And by 1864 there were men who, moved by simple honesty, or alive to the disadvantages of the ideal in the faction struggle, seemed prepared frankly to postulate in its stead the principle of loyalty. In that year the *Empire,* now controlled by Hanson and Bennett, friends of Cowper, found an excuse to attack the old ideal under the pejorative name of 'ratting'. 'It is precisely these political "rats", contemptible as they are, who sway the destinies of contending factions'.[93] Teece attacked the doctrine of independence before the electors in 1877: 'If a member of parliament belonged to no party, then he was a nonentity. You must belong to one party or the other or you can accomplish little or nothing.'[94] In 1881 Parkes quoted Palmerston: '"an independent member is a member who can never be depended upon"', and went on to attack a member who had professed support of his ministry and had yet led attacks on it which had been, 'in one or two instances, destructive of the Administration with which I have been connected'.[95] Similar statements in 1874 had earned Parkes the title of 'Dictator'.[96]

The spectacular exploitation of faction core solidarity occasionally evoked protests in the name of independence,[97] but in the conduct of parliamentary business unostentatious personal devotion was accepted as a normal part of the political process. Indeed, even within the larger combinations which formed around the faction nuclei, honour and a sense of responsibility or commitment to the leader of the group whose parliamentary life the member shared demanded from him a degree of consistency in his political relations that was incompatible with thoroughgoing independence. This became evident on those occasions when notable changes of allegiance took place,[98] and even the ordinary member who changed his allegiance felt it necessary to defend himself against a charge of treachery or 'ratting' by appealing to the alternative ideal of independence.[99]

The practice of caucusing offered the clearest evidence of factional loyalty and commitment and was the hardest to justify by reference to the ideals of liberalism and good government. Caucusing committed members and their leaders to one another, and if they reached any decision on a matter yet to come before the House, it committed them to a particular vote before they had heard debate on the question. And if they considered the composition of a projected ministry, as Martin's and Parkes' followers did in 1870, it was an outrage on the principles of parliamentary government. On that occasion, Parkes himself made a scathing attack on the practice after Martin had decided to take Robertson into coalition in the new ministry. He wrote:

it matters little to the people what set of men may be receiving the rewards of office so long as good government is secured ... It matters very much however by what means Ministers are brought into existence and sustained in power ... A meeting of the Opposition in the Assembly, regularly convened by circular, was held to consider the claims of gentlemen to be raised to the position of advisers to the Crown. Of course, the members at such a gathering would meet on equal terms. The youngest and least experienced would have his voice in the consultation like the oldest and best informed ... Gentlemen whose sagacity had never soared above the points in a breed of cattle or the grazing capabilities of a sheep run, would suddenly have to decide upon the capacity of their friends for statesmanship ... the recognition by Sir James Martin himself of an assemblage of this character was a step towards making Government a delegacy from a mob, a small and privileged mob it may have been, but nevertheless a mob in all the essentials of acting without authority or accountability.

Nothing, he thought, could be devised more contrary to the spirit of constitutional practice and responsible government:

The scheme of Parliamentary Government supposes that a small band of superior men in whose political character and administrative capacity, as a whole, the Legislature has confidence shall govern us so long as they can retain that confidence. The grand security for good government by these men consists in their direct responsibility to a larger body of men, who, in their turn, are responsible to the whole people. But it has never been proposed that these rulers should be elected, directly or indirectly, by the representative body.[1]

Parkes' reference to the 'grand security for good government' that rested on ministerial accountability to 'a larger body of men' was a tacit admission of the ultimate right of the individual member to exercise his independence. At the same time, ministers had to be 'brought into existence and sustained in power'. His prescription for this phase of the governmental process was a negative one: in effect, 'mob' rule could not be tolerated within a faction. In other words, the function of lesser men was not to choose, but merely to support 'the small band of superior men' whose experience and sagacity distinguished them as natural leaders. The unspoken assumption was that loyalty, tempered by judicious independence, and unalloyed by internal democracy, must be the real cement of faction, and thereby of government.

The balance was necessarily delicate, and in the highly individualistic political milieu of the time, the concept of loyalty had to be 'personal'. Though sometimes apparently psychological and imponderable, the personal respect—perhaps affection—commanded by faction leaders had its roots, as we have seen, in members' appreciation of the leaders' ability not only to meet individual expectations, but also to provide 'good government' which would conduce to progress and the general welfare. In this sense faction leaders were in truth recognized, as Parkes would have it, as 'superior' men. Herein lay both their strength and their weakness. Fidelity to 'party' could be used to constrain a motley following, but loyalty was of necessity given to the leader himself, and it operated best when least talked about. Factions did not have the deeper sanctions arising from common aims and ideals, from an organizational and extra-parliamentary life and from power in the constituencies to enable the leaders to insist upon loyalty and to defend it as an ideal in the face of the strong appeal and practical advantages of independence. Possessing no impersonal focus of loyalty, being heterogeneous in composition and lacking sharp boundaries, the factions could be enlarged within limits set only by the acumen of their leaders and the strength of opponents. Leaders had no way of securing majorities in support of their ministries other than by building on faction strength. That their performance brought a high degree of stability was a tribute to their own political skill, to the sense of responsibility possessed by ordinary politicians, and to the aptness of the whole faction system in the existing stage of colonial social development.

CHAPTER THREE

The Formation and Defeat of Ministries

THE CONSTRUCTION of a faction ministry was always a matter of parliamentary manoeuvre and intrigue, conducted in an atmosphere of tension and rumour as the Assembly awaited the outcome. The defeat of a ministry usually exhibited the same characteristics. Each operation called for considerable political skill on the part of the leaders, especially in assessing each other's strength and tactics and demanded of them the most intimate knowledge of the parliamentary struggle and of members' allegiances and antipathies.

The overriding consideration for a premier designate was to find a combination of ministers who could secure the support of a majority. However, after 1863 when the Assembly had become multifactional, no leader could take office on the unaided strength of his own faction. He had therefore to secure as colleagues men who could bring steady supporters with them to augment his own following. But even amalgamation of groups of steady followers was seldom enough to give an administration a majority in the House. It was thus necessary to find a combination of ministers likely to win at the outset confidence or sufferance from an adequate number of uncommitted men. Once established in office a ministry could go on to confirm the attachment of such members and to enlarge its support from other quarters in the House by the use of patronage, by its allocation of appropriations and by its legislative measures.

In the initial phase of seeking as colleagues men with predictable support, coalition was the move most likely to succeed: indeed, this was the only course open to a leader when three or more strong and clearly defined factions existed in the House. At other times, when one or more factions were disintegrating, a leader might find that he could construct his ministry by securing—to use the contemporary term—the 'co-operation' of leaders and spokesmen of small unattached segments of the legislature. Ministries of this kind may be called ministries of accretion. It is worth considering in detail the formation of sample ministries of these types: the Martin-Parkes administration of 1866 (coalition) and the Parkes administration of

1872 (accretion). By examining the outcome in each case it is possible to carry the history of politics in the legislature forward from the point, in 1865, at which it was left in the last chapter.

It had been apparent throughout 1865 that the Cowper ministry was shaky. Three ministers had resigned during the year, and Cowper had failed to win Parkes' alliance by enticing him into the ministry. Towards the end of 1865 opposition attacks, in which Parkes played a leading part, increased in intensity, the Treasurer was forced to resign and the ministry made a drastic revision of its financial proposals. The opposition's onslaught culminated in a motion, put by Parkes, expressing the 'entire disapproval' of the House at the appointment of Marshall Burdekin as the new Treasurer in January 1866.[1] The motion proved fatal to the government.

Parkes had taken the first step towards conciliation with Martin by seeking his support for the attack on Burdekin's appointment, arguing broadly at the same time that a strong ministry was needed. Given the past hostility between Parkes and Martin, caution and mutual suspicion naturally marked the first exchange of letters.[2] Discounting their 'misunderstanding' in the past, Martin made the next tentative move by inviting Parkes to attend a meeting of his followers to discuss the course they should take. Parkes did not accept the invitation, and urged (contrary to Martin's advice) that the motion against the appointment should not be delayed, but proceeded with at once. Martin's faction met as arranged—just before Parkes' motion was passed—and decided that Martin should coalesce with Parkes rather than attempt to form a ministry solely from his own immediate followers.[3]

A week then passed before the ministry resigned and Martin was sent for. In that time Cowper unsuccessfully sought a dissolution from the Governor, Sir John Young,[4] and Plunkett attempted to bring about a coalition between Cowper, Parkes, Martin and Edward Butler who at that time was not in the House. Plunkett hoped to create an all-party coalition that would rise above the battle of the 'Ins and Outs' and be strong enough to attend to the business of the country.[5] In commenting to Martin upon the proposed combination, Parkes committed himself more clearly to coalition, suggesting at the same time that if Martin should be tempted into combining with Cowper instead that would put Parkes in a position to defeat them both. Plunkett's proposal, said Parkes

> means reconstructing the present battered administration by *using* what are supposed to be the best men from the opposition. We are not invited to a coalition on equal terms, but on the con-

trary we are to meet a gentleman who still retains the post of premier and who does not contemplate appealing to his constituents on what he now does after the many strange things he has already done. We however should have to account to our constituents [in ministerial elections] for our share in the transaction which would not appear to the public one of a disinterested character. Moreover, if nothing came of the interview [between Cowper and Parkes which Plunkett suggested] I cannot avoid my suspicions that Mr. Cowper would not be nice in telling his friends that the negotiations were of our seeking and not his. But if we seriously consider such a conjunction . . . what is to become of Mr. Cowper's present colleagues—Messrs. Robertson, Smart and Cunneen? If he is prepared to throw them overboard to meet the exigencies of a new situation, it would not raise him in my estimation, nor make me the more desirous of joining him. Nor is it very clear how they are to be thrown overboard without a resignation . . .

So far as my support in the House goes my friends would from their past sympathies readily assent to my coalition with Mr. Cowper but I am not so sure about your supporters some of whom I know have the strongest possible objection to Mr. Cowper . . . I think the best thing that can be done now is a resignation and then let things take the course which Sir John Young and the natural influences of the situation may give to them.[6]

The 'natural influences of the situation' were in fact the strengths and attitudes of the factions themselves. Parkes was shrewdly pointing out that Martin and Cowper were not in a position to combine without splitting their supporters and giving Parkes the advantage. Next day he explained more fully to his wife where he thought his strength lay. He was apparently still not convinced that Martin would not betray him by some unforeseen manoeuvre:

Mr. Martin has more declared supporters than any other member—that is, supporters who make it plain that they intend to follow him in most things. I have a much larger number of men in the House who would cordially support me if I were in a Government united with one or two others whom they approved, but the larger part of these people do not avow their friendly feelings and support Mr. Cowper while [he is] in office.[7]

He thought too that 'the influences hostile to me' would prevail and that if a seat in Martin's prospective ministry were offered him it would be done in such a way that he could not accept it 'consistently with what I think is my due': a veiled hint that he thought his faction should have more than one office in the ministry. Parkes' gloomy anticipation that his manoeuvres might be defeated did not lack substance. For at some stage in the negotiations of the week Martin appears to have approached Forster with an offer of the lands portfolio. Forster had demanded that the prospective ministry undertake an extensive programme of reform, but this was unacceptable to Martin, and the negotiations had apparently been broken off.[8]

Parkes' own letters, together with an analysis Cowper made of the elections of November 1864,[9] show that Parkes was attempting to build his own following primarily at the expense of the two leading factions in the Assembly. But Parkes also worked to increase his support by getting into the House new men who would be loyal to him. One outstanding opportunity presented itself while the ministerial negotiations were still going on. Robertson, who for private reasons had temporarily resigned from Cowper's ministry in October 1865, returned to office on 1 January 1866. He had therefore to face his constituency again for ministerial re-election, and Parkes saw a chance of dealing the ailing ministry a blow by defeating Robertson and at the same time winning for himself new support which could be decisive in a closely balanced House. This was the occasion on which he engineered Windeyer's nomination and election in Robertson's stead,[10] undeterred by Windeyer's own firm reluctance to be a party to the manoeuvre.[11]

Parkes' success in building his strength—underestimated by Cowper almost to the last minute—is reflected in the numerical balance of factions in the House by January 1866.

Cowper and Robertson and followers (including 2 temporarily out of the House)	27
Parkes and followers	13
Martin and followers	13
Forster and followers	4
Independents	9
Undetermined and doubtful	5

In the circumstances, a Martin-Parkes coalition seemed likely to prosper. Having completed negotiations, the two leaders formally constituted their administration on 26 January 1866.

The price of coalition was legislative delay or inactivity on the very questions that most occupied the attention of the members of the House. Differences of policy between Parkes and Martin were left unresolved. It was agreed that state aid for the clergy should not be a 'government question'. The tariff was not to be altered until the finances of the colony were 'flourishing'. As the ministry proposed no other measures to induce recovery, this meant that Martin's protectionist and Parkes' free trade views were unreconciled. In the circumstances, the new government had very little to offer the House when it reassembled after the ministerial elections.[12] Disillusion among its supporters and scathing criticism from the press[13] were further costs of coalition. John Marks, an old political supporter of Parkes, and a man of some influence in his electorate, indignantly refused to nominate his leader for re-election on taking office, declaring that

> If governments can be formed upon personal contempt and fundamental differences of opinions, it is a perfect farce for electors to squabble about the principles and qualifications of candidates. The only sensible method would be to let [the candidates] toss up for it. I had hopes that you would have either formed or aided in establishing a strong Liberal government.[14]

The coalition must have nonetheless given Parkes considerable satisfaction. He himself had the choice of any office except that of Attorney-General (taken by the Premier, Martin), and he had moreover the 'privilege of nomination of two members of the cabinet'.[15] In a combination of seven ministers, he had a strength of three as opposed to Martin's four. Parkes took the Colonial Secretaryship, a post normally held by the Premier: his followers, James Byrnes and J. B. Wilson,[16] received the Secretaryships of Public Works and Lands. Martin's supporters—R. M. Isaacs, G. Eagar and J. Docker—filled the offices of Solicitor-General, Treasurer and Postmaster-General, Docker being the representative of the government in the Upper House. Parkes and his supporters therefore held three of the four ministerial 'plums': the fourth, the treasury, went to Eagar. These four men presided over departments that comprised the heart of the administration of the colony. The bulk of legislation coming before parliament concerned one or other of them; they spent the greatest part of the money appropriated to the government service; they had under them the largest staffs and a growing complex of sub-departments and special boards.

The personnel of the new ministry suggested that it would be sound. As leading barristers, Martin and Isaacs had professional experience that fitted them for the offices they held, while Eagar seemed well qualified for the treasury by having been long prominent in the Bank of New South Wales and in mercantile enterprises. In addition, he had held office two and a half years earlier in the first Martin ministry. Wilson, a physician and surgeon with a Scottish university education, had also served as a minister under Martin. Byrnes, though lacking previous administrative experience, was a man of private means derived from commerce and manufacturing, who had been mayor of Parramatta since 1862.

But in other respects, the administration was fundamentally weak. One difficulty, about which nothing could be done, arose from internal divisions on matters of policy. There were, for example, disputes early in 1866 between the Treasurer, Eagar, and the Collector of Customs, W. A. Duncan, in which Eagar had to make good his ministerial authority over the customs department. In the course of these quarrels, it became clear that the Customs Act itself was inadequate, that the *ad valorem* system of levying duties was difficult to administer and open to fraud, that the administrative arrangements in the customs offices and on the wharves were far from efficient and that the training of staff could well be improved. The publication of papers on these disputes led to a motion in the House demanding a select committee to investigate the work of the department. The ministry managed to defeat this move, but a month later, by a resolution of the Executive Council, it set up a commission of enquiry into the customs department. The report of the commission[17] implied severe censure of the administration of customs up to that time, and its recommendations included numerous reforms already advocated unsuccessfully by Duncan after he had become Collector in 1859. Eagar had opposed many of these reforms, and now his influence was sufficient to prevent the commission's recommendations being put into effect. There were also hints that the interest of different individuals and groups, particularly commercial firms, in the administration of customs added to the reluctance with which the ministry faced the question. But disagreement within the ministry itself was the most important barrier to reform. An overhaul of the department, especially one which required a new Customs Act and perhaps the abandonment of the *ad valorem* principle, could only be carried through by a ministry united in its tariff policy and strongly supported on this question in the House. The ministry's inability to agree about the renewal of an expiring package duty in 1867[18] showed that it would have been quite unable to agree on the much larger question of a reconstruction of the customs system.

Government support in the House was also weak and uncertain. Six months after Martin had taken office, the Governor observed that there 'is so little coherence in parties that a Ministry may be upset at any moment',[19] and the only major ministerial legislation carried during two and a half years of office—Parkes' Public Schools Bill of 1866[20]—went through the House with the support of two of the opposition faction leaders and eight of their followers. Martin's weakness, implicit in the voting on this bill, was made clear a year later when he brought in a measure to amend the land legislation of 1861. This bill was defeated on the second reading by 32 votes to 30 in a division on faction lines, the pastoralists in the House, who were mostly independents, voting solidly against it. Another defeat was suffered when the House reduced a ministerial loan for unspecified railway construction projects from £3 million to £1 million.

These defeats put new heart into the opposition, which at once began a series of obstructive and probing attacks. But when Martin challenged his opponents to carry a direct vote of censure they failed, and he then argued that the two defeats did not make it impossible for him to continue in office.[21] Behind the scenes, however, the ministry had in fact considered whether to resign or seek a dissolution. Meetings of supporters objected to resignation, and the Governor to dissolution, so both courses had been abandoned.[22] Parkes, according to Belmore, was eager to resign and Martin may well have agreed, but the Governor was anxious not to lose a ministry, and two other members of the administration who 'could ill afford to lose their salaries' were reluctant to go out.[23] Parkes was under increasing pressure from his friends and supporters to break with a combination which they thought was bringing discredit upon him, especially through the financial maladministration, 'ignorance' and 'shuffling' of the Treasurer, Eagar.[24]

Quarrels within the ministry, as distinct from differences of opinion about policy, had also weakened it. At the outset, Parkes had believed that he would 'grow in strength' with his colleagues and that they would all 'pull well together',[25] but before long he was protesting at the failure of other ministers to consult him on decisions affecting departments under his control.[26] He and Eagar quarrelled personally,[27] and Eagar did not speak to him about the proposed £3 million railway loan until the matter was at an advanced stage.[28] Early in 1868 Parkes thought it necessary to write to Martin warning him of the danger to the ministry and imploring him to do something about it.

Our neglect of our functions as a Government is becoming serious ... It seems to me that we have lost sight of our damaged situation [in the House] and to some extent of our existence as an administration, several of my colleagues I have not even seen for the last ten days till I [caught] sight of them for a few [moments] last night and half the public appears to know more than I do of what is being done in other Departments. I suppose the other Ministers jog on in the same kind of Departmental isolation in regard to me

... this cannot last ... What I fear ... is that at the last moment some course will be proposed [in the Assembly] to which it will not be possible to agree and we shall find ourselves in a state of indecision and confusion when everything ought to be decisive and clear.[29]

This was above all an appeal for Martin to give the cabinet strong leadership, and when he failed to do so, the crisis Parkes foresaw was not long in coming. The two groups in opposition, led by Robertson and Forster, mounted an assault on the Treasurer's financial administration and obstructed government business by repeatedly moving the adjournment of the House.[30] The attack was temporarily halted by the arrival of the Duke of Edinburgh in the colony in January and by the dismay that followed his near-assassination by O'Farrell in March. The new Governor, Lord Belmore, judged the ministry to be so weak that he expected them to ask for a dissolution and was in fact prepared to consider granting one.[31] But the House adjourned in April without the request being made. When it reassembled in October, the opposition had new grounds for attacking the ministry in the dismissal of Duncan and the subsequent resignation of Parkes.

Duncan was dismissed because he challenged the Treasurer's control of the customs department. To avoid payment of duty, an importer had undervalued goods worth £64, and had concealed another import on which duty of 3s. 6d. should have been paid. Duncan decided that this was an indisputable case of fraud, and that, even though the sums in question were small, the goods should be seized. Eagar, after agreeing at first, changed his mind: a quarrel followed, but Duncan eventually submitted, and returned the goods to the importer. Duncan hopefully gave the papers on the case to Parkes, but the latter refused initially to intervene on the ground that the matter was entirely within the Treasurer's department and that Eagar's decision must be final for his subordinates. Duncan, however, forced Eagar to take the question further by writing a minute threatening him with correction at the hands of cabinet. Forced to discuss the issue in full, cabinet decided that Duncan should be suspended from duty and asked to show cause why he should not be dismissed. Parkes again refused to take Duncan's part, arguing that he would have 'instantly' suspended a subordinate who addressed remarks to him as insulting and unjustified as those Duncan had used to Eagar.[32] Eventually Duncan apologized unreservedly and sought clemency on the ground of long service. Parkes and Belmore thought that Duncan's submission was satisfactory and that he should be allowed to retire on his pension. But Eagar refused to accept the apology,

and, by threatening his own resignation, forced cabinet to agree to
Duncan's dismissal. Martin had at first thought the dispute could be
smoothed over and regretted Eagar's intractability, but eventually
he agreed that Duncan should go.

At this point, Parkes decided that he could not be a party to the
decision and resigned. He told Martin that he thought the

> decision of the Government harsh . . . Mr. Duncan has not only
> acknowledged himself in the wrong and unreservedly apologized,
> but he has thrown himself on the mercy of the Government, in
> consideration of his long service, his advanced years and his helpless
> family. I know Mr. Duncan to be a man of integrity and unblemished
> life and I cannot view his humbled position as it has been viewed
> by you and your colleagues. Then again, if Mr. Duncan were re-
> moved I could not assent to the arrangements that are to follow
> [to ask Parliament to vote him a pension . . . (is) a job pure and
> simple[33]].
>
> I have failed to give effect to my views in the deliberations of
> the Cabinet and I think I comprehend my own position . . .[34]

More lay behind Parkes' resignation than sympathy for Duncan,
concern that vindictiveness should not mark the relations of ministers
with subordinates and a desire to uphold the principle of collective
responsibility of cabinet. Windeyer had been 'sounded' about the
feeling of ministerial supporters towards the proposed dismissal and
reported their dislike of it. Windeyer was estranged from the government at this time because it had neglected his requests for assistance
to political friends. Bell, Duncan and Lang also wrote to Parkes
expressing the discontent of his supporters. Two of Parkes' faction,
Byrnes and Wilson, remained in the ministry after his resignation,
and another, Tighe, was brought in to take the office of Postmaster-
General, vacated by Docker on his elevation to the portfolio lately
held by Parkes. Byrnes thought of resigning because he was 'no
longer in sympathy with any of the parties [in the ministry] except
Martin . . . ' On the other hand some of Martin's supporters met and
planned to insist, if Martin continued in office, upon a reconstruction
of the ministry to remove Byrnes and Wilson.[35] The unrest of supporters of both leaders in the coalition, when set beside the murmurs of
some of Parkes' followers in 1867, his own thought then that the
best course was to resign, and his later complaints about lack of
leadership and decision, leave little doubt that Parkes was pleased
enough to leave the ministry. The dismissal of Duncan provided him
with an excellent opportunity to resign professing only the most

pure and patriotic motives and without having to refer to the serious tension that existed between the factions.

As soon as the House assembled in October 1868, the opposition moved a censure motion which, with Windeyer's support, produced an even division. The ministry asked in vain for a dissolution, and then resigned. Robertson came back into office. There the matter might well have rested, had not Parkes made a speech at Kiama, in his own electorate, before resigning from the ministry, alleging that he could produce attested evidence that O'Farrell's attempt on the life of the Duke of Edinburgh had been planned and that someone had been murdered to prevent him revealing the plan before the attack was made.[36] The allegations created a great stir. At the time of the shooting, the legislature had passed motions of loyalty and deep regret, together with a savage Treason Felony Act to back them up. But no one then suggested what Parkes now implied: that the shooting was a Fenian plot. Sectarian feeling which had been roused by the Public Schools Act, and had smouldered throughout the decade, now flared, fanned by the Loyal Orange Association and a newly formed Protestant Political Association.[37]

Contemporaries aware of Parkes' political predicament earlier in the year thought they detected here a new and wholly scandalous manoeuvre, perhaps even prepared before the Duncan affair had given him the opportunity to leave Martin and enhance his political capital at the same time. But whether Parkes was seeking to twist sordid sectarian passions to his advantage, or whether his allegations were in fact true, he had offered his enemies an opportunity to damage his political reputation beyond repair. They demanded a parliamentary enquiry into the affair, and a select committee was set up shortly after the new ministry took office. Parkes realized that he was fighting for his entire political future.[38] The committee, dividing along strictly faction lines, brought in a report that condemned him, but he successfully moved that the report be expunged from the records of the House.[39] Though Parkes thus survived, the tension between Protestants and Catholics did not subside and the Orange movement and the Protestant Political Association were roused to take a far more active part in electoral politics than hitherto. Parkes was not allowed to forget the 'Kiama Ghost',[40] and the sectarian feeling he had done so much to arouse in 1868–9 added greatly to the natural complications of the faction game when he carried out the task of forming his first ministry in 1872.

Parkes emerged temporarily weakened from the unhappy experience of coalition with Martin, and had to wait another four years before the turn of the political wheel and his own reviving strength put power again within his grasp. During that time an upheaval occurred which made it inevitable that the first Parkes government should be formed by a process of accretion from a single faction core. The old Cowper-Robertson faction was shattered when Robertson and Martin coalesced; and the realignments that followed made it impossible for Parkes either to join with another major leader or to take office with the unaided support of his own followers. Parkes' solution of this difficulty deserves close consideration: but as a prelude it is necessary to note briefly the outlines of the power struggle between 1868 and 1872.

Robertson took office in place of Martin in 1868, at the head of the old Cowper-Robertson faction and in coalition with Forster and his dwindling band of followers. The ministry underwent a minor reconstruction early in 1870 when Cowper rejoined it, replacing Robertson as Colonial Secretary and Premier. Robertson left the cabinet temporarily because, as in 1865, he was in financial difficulties.[41] But late in 1870 he returned to the lands department, which had meantime been vacated by Forster when a trivial motion had been carried against him in the House.[42] As 1870 wore away, the ministry slowly lost control of the House, to fall at last in December. After two years in office it had even less legislation to its credit than the Martin-Parkes coalition. This legislative weakness, the loss of several supporters by resignation, and the interest of some supporters in a *rapprochement* with Martin had been the chief causes of its decline.

Cowper, now advanced in years, decided at this point to retire, and the way was opened for a possible coalition between Martin and Robertson. Cowper's supporters met in December to consider a number of matters, including the leadership of the faction,[43] and Cowper himself told them that he had decided to take the office of Agent-General. A few months earlier, Cowper had spoken of a rumour that new members wished to form a ministry in conjunction with Martin.[44] Martin too found considerable support for a new combination among opposition members, whom he and Parkes had so far led. Commissioned on Cowper's fall to form a new ministry, Martin met some of his and Parkes' supporters to discuss its composition. The meeting decided to seek the opinion of twenty-six members by circular, asking each to indicate the five men he preferred to see in the ministry.[45] The replies indicated Robertson's popularity: the other favoured candidates were followers of Parkes, although two of them at least had close relations with Martin as well. Martin had said he would be 'led' but not 'bound' by the result of the vote. But after it had been taken he asked Robertson to join him in a coalition. Robertson agreed, and the ministry was formed on 16 December 1870, with Martin as Premier and Attorney-General, and Robertson as Colonial Secretary. The other ministers included Lord, a follower of Martin, Wilson and Byrnes who were primarily followers of Parkes, but members of the late Martin ministry and on good terms with its chief, and Windeyer, another friend of Parkes, but one who had been gravely disappointed in his friendship in 1866–8.[46]

The composition of this ministry, instead of giving it strength, left it weak and ineffective. Parkes and his followers were enraged by the coalition.[47] The old Cowper-Robertson faction was disrupted: of twenty-nine surviving from 1870–1, only ten followed the new ministry, four of them not very steadily. Five of the remainder turned to Parkes, and thirteen formed a block of independents of whom ten were strongly opposed to the ministry. Four of the seven followers of Parkes in the fifth parliament stayed in opposition with him; the others gave the ministry some support. Three of Martin's followers deserted him but remained independent. The net result was to give the ministry twenty-one steady followers, and some support from eleven others, against an opposition of twelve followers of Parkes, ten old Cowper-Robertson supporters, and twelve independents.[48] Parkes was in charge of the largest group led by one man in the House in 1871,[49] and, with friends in the ministry, he had only to win the support of the old followers of Cowper and Robertson to cripple it in the House.

Martin's collapse was delayed by the need to get essential business passed in the remainder of the session, by a four months recess, and by Parkes' absence from the House throughout 1871 while passing through the insolvency court. Without him the opposition was leaderless.[50]

The ministry itself ultimately contributed to its downfall by a serious tactical blunder. During the recess in 1871, delegates from Victoria and New South Wales had quarrelled at an intercolonial conference and failed to agree on terms for renewing the border duties agreement of 1867, due to expire in January 1872. Under the old agreement Victoria had paid New South Wales £60,000 per annum in consideration of duties waived on trade across the Murray. At the conference Martin had insisted that the amount be increased to £100,000. Victoria made a counter proposal for temporary continuation of the old agreement while the actual state of trade across the border was determined, but Martin refused to consider it. After a heavy fight, he managed just before the Christmas recess to persuade the Assembly to pass a resolution supporting his stand. Robertson then rejected a further request that the Victorian counter proposal be considered, and, pointing now to the Assembly's resolution, threatened to begin collecting customs on the border. When Victoria remained unmoved, Robertson took steps to have customs collected as he had promised. The ministry's stand was not wholly unjustified, since a bill levying increased duties had been passed in April 1871. But its action was undeniably impolitic, in dealing both with a neighbouring colony and with a local Assembly in which *ad valorem* duties were generally disliked.

The House reassembled in January 1872, with the opposition eager to do battle. The border duties affair offered a superb issue of principle on which to challenge the government, since a carefully framed resolution condemning its treatment of Victoria might easily wilt the loyalty of a marginal number of wavering supporters. The opposition elected Forster as its leader, and prepared a censure motion for him to move. Forster's elevation reflected the essential disunity of Martin's opponents. Few of the men who chose Forster had more than tenuous obligations to him. His distinct following had in fact dwindled to one or two, and he had moreover gained a reputation, such as no faction leader could afford to have, for independence and cantankerousness as a colleague and for taking impractical doctrinaire positions on issues that he considered to be matters of principle. His elevation now was a measure of the continuing distrust of Parkes, the other obvious opposition leader.[51] But lack of internal cohesion in the opposition was not an impediment to its immediate aim of overturning the government. The censure motion was moved and carried. Several ministerial supporters voted for it, and others absented themselves from the division.[52]

Faced with this defeat, the ministry hesitated about the course to take, and held a meeting of its followers to consider whether to resign or seek a dissolution.[53] The idea of immediate resignation was rejected. A dissolution, it seemed, would in the end be inevitable, since any incoming ministry must be in a minority, and therefore entitled to demand an election. In the circumstances, the most profitable course would obviously be to force a dissolution at once, thus depriving opposition leaders of the advantages of appealing to the electors while in office.[54] The Governor, Lord Belmore, agreed on request to grant Martin a dissolution, in the belief that neither Parkes nor Forster had the strength to take office with a stable majority. It also happened that Belmore was on the eve of retiring, and he was reluctant to saddle the temporary Administrator, Sir Alfred Stephen, with a ministerial crisis and the possibility of a subsequent dissolution. In Belmore's view Martin was not only entitled to a dissolution, but it was also better to leave

> Mr. Robertson at the Colonial Secretary's office during the inter-regnum, even at the expense of a general election, rather than either Mr. Forster who is a very difficult man to work with, or Mr. Parkes who has lately passed through the Insolvent Court.[55]

The elections were disastrous for the government: three of its ministers were defeated and it lost a considerable number of its supporters. The results were as follows:

	Returned			Not returned		
	Opposed	Unopposed	Total	Defeated	Retired	Total
Old members classified by votes in 6th parlt						
Parkes' followers	8	2	10	2	2	4
Martin's & Robertson's followers incl. unsteady	13	1	14	9	8	17
Independents	6	–	6	2	1	3
Independents opposed to ministry	4	3	7	4	1	5
Unknown	10	1	11	–	1	1
New members classified by votes in 7th parlt						
Parkes' followers	11	–	11			
Robertson's followers	4	–	4			
Independents	6	–	6			
Unknown	2	1	3			

The implication is that Parkes had increased his support at the expense of the ministry. But this was not clear at once. That the election result appeared equivocal to contemporaries was amusingly reflected in a series of pseudonymous letters to the press in which Parkes, Martin, and Forster analysed the poll.[56] Parkes predicted that in the new House the ministry would be defeated; Martin argued that it would survive; Forster was less certain but at least made clear his contempt for the calculations—and the principles—of the other two. After the identity of the letter writers had been revealed, W. B. Dalley dryly observed that there had been more to the correspondence than a mere desire to instruct the public about the political situation:

> To the outside public the correspondence . . . between 'An Elector', 'Another Elector' and a 'Third Party' must appear to be a very

lively commencement of the Parliamentary masquerade which, as a matter of course, (like a carnival before Lent), precedes the dreary austerities, late vigils, general pentiential exercises and the very Lenten fare of the eloquence of the Parliamentary session. Enter three dominoes—they circulate among all the characters who have been bidden to this legislative Ballo in Maschera—whispering 'Martin is stronger than he looks', 'Parkes' phalanx is unbroken' 'public good before hustings promises', 'Disraeli is twice as honest as Forster'; and just as the music breaks into a pathetic tarantella the clandestine prompters come forward, and tearing the hoods and satin noses off each other, reveal the three contending chiefs in the battle of portfolios.[57]

In the outcome, Parkes' predictions proved the more accurate. When the House met, he moved censure and the ministry fell, on a division of 36 votes to 11. Forster, who had moved the resolutions which originally led to the dissolution, was commissioned to form a government. He failed, and Sir Alfred Stephen sent for Parkes.

In a burst of optimism at the beginning of 1871, Parkes had written to his sister: 'Notwithstanding the gloom now, in twelve months I shall be Prime Minister. I do not thing [sic] any possible occurrence can prevent it . . .'[58] The boast, wildly extravagant when first made, would still have seemed extravagant enough in the new parliament of 1872. Though Parkes had gladly grasped the Administrator's commission, the auguries for success were not heartening. On 26 January Windeyer had observed that both sides of the House were giving Parkes the 'cold shoulder'.[59] Members in the old parliament who had preferred Forster's eccentricities to Parkes' deviousness remained to leaven the new opposition with distrust. From the late ministerial benches, men who had been the victims of Parkes' triumphant onslaughts could hardly be expected to co-operate with him now; nor could those supporters of Cowper and Robertson who had refused to support Martin and Robertson. A new coalition of major factions was clearly out of the question: none of the existing leaders in the House would play second fiddle to him as Premier and he could expect them to do their utmost to outmanoeuvre him. Parkes had to have the strength to deny them success, and for this he needed a new political combination. In these circumstances he set about the task of forming a ministry by accretion of fragments rather than by coalition.

There had been important preliminaries during 1871 when the weakness of the Martin government was apparent, and Parkes, sensing the coming opportunity, had made quiet moves to secure the confidence of a few leaders of important sectional opinion. In July he had written to J. D. Lang (with whom he had quarrelled in 1868), and to Joseph Wearne, M.L.A. (an influential Sydney Orangeman), urging both to join him in planning for a 'new and thoroughly progressive party'.[60] Later in the year he had raised the same question with two of his merchant friends, G. A. Lloyd and J. L. Montefiore, and had received from the former the gratifying opinion:

> There is a chance now for a Free Trade Party such as has not existed for years and if we only had a man like yourself to take the helm I believe we could . . . establish a ministry that would not only have the vox populi but increasing strength from high moral considerations.[61]

Parkes' wooing of militant Protestants and of merchants came naturally to him, considering his previous course in politics. More striking is the coup he had achieved in 1871 by establishing friendly relations with part of the Irish Catholic group in Sydney. By September, probably through the good offices of his Melbourne friend Gavan Duffy,[62] he had secretly won the alliance of Edward Butler, a prominent and influential local Catholic politician. Butler, having arrived in the colony in 1853, had been introduced to Parkes by Duffy, with whom he had previously been associated in Irish politics. Butler had become an admirer of Parkes and an early contributor to the *Empire* while Parkes for his part had discerned Butler's political promise as far back as 1858.[63] But Butler did not enter parliament until 1869.

By that time sectarian feeling, arising chiefly from the O'Farrell incident, was intense enough to keep him apart from Parkes and to make him in fact prominent in what he himself called 'a separate Catholic party in the House'.[64] But by late 1871 Butler was ready to respond to overtures from Parkes: with sectarian tension easing he felt that 'the good reason was past' for 'any such separate policy', and he was becoming obsessed by his 'dread of the [parliamentary] power of the squatters', whom he thought too influential in the Martin-Robertson coalition.[65] A private alliance with Parkes was thus to his taste. Of Butler it was said that 'if he held up an umbrella his people would vote for it',[66] and there can be no doubt that his assistance proved to be a powerful advantage to Parkes in the elections of 1872.[67]

These incongruous friendships undoubtedly helped Parkes to negotiate from a position of some strength once the task of forming an administration had been committed to his hands in May 1872. He himself wrote two ostensibly complete accounts of the steps by which he managed, when the time came, to construct his ministry: one in his own diary,[68] and the other in a long letter he sent to Joseph Wearne. These narratives exhibit similar characteristics and tell the

same story. Both purport to have been written close to the event
they describe, and both are marked by a carefully assumed tone of
high moral dignity, designed to show Parkes putting the public
interest above personal ambition. But in explaining to Wearne 'the
principles on which I have acted in trying honestly and wisely to
discharge this responsible trust', Parkes admitted—albeit in obscure
and pompous language—that 'public duty' could be only one of a
number of considerations influencing a faction leader anxious to
compose a ministry likely to command the support of a majority in
parliament:

> It seemed to me that it was my duty to the country to construct
> a ministry which would fairly embody the principles that had been
> in controversy and had triumphed in the late elections and in the
> conflicts in Parliament. With this general aim I had to consider
> a number of points in the character and position of individuals—
> such as, the length of public service, special claims, political associ-
> ations, personal fitness, and party fidelity, and to consider these
> things in relation to the state of the House and the tendency of
> public feeling outside.[69]

His subsequent performance offers an intriguing example of these
sometimes incompatible principles in action.[70]

Parkes' first move was to offer a portfolio to Forster, 'on public
grounds, and from a sense of duty and a recognition of his political
standing and ability'.[71] He and Forster had not co-operated in parliament since 1859, when they had been briefly, though inconclusively,
agreed in opposing the nearly defunct Cowper ministry.[72] But throughout the sixties they had been on opposite sides of the House. Forster
bluntly rejected the overture, and Parkes next consulted W. R. Piddington, a leading member of the late opposition. Piddington reported
that he, Saul Samuel and J. S. Farnell had each been offered ministerial
posts by Forster but had declined to join him unless he sought the
co-operation of Parkes. These rebuffs were understood to have been
the chief reason why Forster had been unable to form a government.[73]
All three of them accepted office under Parkes, who explained to
Wearne:

> This strong instance of political fidelity to me behind my back
> and in the face of my personal opponents imposed upon me a new
> obligation which no right-minded man could disregard. It became
> one of my first duties to seek the co-operation of these gentlemen
> who had thus made my co-operation, or at least a fair attempt to
> obtain it, an absolute condition of their joining others. Mr. Farnell
> was also pressed to take office by Mr. Forster and refused on my

account but perhaps I might have expected this from a gentleman who for many years had steadily supported me in public life.[74]

Farnell was indeed a follower of Parkes, but this was true neither of Samuel nor of Piddington. Piddington had been an M.L.A. since 1856, when he had given his support to Cowper. But in the second parliament he had opposed Cowper's ministry and, at least by 1863, he had become a follower of Martin. In 1871 he reacted to the Martin-Robertson coalition by going into opposition. Parkes gave him the office of Treasurer, although before 1872 he had had no special experience beyond acting as Chairman of Committees briefly in 1859–60. Samuel had been Treasurer under Forster in 1859–60 and then under Cowper in 1865 and 1868–70. He had become a steady follower of Cowper and Robertson by 1864, but broke with them when Cowper retired and Robertson combined with Martin. In 1871 he voted with Parkes and his followers in opposition. Samuel had, from Parkes' viewpoint, another advantage besides that of being a steady member of the late Cowper-Robertson faction: he was also a leading member of the 'Jewish persuasion' and 'one of its most trusted political heads'.[75] Under Parkes he became Vice-President of the Executive Council. Farnell, a landowner, was given the lands department.

Of the other members of the team, Innes and Lloyd were old political friends of Parkes, although Innes was a new member in 1872 and Lloyd a member of a little over two years' standing. Sutherland, despite Lyne's comment that he and all the others in the ministry had 'worked together . . . as members of the same party for the same objects',[76] had in fact been a follower of Cowper and Robertson from 1863 onwards and had held office under them as Secretary for Public Works in 1868–70. Beyond a brief phase of unsteadiness in opposition in 1867–8, he had shown no sign of sympathy for Parkes. Innes, a barrister, took the office of Solicitor-General; Lloyd became the Postmaster-General and Sutherland was given Public Works. Parkes himself took the Colonial Secretaryship. Piddington, Samuel and Sutherland, as Cowper-Robertson followers only recently disgruntled by the coalition with Martin, could be expected to draw to their support important fragments of a faction traditionally hostile to Parkes. Furthermore, with Lloyd, they brought to the ministry connections and experience in different segments of the commercial community.[77] They therefore constituted one element of that new 'progressive' party which Parkes had talked of constructing in 1871.

Butler, as Attorney-General, completed the team and provided the link with the Catholics. His appointment had to be explained delicately because, as he told Parkes, he feared that some Catholics 'who have not got quite reconciled to you' might use it to his disadvantage with his Catholic friends. Michael Fitzpatrick, a leading member of the late opposition and a Catholic, had ambitions for office under Parkes (presumably Lands, since he had been Undersecretary for Lands from 1856 to 1869), but after talking with Butler, he decided not to be offended at being passed over because 'in the present temper of the times, two Roman Catholics would not be tolerated [in the cabinet]'.[78] Butler's inclusion had to be explained subtly to the Orangemen too. Only a few weeks before, Wearne had told a meeting of Orangemen that

> Protestant feeling was so ripe just now that any Government that would dare to give the Roman Catholics an undue advantage would be hurled from power immediately.[79]

Parkes therefore wrote to Wearne carefully explaining that he had chosen Butler almost reluctantly, and only from a high sense of public duty.

> In filling the office of Attorney General it seemed to me that my choice was limited to three gentlemen, Sir William Manning, Mr. Darley and Mr. Butler, and it seemed very clear to me that in concurrence of political opinion, Parliamentary standing and popular sympathies, there was no comparison between Mr. Butler and the other two ... The question then arose, was the man best qualified for the office to be excluded from it because he was a Roman Catholic? In accordance with the principles of my whole public life that could not possibly be a question with me ... Rumours for months has [sic] made free with Mr. Butler's name simply *because his name was pointed out to rumours by his undoubted eligibility*. But I give you my assurance that I never spoke to Mr. Butler on this subject until one o'clock yesterday.[80]

He offered a similar explanation to Lang.[81]

But there is no evidence that Parkes included any extreme antiCatholics in his cabinet to mollify Wearne and his friends and to complete the list of linkages with the elements of the 'new' political combination. Farnell[82] and Sutherland were Masons, Lloyd was a Congregationalist, Parkes himself had been described in 1869 as a regular adherent of the Church of England,[83] and the religious affiliations of Innes and Piddington are unknown. It is possible that militant Protestants were content with their influence in the faction through men like Wearne, through Parkes' close association with them over the past three years and through their own electoral strength.

The account of the formation of his ministry, which Parkes gave to Wearne and wrote out in his diary, emphasized the importance of his sense of public responsibility and of obligations to faithful followers as motives for every phase of the negotiations. The ambitions of the Premier-elect himself were not mentioned, and it was implied that the understandings reached during the negotiations were simple, open and devoid of any previous background of intrigue. But on two vital points Parkes' account of the formation of his ministry was inaccurate. He alleged that he was unaware until 11 May (the day after he had been 'sent for') of the efforts of Samuel and Piddington to induce Forster to join forces with him. But, before Forster had even returned his commission, Butler had informed Parkes that opposition members had pressed Forster to approach him and that some of them expected him to refuse. Butler warned against rebuffing the expected overtures in such a way as to give Parkes' enemies an opportunity to claim that he had selfish designs on the premiership.[84]

It is therefore clear that well before he offered Forster a position in his cabinet Parkes was aware of a strong conviction among members of the late opposition that every effort should be made to unite its fragments, and that Forster himself had refused to do this. It was therefore a safe—and clever—tactical stroke for him to approach Forster. After what had occurred, no one as honourable as Forster could have accepted office with Parkes. Yet to offer him a place in the cabinet was to bid strongly for the favour of those who desired unification, and to enable Parkes to appear as a generous and public-spirited man. Parkes in fact made a significant—if guarded—admission of this stratagem in his letter to Wearne. After emphasizing that he had subordinated personal feeling to public duty he added 'of course this step on my part has placed me in a favourable light with all those members who desired our union, but I cannot say that I am sorry that Mr. Forster refused'.

The other inaccuracy in Parkes' narratives concerned his relationship with Butler. It was simply not true that—as he assured Wearne and Lang—his first approach to Butler had been made on 10 March. As far back as 27 January he had written to Butler to ask whether he would accept office as Attorney-General and leader of the Legislative Council in a prospective Parkes ministry: 'I can foresee that such an arrangement would enable the other offices to be filled so as to secure a larger support in the Assembly, while it would give the Government a more influential position in the Upper House'.[85] Parkes had therefore reserved the position of Attorney-General for Butler and had speculated about the composition of a projected ministry more than two months before being commissioned to form one. He had already planned a combination of ministers with an eye less to 'public duty' or even to 'strong instances of political fidelity' than to filling offices 'so as to secure a larger support in the Assembly'. And when formed, his ministry was a combination that brought together not only Catholic, anti-Catholic and varied mercantile elements but also members from each of the clearly defined segments of the opposition: the one-time followers of Cowper and Robertson and of Martin, his own followers and members sympathetic to a union between him and Forster. Such a combination in its incongruity and unexpectedness also had a good chance of winning the sympathy and temporary support of independents while they waited to see what kind of legislation and leadership it would offer.

The result was that Parkes' following in the seventh parliament was as mixed, in terms of its antecedent faction history, as his ministry. It comprised seven men who had supported Martin to the time of his coalition with Robertson or until later; twelve who had been followers of Cowper and Robertson up to the end of 1870; seventeen of his own followers of whom ten were new members; and seven independents. In addition to these he had support for a while from three other members who went into opposition with Robertson before the ministry fell, and unsteady support from two other members. Five of the forty-three steady supporters were lost during the parliament by resignation and five more supporters were gained in by-elections.

It is clear then that behind Parkes' construction of his 1872 ministry, there lay a tangle of personal intrigue directed at winning a majority without coalition with any other faction. Given the membership of the new House, which he had already studied carefully, his hope of securing and consolidating power rested in choosing ministers who through personal merit, political opinion, past record or sectional attachments would, in combination, appeal to as wide a range of politicians and as large a section of the outside public as possible. Obligations contracted through the past fidelity of prominent supporters certainly curtailed his freedom of choice a little. But within these limits, his flair for gauging the tactical implications of information gathered by keen observation and through the confidential reports of friends, combined with unscrupulousness and a readiness to invest the search for power and support with the dignity of a 'public trust', served to open the way for propitiating antagonistic groups and winning acceptance of his tenure of office as 'inevitable'.

Considering the two ways in which established faction leaders

formed ministries—as exemplified in the cases we have discussed—
it is possible to classify each of the ministries up to the early seventies
as one or another of three distinct types: non-faction, faction coalition
and faction with accretions. The ministries of Donaldson (1856), Parker
(1856–7), and Forster (1859–60) were of the first kind. The coalition
ministries were those of Martin (1863–5, with Forster), Martin (1866–8,
with Parkes) and Robertson (later Cowper, 1868–70, with Forster).
The remaining ministries (Cowper's in 1856, 1857–63 and 1865, and
Parkes' in 1872–5), were all based on one faction augmented by the
support of small fragments in the Assembly. Though their method
of formation differed, ministries of all types used the same techniques
to enlarge their support once they had taken office.

The stability of the faction system is indicated by the persistence
of the same methods of forming ministries and gaining support well
into the eighties. The ministries between 1872 and 1887 were of the
same types as those that had been formed in the first fifteen years.
What is more, the whole system survived not only the upheaval of
1870–2, but a further upheaval in 1878 when Parkes and Robertson,
leading the only two factions in the House, coalesced. The seventies
also saw the loss of two other old leaders, besides Cowper: Martin
left politics for the Chief Justiceship in 1873 (the position having
been offered him by Parkes), and Forster retired in 1876. The coalition
of the two factions of the seventies and the loss of old leaders did not
spell the end of the system. Instead, new leaders and new factions
emerged in the eighties. A brief review of the sequence of events in
the twelve years after 1875 will serve to clarify this picture of the
continued operation of the faction system.

Parkes and Robertson alternated in office throughout the mid-
seventies, each leading a following of diverse origins. Their governments did little more than carry minor legislation and business essential to the conduct of the administration and by 1877 neither of them
could secure the support necessary to serve any longer even this
limited function. Both depended to a great extent upon the toleration
of independents. One member, Teece, explained in 1877 that there
were by then three or four 'parties' in the Assembly, one consisting
of only three members and another of four members, a description
that applies to the surviving unabsorbed fragments of the old Cowper-
Robertson faction as identified by the analysis of division lists. When
united, these two, 'though incapable of themselves forming an administration . . . yet were sufficient to turn the scale when acting in
conjunction with the opposition and to defeat one ministry after

another'.[86] It was therefore hardly surprising that although Parkes' and Robertson's first ministries in the seventies each lasted for over two years, their second ministries each fell within four months.

At the end of 1877 a new cabinet, referred to at the time as the Farnell 'Third Party' ministry, was formed. Its title arose more in the expectation that it might serve as the rallying point for a new faction than because Farnell had in fact managed to build one.[87] Before Farnell succeeded in putting together a team of colleagues the confused state of the House had already been reflected by the Governor's having abortively commissioned two relatively minor figures to attempt the formation of an administration. They were S. C. Brown, a member of the old Cowper-Robertson faction, and A. Stuart, a prominent independent who had served in Robertson's 1875-7 cabinet. Since no new leader had emerged, the Farnell ministry was composed of men who had followed Cowper and Robertson before 1870, and of men who had been independents or supporters of Parkes since then. Farnell himself had supported Parkes in both the sixties and the seventies.

The similarities between Farnell's ministry and Forster's, eighteen years earlier, are striking. Both were non-factional and composed of diverse elements temporarily brought together after tangled negotiations and previous failures; both depended heavily on the support not only of independents but of members whose primary allegiances lay with established faction leaders temporarily inactive or in opposition. Behind both ministries lay an impasse which had developed when established leaders were unable or reluctant to respond to growing demands for extensive reforming legislation, notably on the land question in both instances. The result was that each ministry was at the mercy of established leaders and their factions as soon as they saw the chance of taking and holding office.

When Farnell fell at the end of 1878 Parkes and Robertson succeeded in carrying out a consolidating manoeuvre. The coalition government that resulted proved to be one of the strongest ministries before 1887.[88] In its first months, it displayed the strength and stability of its majority by effortlessly passing minor bills and appropriation and loan measures. Then a burst of legislative activity followed. In one year three major measures were passed: the Land, Education and Electoral Acts. The first made a number of changes in the existing law, chiefly with the object of benefiting selectors. The second ended state aid to denominational schools, vested the control of education in a responsible minister and made various changes intended to increase the scope and efficiency of the education system. This Act was subsequently supplemented by a Church and Schools Land Dedication Act which appropriated the income from all unimproved land hitherto reserved for churches and schools to the purposes of the state-controlled educational system. This Act ended a dispute over the lands which had dragged on for over twenty years. The Electoral Act effected a redistribution of seats, enlarged parliament and altered minor provisions of the Act of 1858.

With its parliamentary majority confirmed by the election under the new Act, the government had two more major bills passed in 1881: a Licensing Bill and a Bill to Restrict Chinese Immigration. The former effected a very detailed regulation of the liquor trade and established the principle of 'local option', for which the Temperance movement had been clamouring for years. The ministry came to grief in 1882 when, after defeat of an opposition censure motion, Robertson brought in a measure to consolidate and amend the existing land law without making any modifications of the principles of the Acts of 1861. The leader of the opposition, Stuart, presented a set of counter proposals which embodied radical changes in the law. The tide of public opinion had for some time been flowing strongly against the established system and Robertson's bill was defeated when many of the ministry's erstwhile steady supporters voted against it. The government secured a dissolution and when four ministers were defeated at the polls, it resigned and Stuart formed a new administration.

This was the first of a series of ministries based on a new faction which had emerged in opposition during the last days of the Parkes-Robertson coalition, and its appearance marked the restoration of multifactionalism in the House. With Parkes and Robertson in informal and uneasy alliance, it appeared that the contest for power now beginning would follow well established patterns. It did for a time, but by the mid-eighties there were signs of change which threatened to disrupt the faction system altogether: the appearance of a new type of pressure group inside the House and of new forms of organization without, both emerging in conditions of crisis likely to strain traditional faction loyalties to breaking point. These important matters will be discussed in detail in chapter 6.

We have seen in the detailed account, given above, of the origins of the Parkes-Martin coalition of 1866 and the Parkes administration of 1872 something of the faction manoeuvring that normally shaped the process of cabinet formation. As the connecting survey-narrative implied, the business of overturning a ministry normally had similar general characteristics, though, one might say, it was directed from the opposition benches and conducted in reverse. Opposition was always a matter for manoeuvre and intrigue, designed to harry and test leaders in office and to secure majorities, frequently ephemeral, for motions of challenge and censure. Of course, in many cases circumstances largely beyond the control of opposition leaders prepared the ground for delivering a *coup de grâce*. A ministry normally suffered attrition of its majority by absenteeism, death or resignation of supporters and the defeat of candidates sympathetic to it in the subsequent by-elections; by losing the confidence of independents and by a loss of supporters to new leaders or by defection to former leaders. Examples of each of these weakening factors have been mentioned in the preceding discussion.

Competing leaders also gained strength at the expense of ministers when the latter were unable to carry, or simply failed to see, the legislation necessary to hold or enlarge support, particularly from non-faction quarters in the House. The demise of the Parkes-Robertson coalition in 1882, for example, was only the most dramatic of a number of collapses which followed the failure of governments to devise reforms in land legislation to meet increasing expectations and pressures from supporters and independents. More typically, erosion of power occurred quietly and as a consequence of the heterogeneity of the following a leader in office had to depend on: as witnessed, for example, by Martin's fall in 1864 after failing—by a series of misadventures—to satisfy groups of members who had expectantly supported him when he took office. Coalition ministries were subject to dangerous internal tensions which if unrelieved—as the break-up of the Martin-Parkes administration showed—could bring fatal weakness, both through ministerial dissension and because it might lead to a truce on contentious legislation for which in fact important elements of a following might be anxiously waiting.

To overturn a ministry weakened in these various ways was not difficult for opposition leaders skilled in the usages of the House, having the necessary instinct for correct timing, and equipped with an intimate knowledge of the views and attachments of the individual members whose reactions would determine the success or failure of the final coup. Parkes and Forster displayed finesse in exploiting the border duties issue in 1871-2 to oust the Martin-Robertson government, but the ground had been well prepared for them by the tensions that the original coalition had created, and the government's subsequent loss of prestige. Again, Parkes' censure motion which removed Robertson from office in 1877, though well timed and delivered with *élan,* was hardly likely to fail, considering the serious diminution of support already apparent when the ministry suffered four defeats in the Assembly within one week.

The outcome in such cases seemed inevitable, though even a weakened administration might hope for reprieve if it played its cards skilfully, or if its attackers blundered. By contrast, the power of intrigue and manoeuvre in the hands of master faction tacticians was best demonstrated when used to overthrow a government at the full height of its power. The most striking example of this was the unexpected victory of the then opposition over Parkes in 1874. Though his government appeared formidable—it had a steady following of 44 per cent of the House—Parkes succumbed to assault on an unforeseen issue which bore no relation to his declared policy. The occasion for the attack arose out of the Governor's decision to pardon an ex-bushranger, Gardiner. Utilizing widespread uneasiness at the release itself and at the Governor's tactless handling of petitions expressing the public alarm, Parkes' opponents manoeuvred him into the position of defending the Governor. A naïve opposition member, who specifically denied any wish to do more than register a complaint against the Governor, moved resolutions of protest. But he had been privately persuaded beforehand by a leading supporter of Robertson to move his resolutions as an amendment to a government motion to consider Supply. This automatically constituted censure, and with a number of members supporting the resolutions as a matter of conscience they were carried and the government fell.

Observation of the circumstances in which ministries were constructed and overturned serves to emphasize the extent to which the struggle for power was located in the Assembly. Parliamentary warfare was real and had its own rationale, whose twists could rarely be predicted, or even affected significantly, by pressures emanating from extra-parliamentary sources. No leader commissioned to form a ministry came to the task because he had won a ready-made majority in an election. An election might occasionally increase the strength of a ministry in office. Alternatively, it might administer the final blow to a ministry which had appealed to the country after its support in the House had dwindled and it had been defeated; but an election of this kind did not necessarily define for leaders a new majority. Many electoral contests were isolated struggles, deeply influenced by local issues, personalities and cliques. Calculations of the general outcome before parliament had assembled usually appeared very difficult. This did not, however, mean that faction leaders accepted the apparent uncertainty of the electoral process, supinely waiting to marshal their forces until they knew the personnel of a new House.

The dissolution of a parliament did not herald a truce in the political struggle: rather, the faction leaders briefly moved the focus of their attention from the Assembly into the constituencies. In so doing, they transferred to another arena their interest in tactical manoeuvre and intrigue, reshaping their methods to suit different circumstances, and cloaking them with a secrecy which hid their operation from the generality of electors. Rarely adjudged by contemporaries and difficult now to assess precisely in its effects, electoral manipulation was regarded by faction leaders as a useful weapon in the making and breaking of the majorities on which ministries depended. An examination of its operation is necessary, as much to clarify the relationship between the Assembly and the electorate as to identify one essential part of the political process of the time.

CHAPTER FOUR

The Electorates and Faction Politics

THE PARLIAMENTARY FACTION leaders had one overriding interest in elections: to use them to secure increased support or to preserve the support they already had. They continually intervened in the political life of the constituencies, to assist favoured candidates, to manipulate nominations, and generally to build up local networks of influence. Operating chiefly through resident agents and partisans, such networks could outlast particular campaigns.

The leaders of what became the liberal faction in the first parliament made the first tentative steps in this direction in the election of 1856. Most of the contests in that election were isolated or unrelated struggles arising when local men of influence disagreed as to the man who should represent them in parliament, when new or growing occupational groups in electorates, feeling that they had been shut out from political influence by the local leaders, decided that the time had come to challenge them, or when someone with ambition resolved to try his fortune at the hands of the electors and perhaps enhance his local prestige by winning a seat in the new parliament. In contests of these kinds the questions disputed by candidates were chiefly of local or even personal interest. Matters affecting the colony at large were of course discussed, but often only in their local bearings or with an air of vagueness, uncertainty or dutifulness that deprived them of much of their immediacy.

The liberal leaders in 1856, after being themselves elected in the four-member constituency of Sydney, took an interest in the nominations and campaigns of at least five other electorates ranging from Argyle in the Southern tablelands to the Northumberland Boroughs in the Hunter River Valley. In one of those contests (South Cumberland) a candidate they had nominated was successful, and in the next few months they managed in addition to win three by-elections.

This electoral intervention by leaders in parliament and at the head of the opposition was intended to increase their strength and improve their chance of winning and holding office.[1] Almost accidentally, they had broken through the established pattern of elections. The

men on the committee set up to secure the return of the liberal leaders
in Sydney were employed not only in other elections at that time,
but in the later by-elections in which the parliamentary leaders took
an interest. G. C. Reid was one of these men, working as a lieutenant
under the general direction of Parkes, who played the most active
part in arranging electoral matters for the liberals. In 1851 Reid had
assisted in the election of Rev. J. D. Lang to the old Legislative Council;[2] in 1856 and 1857 he was one of the committee men who did the
arduous work of getting signatures to requisitions in support of
candidates, putting up posters, assisting in the preparation and
conduct of campaign meetings and the door-to-door canvass of
electors and getting voters first on to the rolls and then to the polls
on election day.

Reid took part in at least four of the elections in which the liberals
intervened, and later he played an important role in the Land and
Electoral Reform Leagues, both of which had close relations with the
liberals in parliament, before being given a minor post in the customs
department by the Cowper government.[3] The survival from one
election to the next of the original liberal committee for Sydney,
reconstructed as a central committee with subordinate local committees under it, its participation in making nominations, and its
interest in elections of more than one candidate—especially in constituencies outside that for which it was originally set up—distinguished it from the traditional personal committee of the candidate.
Its development provoked alarm and bitter attacks in the press,[4]
as well as an admission from Parkes that its methods were new and
had alienated many voters.[5]

In the next ten years, similar intervention by parliamentary faction
leaders became an established feature of all elections. But constituencies continued to be extremely suspicious of the intrusion of outsiders into their affairs, and in country areas especially there was
resentment at the attemps of parliamentary leaders in Sydney to send
out non-resident candidates. Reactions of this kind, as well as the
stress conventionally placed on the virtues of 'independence', forced
the faction leaders to conceal their intervention by working privately
through local residents. This secrecy, which now makes it difficult
to unravel many individual contests, did not prevent contemporaries
distinguishing clearly between the traditional influence of local men
of property or profession and the newer influence of faction leaders
and their agents. District Court Judge, H. R. Francis, in giving
evidence in 1872[6] on local appointments in the administration, spoke
explicitly about influence from each source and explained that it

counteracted the advice the judges could give about appointments to clerkships of petty sessions and the police magistracy.

The evidence which survives to attest to the intervention of faction leaders in elections is thus fragmentary and incomplete, with the exception of that to be found in the Mitchell Library's Parkes Papers. Numerous letters in this collection reveal Parkes as having been indefatigable and extremely skilled in the art of finding or placing and getting support for candidates likely to follow him in parliament.[7] But he was by no means the only faction leader who employed these political techniques.

When the Martin and Forster coalition secured a dissolution in 1864, their concern for their strength led them to search for a candidate to contest Maneroo. Forster indirectly approached W. A. Brodribb, a pastoralist who lived in the constituency, asking him to stand for election. Brodribb agreed on receiving the assurance that he would have support from the ministry itself.[8] In an address to the electors in the local paper he claimed that he had come forward 'in deference to the wishes of many residents', and during his campaign he declared that he had originally been invited to stand by G. P. Desailly, who had promised him the support of a number of electors. Desailly, a J.P. and the lessee of over a million acres of Crown land in the Riverina, was a prominent member of the Riverine Council, which had given dinners to the ministry and its friends when it came into office. There can be little doubt that Desailly was acting as intermediary between Forster and Brodribb. His arrangements were upset when Martin himself, in search of a seat after two defeats in the election, was forced to enter the contest in Maneroo, displacing Brodribb at the last minute.

The leaders of the opposing faction, Cowper and Robertson, were also engaged at this time in manoeuvres to forward candidates disposed to support them in parliament. In the nomination proceedings at Tumut in 1863 Henry Hayes reluctantly admitted under criticism that 'he was the representative [of] the Cowperian party' in the electorate.[9] Charles Cowper Jun. had held the Tumut seat briefly before resigning it in order to oppose Martin in his ministerial re-election in Orange. Cowper won the contest and Martin, returning the compliment, contested Tumut and won it against a candidate O'Connell, whom Hayes had helped to nominate. Cowper Jun. did some of the organizing work for his father's faction besides standing as a candidate on its behalf. In 1856, he had supported J. W. Chisholm in Argyle and managed his campaign after Chisholm had been brought forward by local families.[10] Cowper made it plain that Chisholm was not liberal enough, but that he was the best man available to oppose J. H. Plunkett who, after defeat by Cowper Sen., Parkes and their friends in Sydney, had been offered the nomination in Argyle.

A few years later Cowper Jun. appeared in another electorate, Camden, assisting a candidate, Morrice, who supported the Cowper-Robertson faction and its land policy.[11] The electorate was one of many at this time in which agricultural settlers anxious to obtain more land or freehold land were beginning to challenge the influence, over nominations, of men of substance. The Macarthurs had nominated H. M. Oxley and W. V. Wild, both opponents of the liberal leaders and their land policy, and Morrice's supporters, who had once supported James Macarthur himself, decided when he retired to 'seize the opportunity and select their own man'.[12]

If press reports are to be believed, Cowper's activity in 1863-4 in Tumut and in Orange was at this time only part of a widespread liberal network. The *Sydney Morning Herald* claimed that Cowper Jun. had been returned in Orange by the faction leaders' influence there.[13] The *Tamworth Examiner* added darkly that it had been 'informed that the "unseen influence" which . . . both planned and effected the return of Mr. Cowper Jun. for Orange is one which is neither unknown to, or unfelt by, the Northern electorates', and that it was guided by the 'magnates of the Victoria Club', that is, Cowper and Robertson.[14] This 'unseen influence' in the northern electorates had been revealed in 1859 when the Cowper-Robertson ministry appointed three men as magistrates after they had helped in the election of one of its supporters.[15] In Mudgee in the north west, the 'Cowper party' unsuccessfully put Innes in nomination in the general election a year later.[16] In this election in 1864, F. A. Bell worked 'for free trade members for Cowper' and claimed that he had 'worked the oracle well'.[17]

Bell was the secretary of a Free Trade Association set up early in 1864 to agitate against the Martin ministry's tariff proposals.[18] The opposition, led by Cowper and Robertson, had been closely connected with the formation and work of the Association; but it became inactive when Martin's proposals were defeated in the House soon after its foundation, and Bell was left in close relations with the faction leaders. A few years later, still speaking in the name of the now entirely vanished Free Trade Association,[19] Bell had become Parkes' electoral agent in the Port Macquarie area where he had a sugar plantation and considerable property.[20]

The character of a faction agent's work is summed up in one of Bell's letters to Parkes at the time of the elections in 1869, a letter which incidentally reveals the editor of the *Empire* in Sydney as a roving electoral agent for Robertson. Parkes and Martin were in opposition to Forster and Robertson at the time.

> Bennett of the Empire arrived here [today], he says to see the progress of the Sugar Industry, but Chidgey, the Telegraph master informs me that there are a swarm of *electioneering* men come with him—he had written to *me* . . . saying that he had intended to go to Kiama and Shoalhaven but he had altered his intention. [He had planned to stay with Bell but] several that came with him have learned that I am anti-Forsterite and Jackite [Robertson] and therefore that no consultations can be held here . . . Forster has lost so much ground that he could be easily upset. Now if Sir James Martin would allow himself to be nominated for here, I would propose him and I feel sure of returning him at the top of the Poll . . . if this is refused you must send us a good name, but as I said before *Mr. Palser would not do.* Is Charley Lyons going in again for Central Cumberland? If he is not—here the election would cost him a trifle in comparison, not much more than travelling expenses. There is a young barrister of the name of Pilcher—he has plenty of sense and a goodly quantity of *brass* and I understand speaks well and fluently [and] *if* he is *not* a Robertsonite then he should be looked after : . .
>
> If Mr. Montefiore goes to England you will need to get Alexander Campbell, M.L.C., or Mr. Tighe could read up for the Treasurership.[21]

The electoral work of an agent on behalf of his leader had a number of aspects which, in their detail, are most fully revealed in the Parkes Papers.[22] The most important task of the agent was to assess the disposition of power among the known groups within the electorate and the variations that could be expected to take place in the balance of influence when a campaign was in progress. He was then able to suggest the type of candidate most likely to succeed: information that was indispensable if 'outsiders' (the firm supporters of a faction leader), were to be brought forward in the electorate. In such a case, immediate steps had to be taken to announce and support the chosen man.

Alternatively, the agent and his local friends could assess the balance of forces and select a candidate from among the local inhabitants well before a campaign began, or where neither this nor the promotion of an outsider was possible, it was still practicable to choose the most likely of the candidates independently entering a

contest and to seek to extract a pledge or at least an implied promise
of support from him.

The local resident acting as agent or friend of a faction leader
commonly undertook on behalf of his leader other work not closely
connected with elections. In East Maitland in the sixties, Parkes had
the usual electoral assistance from J. N. Brunker,[23] who, as a stock
and station agent, was in an occupation admirably suited for gaining
information and friendships useful in the work. When Parkes became
Colonial Secretary, Brunker kept him informed about local administrative matters of official interest, and, when Parkes' Public Schools
Bill was before parliament in 1866, Brunker not only prepared and
circulated petitions to parliament for signature in the vicinity of
Maitland but also kept Parkes informed of the attitudes of local
members, Dodds, Eckford and Burns and put steady pressure on them
to be in the House to support the Bill with their votes.[24]

The local assistance given to a faction leader was frequently re-
warded in various ways. When J. A. Portus, another old political
agent of Parkes in East Maitland, was out of work in the sixties,
Parkes found him an appointment as clerk of petty sessions[25]—an
appointment of the type Judge Francis later objected to. Again,
Parkes had a number of friends in his own electorate of Kiama who
could be relied on to conduct elections on his behalf and to whom
he was able, for example, to recommend a new candidate, J. Stewart,
when he himself decided to sit for another constituency. This small
group of men, including Joseph Weston, the editor-proprietor of the
Kiama *Independent*, were repeatedly active in opposition to S. W.
('Poodle') Gray who was a supporter of Cowper and Robertson and
had held the seat until 1864. Their reward for their services is to be
found in Parkes' achievement in placing a bridge and a wharf for
the area on the estimates in 1868.

From the viewpoint of the country constituency itself these benefits
were not simply rewards, or as the press was inclined to put it, corruption.[26] They were rather an appropriate attention to the needs of
the district.[27] The rudimentary state of public services in many
isolated country electorates gave the local people a lively interest in
the immediate, if small, benefits to be won by helping politicians in
search of votes and seats and therefore laid them open to exploitation
by the faction leader and his agents, despite the customary suspicion
of 'outsiders'. Quarrels of purely local character in an electorate,
which might arise, for example, from ambition for prestige or from
religious feeling,[28] could give the faction leader another opportunity
for manoeuvring to build influence.

The importance of manipulators who exploited local antagonisms or (as in the case of Charles Cowper Jun.'s work in Camden) the desires of growing occupational groups for reform and greater influence, was enhanced by the fact that elections were rarely fought in terms of sharply defined positions on general questions. A parliamentary struggle dominated by factions was scarcely calculated to produce national issues to override petty conflicts, local feeling and jealousy of Sydney. More generally, the social and economic life of the colony was fragmented by the geographical isolation of many country settlements, and local social solidarity drew strength as a result from community rather than from class, occupation or interest group.

The isolation may be inferred from the fact that in 1856 the whole colony, divided into thirty electorates, had only 42,300 enrolled electors, of whom one-third were in the metropolitan electorate, Sydney. In the sixties and seventies, the enrolments grew steadily, first when adult male suffrage was introduced in 1858 in place of a suffrage limited by various property qualifications, and then as the population itself grew. The smallest electorates of the colony in 1856 and 1889 had respectively 294 and 1150 enrolled voters.

Numbers of enrolled electors and electorates, 1856–1889[29]

Year	Total enrolled electors	Number of electorates	Average number of electors/electorate
1856	42,330	30	1411
1861/2	101,826	60	1697
1871/2	147,934	60	2465
1881/2	192,213	72	2670
1885/6	232,190	72	3230
1889/90	290,314	76	3860

The consequence of isolation was that the influence possessed by faction leaders because of their power in the centralized political and administrative institutions of the colony could not be decisive in the internal politics of most country electorates. The faction leaders and their agents simply had to come to terms with the local people and do it covertly.

The ineffectiveness, before the late seventies, of extra-parliamentary political organizations also suggests what obstacles politicians faced when seeking electoral power and support. In the elections themselves, by tradition, all candidates had their personal committees, and these were the only open organizations normally employed in their campaigns. These committees seldom survived the campaign for which they were set up, although the men most active in them frequently stayed together and reconstituted the committees for subsequent contests. The committee usually conducted the routine work of canvassing, organizing meetings, raising money and paying expenses. Meetings and the canvass were particularly important because throughout the period voting was not compulsory. While open voting was in existence—from 1856 to 1858—the committees had complicated tactical tasks to perform on voting day, but even after the secret ballot was introduced, getting voters to the polls was one of their important jobs. Personation, conveying and, more rarely, intimidation and obstruction inevitably accompanied these activities, as they did in England. The committees also had more subtle functions. The publication of the names of committee men was an announcement of the local support a candidate had received. If he was an outsider or a known supporter of a faction leader, the committee was therefore the outward sign, to those who knew how to interpret it, that the candidate had come to terms with the local people.

Extra-parliamentary organizations were, of necessity, unable to work behind the façade of the candidate's committee as did the faction leaders and their agents. A number of organizations emerged in the later fifties with the aim, among others, of attempting to influence legislation by building support for their causes in the electorates. They were all formed in Sydney and played out their brief parts in the metropolitan area, where the processes of social change, as a result of economic development and urbanization, were most advanced. The number of voters was far larger in Sydney than in any country electorate and, being physically concentrated and easy to reach by meeting and pamphlet, afforded to organizations opportunities that no country electorate was to give them until the eighties.

Still, they were all singularly ineffective and short-lived. The Electoral Reform League, for example, set up in support of the reforms carried into effect in the Act of 1858, confined itself to agitation and made no attempt to nominate candidates. Its contribution to the passing of the Act, though hard to assess precisely, was unquestionably small. The Land League was established at about the same time [30] to support radical land reforms similar to, but more extensive than, those advocated by Robertson. It had a minor success in 1858 when its two candidates defeated men advanced by the Cowper ministry in Sydney. In 1859 its president, John Black, became Forster's Secretary for Lands after being elected, along with Pemell, as the League's candidate. But early in 1860 it ceased its activity and faded out of existence without playing any important part in stimulating the rising tide of support for Robertson's land policy or in the election of December 1860.[31]

In the sixties no marked change took place. Protectionism, advocated in the later fifties by a Protection League which was more a name and a handful of enthusiastic agitators than an organization,[32] had no success at all. The Free Trade Association of 1864, after elaborating an organization suitable for permanent electoral activity and parliamentary lobbying,[33] lapsed into silence later in the year. In the country, the Liberal Political Associations of 1858, intended to bring together the liberals in each of five towns for electoral and parliamentary purposes on a wide range of questions, came to nothing.[34] The Riverine Council, in which pastoralists of the southwestern electorates predominated, was set up early in the 1860s to advocate the separation of the entire western half of the colony as a new entity and to secure minor reforms in the administration of the area. Its influence, even on a ministry which needed its support, was negligible and there is no evidence that it played a part in elections in its area. The faction leaders never committed themselves publicly to these organizations,[35] and although some of their followers were active in their committees, most members of parliament did not associate with them. Parkes, whose instinct for the sources of political strength was unrivalled, was occasionally to be detected in the shadowy world of influence behind them, but never, despite his constant need for support, in the forefront of them.

By the end of the sixties at least one organization had managed to build some branches in the country as well as in the city and to enrol a considerable number of members. This was the Protestant Political Association, formed when sectarian passions flared after O'Farrell's attempt in 1868 to assassinate the Duke of Edinburgh. Shortly after the formation of this Association, it was reported to have thirteen branches, many of them in the country electorates, and to be establishing more.[36] Representatives of the branches attended a general council meeting in 1869.[37] According to the secretary, the P.P.A. then had 2,000 members [38] in the metropolitan area and could command 3,000 votes with all its branches considered.[39] In 1872, it issued a series of nomination orders from its headquarters in Sydney to its agents in country electorates.[40]

It is probable that the Loyal Orange Lodges, established for twenty years or more and enjoying a revival in the late sixties, provided the Association with the means for establishing branches and recruiting members so rapidly. In Sydney it had close relations with one of the Lodges.[41] Several of the more prominent members of the Association were Orangemen,[42] and candidates who made no secret of their Orangeism were supported by committees whose leading figures were Orangemen and members of the Association.[43]

The political activity of the P.P.A. was almost exclusively electoral. It had some success in the metropolitan area: its president, John Davies, 'fairly ruled the political and aldermanic roosts in Sydney' for some years through it, the temperance and 'other' unspecified bodies, if E. W. O'Sullivan is to be believed.[44] Robertson himself admitted in 1869 that Davies' election organization was superior to his own and gave it much of the credit for the defeat of Cowper in East Sydney in that year.[45] It is possible that the Association's influence outside Sydney was gained not only through its own branches and the Orange lodges, but also through relations behind the scenes between Parkes and its leaders, which gave each the benefit of the influence commanded by the other. In 1868 it intervened in an election in The Hastings constituency to support Palser against Forster, who was seeking re-election after taking office with Robertson.[46] A year later, Parkes' agent in the area, F. A. Bell, advised him that Palser was unsuitable as a candidate to oppose Forster in the general election, speaking as if Parkes had in fact been advancing him.[47]

The secrecy with which the Association worked makes it extremely difficult to assess the significance of its political activity. If its secretary and other contemporaries are to be believed, both its organization and its activity were centred in the metropolitan area and met with most success there. The Association lasted for four years and then faded completely from the public record. The implication is that its influence was probably limited not only by its sectarianism, but by localism outside Sydney and by the dispersion of limited staff and funds[48] in an attempt to build branches over a wide geographical area. Its influence in electorates, when compared with that which faction leaders had long since won, was almost certainly ephemeral and incidental despite the fact that long after 1868 sectarian tensions continued to offer the political manipulators an ideal field for exploitation.

Repeated failure of early interest group organizations did not stifle the impulse to form associations for political action. While the faction leaders in parliament manoeuvred for office in the seventies, a number of questions became the subject of burning political dispute outside the House and new associations were formed, some for simple agitation and propaganda work and others to secure detailed legislative remedies for grievances. The Public Schools League, which agitated with considerable effectiveness for free, secular and compulsory education was one of the first kind. Temperance organizations were another. These associations, although they lasted longer than earlier bodies, were not as radically different from them as the most notable of all the political groups in the seventies, the Free Selectors Associations. The latter made a new and, for the first time, relatively successful attempt to secure direct representation in the House and to do it by building on electoral strength. This strength came from a section of the population which, although of diverse character,[49] had a sharp unifying sense of economic grievance corrosive of the old bonds of local solidarity in the country electorates.

The free selector organizations were formed in country areas as a wave of dissatisfaction with the Robertson Land Acts gathered momentum in the early seventies. The first Selectors Association was formed at Yass in 1873 and it was rapidly followed by the establishment of similar bodies in other country areas.[50] Occasional country conferences of representatives from these Associations were an early feature of the movement. One of the first of these conferences, held in 1873, passed strong resolutions in favour of ending the sale of Crown land at auction and of crediting interest payments to balances owing on conditional purchases,[51] demands which were to become basic elements in all programmes devised by the movement as it grew.

While the Land Bill of 1875 was under consideration, selectors' organizations inundated parliament with petitions setting out their claims.[52] Late in the same year delegates from the country Associations joined with sympathetic members of parliament in establishing a Land Law Reformation League in Sydney[53] to stir up public support for the reforms demanded by selectors. Beyond organizing a few public meetings, the League's influence was limited and short-lived, but its coming caused a stir, on the ground that it was aiming to exert a blatant 'class interest' in politics.[54]

Within two years, the Free Selectors Associations had sent delegates to a central conference in Sydney,[55] and similar gatherings were then held annually until 1883. The first conference agreed to a long list of demands for detailed reform of the land law, and embodied them in a manifesto,[56] which concluded with the resolution that

> this conference of delegates pledges itself not to support any candidate at the forthcoming election, unless promising to carry out the above programme.

Twenty-seven country Associations sent delegates to the conference and at least one of them instructed its delegate beforehand.[57] After the conference, some of the Associations held meetings to select candidates or to support candidates with acceptable views who were already in the field in the general election of 1877.[58] The selectors thus entered the political struggle at the electoral level, after four years of organized struggle which had its origin and its strength in country electorates, and they accepted a method of political warfare which, although glimpsed as a possibility by earlier organizations, had never before been practised successfully.

It is difficult to assess the extent of the influence these bodies wielded in their own electorates. Since they represented an important segment of the known vote—in some areas the decisive one—they became one of the more important factors to be reckoned with by individual candidates.[59] In addition, selectors had individual champions in parliament, men like G. Day and R. Barbour, some of whom no doubt owed their positions to the electoral work of the Associations, while others, though not ostensibly supported by them nor even of the selector class, stood to gain from any legislation favouring it. As a result, the legislature of the mid-seventies had a strong pro-selector tone and some concessions were made to their demands in the Lands Act Amendment Act of 1875.[60] Selector influence in parliament contributed to the difficulties faced by the Robertson ministry in 1877, difficulties which came to a head when Garrett, the Minister for Lands, attempted to have cabinet accept far-reaching pro-selector reforms, and was forced to resign when Robertson refused to consider them.

The abortive Farnell Land Bill of 1878 showed even more clearly how influential organized selector opinion was becoming. Farnell's ministry, lacking the support of an established faction, had to place particular reliance on its measures as a source of popularity. Robertson's failure to reach a compromise with members sympathetic to the selectors had alienated many of them and indicated clearly one group which Farnell had to propitiate. His Bill made extensive concessions to selectors along lines advocated by their organizations.[61] During the debates on the measure, a number of members frankly admitted their position as the political servants of the Selectors Associations.[62] This had been obvious even after the election in 1877 and had provoked protests in the name of 'independence' against 'class representation' and 'delegation'.[63] The Bill failed in the face of bitter resistance from the pastoralists in the House, and from the misgivings of those who felt that the measure smacked too much of class bias.[64] The Farnell ministry resigned, to be replaced by a coalition of the Robertson and Parkes factions which proved for some years to be more than strong enough to outweigh the influence of the free selector champions.

The Free Selectors Associations, although the most notable, were not the only bodies to try to gain direct representation in parliament in the seventies. The Trades and Labour Council was successful in having Angus Cameron elected to represent working class interests in 1874, and paid him a salary for some time. But before long the connection was severed, when Cameron asserted his independence by claiming that the 'Council should not control him but he should speak and vote as his conscience dictated'.[65] The Council's political experiment was thus a 'comparative failure' and for a time it 'withdrew from direct political activity and proceeded to concentrate on the consolidation of the industrial base of the Labor Movement'.[66] Nevertheless in the general election of 1880, it embarked once more on a search for candidates for several electorates, and questioned the chosen men carefully on their attitudes to its platform before committing itself to supporting them.[67]

There had of course always been organizations outside parliament which sought to secure favourable treatment whenever bills affecting their interests were before parliament. The Chamber of Commerce[68] and the Licensed Victuallers Association [69] were of this kind. But the main activities of such bodies were domestic or internal, and none of them seriously undertook to choose and promote candidates for parliament. Occasionally they tried endorsing someone[70], but members able and willing to express their attitudes tended to reach the House without their overt and organized support. The pastoralists were in a somewhat similar position. Always well represented in parliament, they usually showed their hand in relation to limited and concrete issues. Most frequently when acting as a group they were on the defensive. When they resorted to organization it was of a limited and semi-confidential nature.[71] They remained to a large extent a closed fraternity, depending for electoral strength on their social prestige in the areas from which they came.[72]

The political activity of the Trades and Labour Council and the work of the Free Selectors Associations were not the only signs of a growing tendency towards political organization by men who felt their views were inadequately represented. In 1877, at the time of the free selectors conference, a Working Men's Defence Association was active in the metropolis, and there were reports that it had branches at Braidwood[73] and Bathurst,[74] as well as in the Sydney area.[75] It was a distinctive organization in several respects. It aired its members' views, not on a single issue, but on several,[76] and both working men and employers took part in it.[77] Besides agitation, it also took some part in the elections of 1877.[78] More important, as a sign of what might come in future, it sought an alliance with the Free Selectors Associations, though this was refused.[79] The *Sydney Morning Herald*,[80] commenting on the activities of the W.M.D.A. at this time, observed that working class agitation had one desirable feature: it countered localism.

Early in 1878, the W.M.D.A. transformed itself into the Political Reform Association[81] announcing in its constitution[82] that it intended to 'infuse new vigour' into parliament and to raise the colony from the apathy into which it had fallen by publishing information respecting questions of public policy and by returning 'to Parliament gentlemen whose opinions are in harmony with those of the Association and who pledge themselves to their advocacy and support'. It further planned to supervise 'the electoral rolls with a view to secure the registration of every elector'. Its programme embraced reforms in the land law and the electoral system; more rapid extension of public works; protection to encourage local industry; amendments to the liquor licensing law and the Public Schools Act; supervision of immigration and 'stringent restrictions' on the entry of Chinese; a bill to promote mining; a special tax on the property of absentee owners, and support for federation. A similar impulse produced the Political Reform League at the same time.[83]

But these early associations, though the predecessors of the more successful Protection and Political Reform League, formed in 1881, met with little success in the short run. Lacking a clear point of focus, their broad programmes contained the seeds of defeat, and they either dissipated their energies in 'extraneous' controversies, (extraneous that is to the 'coming' question of protection) or died of 'sectarian strife and inertia'.[84] If they survived, it was to be caught up in the intellectual ferment of the early eighties,[85] and to be shaped and reshaped under pressure from protectionist enthusiasts or the defenders of free trade.[86] But this is to run ahead of the story.

The importance of these organizations and of the movements which lay behind them slowly became clear to politicians in the eighties, but the faction system was not destroyed overnight. Each association represented limited class and economic interests and men with limited enthusiasm for sustained political action. None of them threatened any immediate change in the character of the political process in parliament, because they could not hope to secure enough support to enable them to form ministries. Even in the electorates, the Free Selectors Associations did not greatly affect the operations of faction leaders during the seventies. They were, for a long time, simply another type of group with which such leaders had to come to terms. Admittedly, since they cut across the bonds of local solidarity and the isolation of electorates, they were groups whose existence complicated the task of manipulation but on the evidence of the Parkes Papers, the faction leaders' activities in constituencies continued much as before.[87] In the House, the members connected in one way or another with the Free Selectors Associations and similar organizations had to be taken account of when faction leaders were assessing and manipulating the balance of forces there and they proved susceptible to the methods so long employed in constructing majorities. The activities of the Trades and Labour Council and the efforts to write comprehensive programmes and to build alliances foreshadowed the growth of more powerful, and far more autonomous and disrupting political organizations. In the meantime the faction system was stable enough to absorb the new methods of political activity.

CHAPTER FIVE

The Cabinet

O N 9 March 1880, Henry Parkes, as Premier of New South Wales, wrote and initialled the following minute:

The Cabinet, after consideration, concur in the views of the Minister for Justice, and approve of effect being given to them accordingly.[1]

Behind this and many similar surviving minutes lies the story of the development of the cabinet in New South Wales, long before political parties emerged in the colony. It would be easy to suppose that this institution, if it existed at all before the end of the century, must have been but a shadow of its English counterpart, deprived of real collective responsibility and unity in action by divisions of opinion within coalition and *ad hoc* ministries, and by the effect on such ministries of faction manoeuvres in the legislature. But a supposition of this kind, resting on the premise that party government is essential to responsible government, would be wide of the mark. In writing the minute quoted above, Parkes was following a procedure which had been first worked out in 1856 and which was intended at the time to make cabinet an institution distinct from the Executive Council and to ensure that it did act collectively.

The Executive Council was a body of advisers selected and appointed by the Governor according to his commission and instructions.[2] With some exceptions the Governor was required to consult with the Council in the exercise of all the powers given him in his commission and instructions, and he was expected to be present himself at its meetings. Nothing in these instruments or in the constitution itself specifically enjoined that a cabinet be set up in addition to the Executive Council. It was nonetheless accepted without question that under the new system of government the Governor would select as his Executive Councillors the members of the legislature chosen by the premier of the day to form the ministry, and appointed by the Governor, on the advice of the premier, to the offices in charge of the main departments. The cabinet was established in the shadow of this Executive Council under the influence of Governor Sir William Denison.

Denison had two aims: to ensure that the change in the system of government did not weaken the executive power, and to make arrangements that would at least reduce the possibility of political conflict between himself and his ministers. He recognized at the outset that although he would occupy a 'sort of indifferent position'[3] in the new system—indifferent in not taking sides on matters in dispute in the legislature—he still had a responsibility to the Crown and the Imperial government that could not be transferred to his ministerial advisers. This responsibility had to be reconciled with the latter's responsibility to the legislature if conflict was to be avoided or minimized. Denison also feared that the executive arm of government would be weakened once the ministers became dependent on majorities in the Lower House for their tenure of office, their legislative measures and their finance. He saw the Assembly as a source of pressures for hasty and ill-considered legislation, and for measures for strictly local and material benefit. He doubted whether ministers drawn from, but unable to control such a body by deploying a strong party within it, would be powerful and experienced enough to give the strong and balanced executive leadership that he thought the administrative arm of the government needed. He aimed therefore to give the Governor a powerful voice as an adviser to the ministry in the new system, but to arrange matters so that his voice should be 'non-political' or 'indifferent' and the entire responsibility for advice tendered him formally by his Executive Councillors should fall on the ministry of the day.[4] The same arrangements would make possible the reconciliation of the two distinct responsibilities of the Governor to the Crown and of the ministers to the legislature.

Denison could not openly avow his intention of strengthening ministries by lending them the Governor's experience and advice, but had to proceed more indirectly. Thus, when first raising the question with the Premier, Donaldson, in July 1856, he presented it simply as a matter of finding a procedure that would prevent clashes between the concurrent responsibilities of the Governor and the ministry. The analogy, he argued, which had been freely drawn in the press between the Governor and the Sovereign—an analogy which seemed to show that the Governor would be a 'cipher' or 'rubber stamp' under responsible government[5]—was not in fact so close that the Governor could model his conduct on that of the Queen.[6] He proposed at first that the ministers should not submit bills to parliament without having first laid their legislative proposals before the Executive Council. He made no explicit claim for a voice in the formulation of legislation at this stage, but it was apparent that any procedure to bring proposed legislation to the Council would give him the opportunity to see it and to make his views known to ministers. In this way, possible conflicts between the Governor and ministers could be ironed out before either party had become publicly committed to a particular position.

Donaldson's ministry was at first less interested in the questions raised by Denison than in proposals for reorganization of the entire administrative structure, especially at the top, to achieve two aims: to reduce what was considered to be the excessive centralization of the old system and to allocate the work of different departments quite distinctly, so that each minister might be held individually responsible for the departments placed under his control. When plans for administrative reorganization to accomplish these ends had been agreed on in the Executive Council in August[7] the ministry brought them up for discussion and approval in the Assembly. Parker, in reply to a demand that ministers be held individually responsible by the House, insisted that a ministry must have a 'united responsibility'.[8] Denison had meanwhile sought the opinion of the late Colonial Secretary, E. Deas Thomson, the chief administrative officer of the old system of government, who agreed that the administration had to be reorganized and went on to emphasize that a cabinet would be a vital part of the new system. With Thomson's advice available to ministers,[9] Denison then brought forth his own detailed plan of the procedural relations that should exist between the Governor, the ministers and the Executive Council. This plan, modified somewhat by the ministry, was adopted by the Executive Council.[10]

The procedure Denison recommended included weekly meetings of the Executive Council at a fixed time; and prior circulation of departmental documents through the minister concerned, to him and then to the other members of the Council through its clerk, before they were brought up for decision in the Council. No one disputed Denison's claim that he should have a voice in the formulation of government policy, even on matters which were not required by law to go before the Council, although the Attorney-General, Manning, did question whether the action of the Governor and the ministry should of necessity be 'concurrent', as Denison had put it.[11] Denison replied to this criticism that he knew he was bound to accept ministerial advice or, if he insisted on a course opposed by ministers, to have them resign and be forced to find others, so that he could insist only when he knew he could find other ministers with the support of a majority.[12]

The ministry added to the plan the recommendations that cabinet should concert its policy before advising the Governor in Council and that it would be represented collectively in its relations with him by the 'first minister'. The Governor was also given a voice in discussions when the law did not require ministers to consult him. It was agreed that he should 'approve' cabinet's decision on such questions and that the decision should be formally taken and recorded in the Executive Council.

Denison therefore secured all he had wanted and in the process he helped the Donaldson ministry clarify its attitudes about cabinet and accept procedures which made it necessary for ministries to establish a cabinet almost as soon as responsible government was put into operation.

By the end of 1857 the procedure was established. As Denison explained in an admonitory letter to Cowper, the then Premier:

> The rule on which we have hitherto acted is as follows. Any member of the Government who may wish to introduce a Bill will first obtain the assent of his colleagues to the principles of the measure. Having done so he will forward an outline of the measure to me for submission to the Executive Council, and this is done as a matter of course unless I should think it advisable to suggest any alterations or modifications; should I do so it is returned to the officer for reconsideration; should I have no remark to make the assent of the Council follows as a matter of course . . .
>
> There may . . . be subjects upon which the advice or opinion of the Governor may be of use in settling the principle of a measure and it is evident that this advice . . . should be available before the Bill is introduced . . .[13]

This letter suggests that the procedure was not always strictly adhered to, and occasionally Governors did complain[14] that they had not been given an adequate opportunity to express their views on ministerial legislation before it was presented to the Assembly. But the minuting on documents in the archives leaves little doubt that the procedure was usually followed, and that, as a result, Governors could and did comment in detail upon the general policy and precise form of the measures ministries proposed to put to the Assembly. Denison, for example, discussed the Cowper ministry's Land Bill at length both in a letter and in a minute to Cowper,[15] and he later discussed a number of the Forster ministry's measures, making especially severe criticisms of its proposals for land legislation.[16]

The core of the early cabinet, enlarged by the creation of new ministerial offices as time went on, consisted of the colonial secretary, the treasurer, and the secretaries for lands and works (after those two departments were separated in 1859). The premier usually became colonial secretary, although James Martin took the attorney-generalship in his ministries, and Farnell and Robertson, in their ministries of 1860 and 1877 respectively, took the lands portfolio—on each occasion at a time when the work of the lands department was of particular political importance. The colonial secretary's office, central and pre-eminent before 1856, retained a great deal of its prestige, and in each of Martin's coalition ministries it was taken by the leader of the group whose alliance Martin secured. The ministry as a whole normally included the attorney-general and, until 1873, the solicitor general. These men were commonly, but not always, of cabinet rank although their offices were not of major political interest to the members of the Assembly.

The creation of new ministerial offices enlarged cabinet a little. The postmaster-general's office created in 1865,[17] the ministry of justice and public instruction created in 1873 and divided into two in 1880, and the secretaryship for mines created in 1874, brought the number of cabinet posts to nine in the eighties (ten if the office without portfolio of vice-president of the Executive Council is included, although it was occasionally not filled as a ministerial post). With two minor exceptions[18] the vice-presidents were members of the Upper House and had cabinet seats because they represented the government there. The Legislative Council demanded and the ministries readily admitted that the ministerial representative in the Upper House should be a member of cabinet. The work of ministerial representative fell as a rule upon the vice-president or one of the less important ministers, such as the postmaster-general.

The arrangements made in 1856 to define the relations of the Governor, the ministers and the Executive Council gave premiers a strong inducement to insist upon the collective responsibility of ministries, for both policy and administration, in their relations with the legislature as well as with the Governor. In Britain the principle that ministers were collectively responsible to the House of Commons and to the King had been established well before the mid-nineteenth century,[19] slowly circumscribing the limits of individual ministerial responsibility.[20]

The Donaldson ministry had the clear advice of E. Deas Thomson on the need for collective responsibility, assuming that cabinet practice would be modelled on that of the contemporary British cabinet. He had proposed, in a widely published memorial on administrative reorganization, that each minister would be 'held responsible to his colleagues' for departments under his control and that there would be ministerial consultation[21] 'on all matters requiring their joint action'. He quoted *Murray's Official Handbook of Church and State*[22] on the position of cabinet in Britain and the procedures by which its collective action was secured. Denison also assumed that before any proposals reached him they would have been already agreed on by the ministers in 'private meetings or cabinet councils'.[23]

The procedure for bringing matters from ministers to the Executive Council made it necessary for cabinet to elaborate its own procedure. Some of the elements of a secretarial service were in effect provided by the arrangements made for circulating documents prior to Council meetings. It appears, however, that some of the secretarial work of cabinet, at least from the sixties onwards, was conducted out of the colonial secretary's office by the under secretary.[24] Many, if not all, of the cabinet's decisions were recorded on the documents that issued from departments over ministers' signatures, either as minutes for the cabinet, or as minutes for the Executive Council. The cabinet minutes were almost always made and signed by the premier of the day and, being merely marginal notes of the kind quoted at the beginning of the chapter,[25] they are now dispersed throughout the archives of the departments. Some of them are, however, long statements of the collective opinion of the ministry, occasionally prepared for the information of other people,[26] and minutes of this kind, as well as brief notes attached to departmental papers, found their way into print in the official record of the Assembly, its *Votes and Proceedings*,[27] when the House called for departmental papers. Another small group of minutes survive in which cabinets gave their collective advice to the Governor that he should, for example, dissolve the Assembly.[28]

Cabinet secrecy meant a good deal less in the colony than it did in England,[29] given that cabinet minutes were made public when the Assembly called for papers, but it was recognized as a necessary part of cabinet procedure.[30] When cabinet minutes were published, no attempt was made to argue that this should not have been done or that the permission of the premier should have been obtained first, as was customary in England. But secrecy appears to have been broken only after a decision determined in cabinet had been carried out.

Little is known of procedure at cabinet meetings, but Robertson gave one glimpse of it when questioned during an election about how far cabinet members were committed to his Land Bill. He explained that proposed legislation was discussed in cabinet clause by clause and that each question was decided by majority vote, the

minister in whose department a particular measure fell having two
votes. Then 'all the members of the Cabinet are bound to vote for
the measure as it stands, when it comes before the Parliament, unless
it has been agreed to leave any particular clause open . . .'[31] Other
ministries undoubtedly did not follow the exact procedure Robertson
described, but the existence of recognized 'open questions' within a
ministry[32] and the solidarity shown by ministers in voting in the
House both indicate that, however decisions were taken, the collective
responsibility of ministers was accepted as necessary for cabinet'
existence and that some, at least, of its procedure was designed to
secure this.

The resignations of ministers and conflicts within ministries show
even more clearly that the collective responsibility of cabinet members
was an established fact as well as an ideal. In 1858 James Martin resigned from Cowper's ministry at the Premier's request after Cowper
and his colleagues had decided that they would no longer defend
Martin's conduct in the House and that they would not resign when
the House had carried a motion against them. The motion criticized
the ministry for not having obtained certain returns of insolvency
that had been ordered by the House seven months before.[33] It was
Martin's responsibility to see that the returns were furnished and he
had failed to take the necessary action despite the remonstrances of the
Premier, Cowper.[34] During the debate in the House, the ministers conferred and decided not to treat the vote to come as a vote of censure.

Martin had joined Cowper in 1856 solely in order to help put the
Donaldson ministry out of office and despite admitted differences
of opinion between them on the leading political questions of the
day. Cowper, though he had been glad enough originally to accept
Martin's support, was becoming much more independent by 1858.
The ministry's Electoral Bill had now been passed with large majorities, and it was thought likely that, after an election, the ministry
would succeed with a proposed land bill. Martin was opposed to one
of the main features of the latter—free selection before survey—
which Cowper had accepted when taking Robertson into the ministry
early in 1858. It is therefore probable that the ministry had decided to
rid itself of Martin, since it was no longer so dependent on him,
before settling down to the task of drawing up and defending a new
land measure.

Martin had also frequently absented himself from cabinet meetings
and criticized the view that cabinet ought to discuss and decide the
'trivia', as he regarded them, of the administration. 'United action',
in his opinion, 'should only be required where some great principle

were at stake'. Regular cabinets were unnecessary 'red tape'.[35]
Martin and his colleagues differed on a considerable range of 'great
questions'. He had been opposed to secret voting and to adult male
suffrage, two leading principles of the recent Electoral Act, and had
disapproved of a Stock Assessment Act recently carried by the
ministry. He also disagreed with their freetrade policy and their
readiness to abolish state aid to religion, and he differed from Robertson
in particular on the question of the Upper House. Martin denied
that these differences of opinion were of any consequence, as he
had always voted with his colleagues. But he did not often speak
in support of their measures, and his views would almost certainly
have embarrassed the ministry in the impending elections had he
still been a member of it.

Cowper and Martin aired their dispute in the House, quoting the
letters that had passed between them. In a letter informing Martin
that his colleagues would no longer defend him, Cowper admitted
that Martin's conduct had 'alienated, in a great degree, the best
friends and supporters of the Government'.[36] He went on to argue
that 'there would be no unity of action [of cabinet members], there
would be no confident reliance upon the soundness of measures, if
each individual [minister] was allowed to act for himself in this
[Martin's] way'.[37] The speeches made it plain that Martin's mechanical
support of the ministry in the House was not sufficient for cabinet
solidarity, even though it was given in deference to the principles
of collective responsibility. Furthermore, support in the House
depended, in part, upon cabinet solidarity, and the ministry had no
alternative but to rid itself of Martin once it had decided that it would
neither resign nor defend him. Martin's assumption that ministers
could be individually responsible to the Assembly for the details of
their administration was in direct conflict with the principle of collective responsibility, and, as Cowper recognized, ministers stood or
fell together on everything for which they were responsible to the
House and not merely on major policy and legislation.

The solidarity of cabinet was once more at issue a few years later,
when William Forster resigned from a ministry led by Martin. The
ministry, although it knew it was on the point of defeat in the Assembly and about to resign, advised the Governor to make two appointments to the Upper House. Sir John Young refused and when the
ministry did not resign, Forster did. In a letter to Martin, he explained
that he felt he had no alternative. The decision to advise the appointments 'was not my individual act but had been agreed to by the
Ministry in general and in particular by yourself'. Forster had been

given the task of informing the proposed appointees, on the understanding that the Governor had agreed.[38] When explaining his
resignation to Sir John Young, Forster also argued that, in refusing
to make the appointments, the Governor had in effect favoured the
political opponents and predecessors of the ministry.[39] Such an argument implied that the Governor should have no independent power
of refusing advice to make appointments if he wished to maintain
a position of impartiality in relation to his ministries, and this independence was precisely what Young did claim.[40] The rest of the
ministers accepted Young's refusal. They had no power to resist
in the face of a vanished majority and they did not agree that Young
had shown partiality to their predecessors. They made no statement
on the question of whether the making of appointments to the Upper
House was a special matter, exempt from the ordinary conventions
of responsible government. Since Forster disagreed with the claim
Young made, and had been a party to a collective decision, he could
not continue in office when his colleagues had failed both to uphold
that decision and to resign at once when it was not carried out.

The collective responsibility of cabinet was once more severely
tested in the coalition government of Martin and Parkes between
1866 and 1868. The quarrels and disagreements within this ministry,
reviewed in chapter 3, had eroded its solidarity before 1868, and
Parkes and the Governor had both noted the resulting tendency
towards departmentalism. Martin seemed scarcely aware that the
agreement to differ, on which the coalition was founded, left cabinet
little to discuss if only the 'great questions' were to be brought before
it. Their differences on some of these questions were not counteracted by agreement on others because their legislative programme
consisted almost wholly of straightforward administrative measures
and minor bills. It is also possible that Martin had attempted to
follow his own view, expressed in 1856 and again in 1858, that the
trivia of administration should not be discussed in cabinet but left
to the decision of individual ministers. The disunity of cabinet could
no longer be concealed when the quarrel between Eagar and Duncan
about the administration of the customs department led to Duncan's
dismissal.

Yet Martin himself also entertained the orthodox view that cabinet
was jointly responsible for all that was done in its name by individual
ministers. Two years after Duncan had been dismissed and Parkes,
refusing to share responsibility for this action, had resigned, Martin
told Parkes that

for all official acts of yours as a member of the Government of which I was the head, I and all our then colleagues are just as responsible as you are. All those acts had our fullest concurrence.[41]

The difficulty in maintaining this view along with the opinions Martin had expressed earlier about the matters cabinet should discuss, was that ministers could not take the concurrence of their colleagues for granted in lesser matters when their strength in the Assembly rested on the steadiness of followers interested far more in those matters than in the 'great questions'. If disputes like that which eventually brought about Parkes' resignation and the ministry's defeat were to be avoided, concurrence on lesser matters had to be worked out in cabinet.

Differences of policy, as distinct from differences of opinion within a ministry, were not the sole decisive factor in any of the three cases so far discussed. A fourth case may be adduced therefore to show the operation of the principle of cabinet solidarity when ministers disagreed about policy. In 1877 the Robertson ministry lost its Secretary for Lands, Thomas Garrett, after he had disagreed with Robertson about the extent and character of proposed amendments to the land law. Garrett had first entered parliament in 1860, and from the beginning had steadily supported Robertson. He had, in fact, been the whip for the Cowper-Robertson faction in the Assembly for some years in the sixties, and in the seventies he had held office as Secretary for Lands under Robertson from 1875–7, resigning in February shortly before the ministry itself collapsed. When it came back into office a second time in 1877, Garrett was again Minister for Lands.

Robertson's ministry had made some concessions to the demands of free selectors and their friends two years before in the Amending Land Act of 1875. Now, in a precarious position in the House and under growing pressure from the free selectors who were about to hold a conference in Sydney, the ministry agreed to consider new amendments to the Acts of 1861. According to Robertson, the ministry had already agreed to some reforms of the kind demanded by free selectors, although not to all of them. A few days before the free selectors' conference began Garrett and Robertson fell out over the extent of the proposed amendments. Garrett insisted on reforms that were virtually identical, he said later,[42] with those demanded by the free selectors and threatened to resign if the ministry did not accept them. Robertson was not to be bullied. He told Garrett that some of the proposals were unacceptable to him and that he would therefore not submit them to cabinet as the 'question of their adoption or rejection would mean your or my retirement' from the ministry.[43] Garrett seems to have extended the list of reforms he thought advisable after the question had been submitted to cabinet and Robertson apparently found these further items unpalatable.[44] Garrett resigned office after being returned in the elections that followed shortly after the quarrel, and the proposed reforms fell to the ground when the ministry itself was defeated and resigned a month later.

The principle of collective responsibility was tested in situations of another type which had to be faced on several occasions in the first years of responsible government. Premiers sometimes had difficulty in finding a man to fill the office of attorney-general. The attorney-general was made responsible to the Assembly for all judicial establishments and for the administration of justice in the departmental reorganization of 1856, and he was required to advise the ministry on all legal questions and to assist in the preparation of bills. However, he also had the duties of Crown prosecutor and grand juror in the colony. Many people thought that these could not be performed by an officer politically identified with any government. Two alternatives presented themselves as a result—to make the attorney-general 'non-political' as the auditor-general had been in 1856, or to divide the duties of the office and give the work of Crown prosecutor and grand juror to a non-ministerial officer. But although these alternatives were repeatedly canvassed, no ministry seriously concerned itself with the question in the fifties and sixties. Instead Cowper in 1858 and Forster in 1859–60, simply refrained from giving their attorneys-general seats on the Executive Council or in cabinet.[45]

A second difficulty arose out of the first. The duties of the office made it essential that it be filled by a man of considerable legal standing and experience, and by 1856 it had become something of a tradition that the appointee should be a leading barrister. The barristers themselves were jealous of the social and professional precedence that the office gave to the man who held it, but they were at the same time a conservative body of men. As a result premiers of liberal ministries twice had difficulty in finding appointees who had enough experience and standing not to rouse the professional jealousy of the barristers and who were at the same time liberal enough to be included in their cabinets as responsible officers. In 1856, the profession was angered when Cowper appointed Martin Attorney-General only a few days before he was admitted to the bar. Cowper claimed that he had 'exhausted' the bar in a search for someone of liberal opinions, which Plunkett, a leading barrister himself, denied.[46] The bar petitioned the Governor against the appointment,[47] making plain their jealousy if not their conservatism. Denison told the barristers that he could not refuse to take his ministers' advice.

In 1865 when Cowper asked Manning to accept the office in place of Darvall who had resigned, Manning refused on the ground that he would feel out of place in the government.[48] The Governor, Young, observed that the leaders of the bar were 'one and all opposed to the policy of the liberal party and refuse to take office with or under it',[49] and he finally induced Plunkett to take the office until a younger and more suitable man could be found.[50] The appointment was a makeshift that was scarcely compatible with the principle of collective responsibility, but it was tolerated because many people believed the attorney-general should not be a member of cabinet. So long as the duties of the office remained unchanged it was one to which the principle could not be rigidly applied and it was therefore easier to overlook discrepancies between the political views of attorneys-general and those of other ministers. A different procedure was adopted in 1860 and 1868 to overcome the difficulty in filling the office. Manning accepted it on both occasions on the understanding that he would not be a member of cabinet.[51]

Neither Manning nor Plunkett was under any pressure to take office as were the leaders of a faction in the Assembly. They both had seats in the Legislative Council after 1861 and were independent of the political struggles in the Lower House. They were therefore free from any necessity to modify their political opinions or to reconcile them with the opinions of others. Manning recognized that differences of opinion within a ministry, especially if they were as great as his differences with Cowper and Robertson, were a grave disadvantage to it. So did Robertson, who in 1860 wanted the 'active political support of his Attorney-General as well as his legal advice'.[52] He was therefore as unwilling as Manning to continue the arrangements Forster had made a few weeks earlier to exclude the attorney-general from political responsibility. These arrangements were all evidence not only that the collective responsibility of cabinet was recognized as an essential principle of the new system of government but that it was thought necessary to protect it by special agreements in exceptional circumstances.

Another special arrangement was entered into in 1887. On taking office, Parkes and his colleagues were aware that there was growing pressure in the Assembly for a bill to provide for payment of members. They were divided among themselves on this issue. Parkes was opposed and at least two ministers were strongly in favour. They therefore agreed that it should be an open question.[53] But in May and June, Fletcher, a member of the opposition, successfully moved for a resolution asking the Governor to provide for payment of members in a bill,[54] and ministers voted on both sides of the House. The ministry, however, had to take part in the business of bringing in the bill, because money bills could only be introduced by a message from the Governor to the Assembly and the Governor could not act without advice from ministers. The cabinet discussed the matter, and rather than be 'asked to bring down a message to cover a bill in the hands of private persons', it decided that 'a Minister who agreed with the principle should bring in the bill'.[55] The cabinet therefore collectively agreed that the bill should be brought in, but only on condition 'that the principle should come into application in the next parliament'.[56] Garrett, the Secretary for Lands, undertook to bring in the bill and Parkes, explaining what cabinet had agreed on to the Governor, told him that Garrett would apply to him for the necessary message 'with my knowledge and consent; and on behalf of the Government. I accept the responsibility of the advice so tendered.'[57]

Fletcher's raising the question was a palpable tactical manoeuvre. He was acting on behalf of a section of the opposition which had been trying for some time to obstruct business in defiance of its own elected leader.[58] Since the ministry would be bound to advise the Governor before the necessary message could be sent to the House, it seemed that it would be forced either to oppose the principle and defend its opposition in a House in which a considerable majority drawn from both sides favoured it,[59] or to support the principle against the well-known opinions of the Premier himself and of several other ministers. There was in Fletcher's motion a further catch that can hardly have escaped the ministry. If it allowed itself to advise that the message be sent simply on Fletcher's initiative, the precedent would be created for endless resolutions calling for messages recommending appropriations. The ministers therefore had to do two things. First, they had to make a distinction between the introduction of the bill—for which they could all be collectively responsible—and its substance, which they had already agreed should be an open question. Second, they had to take the introduction of the bill out of Fletcher's hands and give it to one of the ministers, Garrett. It is probable that Parkes was confident that the Upper House would reject the bill—which it did at once—and that this made it easier for him to agree to the counter-stratagem.

These incidents all lead to one conclusion: that solidarity in cabinet was as important to ministries depending on faction support in the Assembly as it was to ministries depending on party support in the

House of Commons. The principle of collective responsibility was invoked from the outset and maintained, partly by expedients, with considerable success throughout the period as the one way of securing cabinet solidarity. Parkes himself made a statement in 1887 which serves as a summary of the argument. He reminded members of his new ministry of the need for solidarity and brought the English cabinet, as explained by W. E. Hearn and Gladstone, to their attention as the example to be followed:

> Of course we must copy the English model as closely as we can and depend upon it our safety as well as our usefulness as a Government consists in concert of action and this can only be maintained by the Head governing the Body.[60]

Parkes was very anxious here to argue that he as Premier should be accorded a pre-eminence in cabinet that in his opinion followed of necessity from its 'nature', but the important thing is that he referred to the 'safety' and 'usefulness' of the government depending on concerted action. These words refer unmistakably to the fact that a government that was internally divided and unsure of its action, like the Martin ministry in 1866–8, was open to embarrassment or defeat in manoeuvres such as the one involving payment of members.

Parkes added that there were also administrative reasons for solidarity and for granting the Premier pre-eminence:

> I must make it a rule to be made acquainted with any new or unusual proposal before it is even submitted to the Cabinet. Oneness of consultation and action, if I may use the phrase, is more necessary with us than in England. Here most of us are men untrained in public affairs . . .
> I must trust to your good sense not to put a wrong construction on this communication. All that I want is to hold the Government together in a manner that will enable us as a body to be useful and at the same time be creditable to all of us individually.

The phrase 'oneness of consultation and action' describes exactly what the conventions or rules of collective responsibility achieve. These rules, defined by Jennings in his examination of cabinet government in England,[61] are, as Encel points out,[62] 'facets of the one central principle of cabinet solidarity'. If it is assumed, as it commonly is,[63] that unanimity of opinion within a ministry, at least on 'fundamentals', is essential if it is to have any stability or solidarity, the colonial ministries before 1889 must remain a paradox. 'Fundamental' political principles were rarely distinguished and were seldom at the basis of political divisions in the colony, and agreement about them did not provide the cement of ministries. Ministers quarrelled about 'incidentals', as Jennings calls them, just as often as they reached compromises concerning them. Yet Jennings concludes that agreement on 'fundamentals' and compromise on 'incidentals' are essential if ministries are to survive as collectively responsible bodies. It is true that some of the rules he describes—for example, that a minister not prepared to defend a cabinet decision must resign—were not broken in the colony, but these rules do not necessarily establish unanimity of opinion; they are rules defining the conditions of united action and this unity need not depend on an agreed opinion. Even English cabinets, as Jennings himself shows, did not always achieve unanimity of opinion, but they did have unity in action.

It would therefore be hasty to conclude that the talk of collective responsibility in the colony was no more than talk. On the surface it seems that factionalism and coalition should have strained the principle to the point where it meant little, and it must of course be conceded that the solidarity of colonial ministries was tested severely by differences of opinion. But the political necessity of presenting a united front in the Assembly if ministries were to hold their majorities forced them to act with unity, and this tendency was reinforced by the close relations of the ministries with the Governors and the Executive Council. The unimportance of 'fundamental' questions to ministries and majorities, far from making collective responsibility impossible, undoubtedly made it easier for ministries to maintain the solidarity they needed in their relations with the Governor and parliament.

CHAPTER SIX

The First Parties

I~N~ 1887 the patterns of politics established for thirty years were disrupted. Of the two things which had so far channelled the political life of the colony, the parliamentary institutions and the faction system, the latter gave way in a crisis and was transformed. A year or two before, Forster and Froude had gloomily doubted whether the institutions themselves would survive. Froude thought that parliamentary government would probably 'prove but a temporary expedient in imitation of English institutions but incapable of permanence',[1] while Forster had argued that what was to be feared from faction politics in colonial democracy was the 'apotheosis of the individual'.[2] Neither of them guessed that parties might yet develop and transform the system.

In the general election of 1887, two distinct political bodies—the freetrade and protectionist organizations—played a new and leading role and it seemed that the faction system was about to be replaced by a power-struggle between two groups which can only be called parties of principle, formally organized and overtly managing currents of pressure and opinion. This dramatic change followed a period of governmental disorganization and uncertainty in the faction struggle, played out against a background of general economic crisis in the colony. It stemmed, on the one hand, from the conviction of some pressure groups in the electorate that traditional policies and the men and methods that sustained them were outmoded in the colony's changing circumstances. It was partly stimulated, on the other hand, by the eagerness with which leading faction politicians—always alive to the main chance—were to seize upon new currents of feeling and seek to adapt them to their own purposes. Elements of change and continuity were thus intermixed: the new parties at once represented a reaction against the old faction system and a redirection of many of the techniques on which it had rested.

Until the early eighties 'protection' was never a viable cause in New South Wales. The lesson had been driven home in the defeat of Martin's tariff proposals in 1863–4, and thereafter 'Freetrade' was

taken to be an essential element of the colony's dominant 'liberal'
orthodoxy. In 1872 the *Sydney Morning Herald* could wither a politician
who dared to deliver a protectionist harangue in parliament by
laconically speaking of his incursion

> into a forsaken arena, where he could only fight with the remains
> of the departed . . . Like the noble hero whom madness had touched,
> he ran round the filed challenging the victors who had already
> triumphed and were gone.[3]

The mercantile strain in the colony's 'liberalism' was one obvious
explanation of the strength of freetrade dogma; the extensive revenue
derived in New South Wales from Crown lands was another. The
custom-house was habitually resorted to as a source of state income—
more extensively, indeed, than those who boasted of their freetrade
principles often cared to admit—but New South Wales had never
faced financial difficulties analogous to those which made politicians
depend on tariffs and turn to protectionism in Victoria. The seventies
witnessed dramatic increases in the volume of land sales in New
South Wales and in 1873, with great éclat, the Parkes government
'simplified' the colony's tariff by removing a number of duties imposed
in 1866 and 1871 to meet temporary budgetary difficulties.[4] Parkes
received a gold medal from the Cobden Club and became henceforth
the high priest of free trade in Australia. The revised tariff schedule
still contained fifty-five articles and in fact the colony's income from
the customs remained at over £1 million sterling.[5] But the 'protective
incidence' of the tariff was negligible: in contemporary opinion the
freetrade honour of the colony had been vindicated.

In the late seventies and early eighties, however, spasmodic instances of protectionist agitation began to disturb some traditionalist
politicians. As we have seen, the Working Men's Defence Association
included protection in its platform in 1877 and unsuccessfully tried
to use it as the link for an electoral alliance with Free Selectors Associations. In 1880 temporary but severe unemployment led a few
enthusiasts to look to protection as a possible means of relief: resolutions in favour of tariff reform were brought forward by a protectionist
in the Assembly,[6] and a League for the Encouragement of Colonial
Industries was formed by a few men who had been prominent in
the New South Wales Political Reform League (an evanescent organization representing breakaway elements from the old Working
Men's Defence Association).[7] The parliamentary resolutions were
overwhelmingly defeated but the old politicians stirred uneasily:

'I fancy', wrote F. B. Suttor to Parkes, 'the day is not far distant when the battle of Free Trade and Protection will be fought out in this Colony'.[8] The League for the Encouragement of Colonial Industries was disbanded in February 1881 but four months later some of its members formed the Protection and Political Reform League. This body was directed by R. C. Luscombe and W. Richardson, and had among its prominent supporters N. Melville and D. Buchanan, two of the earliest protectionists in the Assembly. Insignificant at first, the League was later to win some support from manufacturers as well as from workingmen, and to be the only protectionist organization to have a continuous history throughout the decade.[9]

During 1883 a correspondent to the *Debater*—an ephemeral 'liberal' Sydney weekly—noted that 'a slight wave of protection . . . [was] now . . . rippling on the social horizon of the colony'. He identified four 'classes' as its supporters: manufacturers, 'needy politicians burning for notoriety', artisans, and 'young natives . . . who . . . look upon their native land as one of the "boss" nations of the earth, charged with a mission to breathe defiance to all other communities'.[10] But the wave was indeed still a ripple: though there were perhaps five noisy doctrinaire protectionists in the Assembly, they were regarded merely as amusing oddities, and outside parliament they could call no effectively organized body of opinion to their support.

By 1884, however, an incipient protectionist 'movement' had begun to take shape. Protection was a subject for discussion in many of the petty associations and debating societies whose activities made that year a 'time of mental upheaval' among many of Sydney's young journalists and self-educated radicals.[11] For eager iconoclasts free trade stood as an obvious symbol of the *status quo* in New South Wales, while a glance across the border at Victoria suggested readily enough—at least to the excited superficial observer—that 'protection' and 'democracy' were, in the proper order of things, synonymous. Appropriately enough E. W. O'Sullivan, a Victorian expatriate, became by 1884 the leading Sydney advocate of organization to concentrate and direct current social criticism under the banner of protection. Printer, journalist and trades union official, O'Sullivan cherished the memory of having served as one of Graham Berry's 'lieutenants' in Victoria during the campaigns of the seventies. A devout Catholic, he was moved by generous social impulses and was convinced, both by temperament and experience, of the efficacy of organized propaganda as a weapon for reform. In association with other doctrinaire protectionists, mostly drawn from Sydney's 'debating-society, hard-reading crowd', he took the lead in founding as twin radical bodies the Democratic Alliance and the Land and Industrial Alliance.[12] The first was directed at workingmen—its objectives included payment of members and abolition of assisted immigration—and the second was designed, as O'Sullivan himself put it, 'to combine the farmers with the workers in the city and towns, as a democratic movement'. Protection, the crying need it was said, of workers, farmers and manufacturers was to be the cement for a new coalition of classes in New South Wales.

It is difficult to judge how much support these organizations won in their early days. In his recollections O'Sullivan claimed that the Democratic Alliance had soon boasted six hundred paid-up supporters, though he also remembered—perhaps with sardonic exaggeration— that the Land and Industrial Alliance long languished with only three members: a President, a Vice-President and a Secretary. But the noisy tactics of their officials kept these bodies before the public eye: they became adept at interrupting public meetings with their amendments, they wrangled loudly with other radical agitators, and O'Sullivan saw to it that their own meetings—however meagrely attended— were impressively reported in the *Daily Telegraph,* for which he was at the time writing.[13]

But whether their organizations were initially successful or not, the instinct of O'Sullivan and his friends that protection might be made the spearhead of a reform movement in New South Wales soon appeared to be reasonable enough. In July 1885 the Land and Industrial Alliance organized a 'Political Conference' in Sydney to test the potential strength of the radical forces its sponsors dreamed of amalgamating. The results were impressive: over forty different organizations sent delegates. Fourteen of these claimed to represent country branches of the Land and Industrial Alliance itself, thus apparently testifying to intensive missionary work by those who had founded the parent organization scarcely a year before. Other country men included the representatives of six Free Selectors Associations and five Farmers' Unions. Sydney trades delegates (bootmakers, coachmakers, ironworkers and stonemasons) attended on behalf of their respective unions, as did country artisans representing the Lithgow Protection League, the Western Miners' Association and the Eskbank Ironworkers. A prominent part was also taken by the men of the Protection and Political Reform League. At the Conference there was much wild denunciation of 'a dominant class of monopolists, who have ruled our country too long', perverting the land laws in favour of squatters, recklessly squandering the public revenue, and maintaining a freetrade tariff in the interest of merchants. Conference unanimity could be maintained at this level of generality, and there were no dissentients to the resolution:

> that in order to confront the dominant influence of the pastoral and importing interests, the farmers, manufacturers, miners and industrial classes should combine in political unions for self defence and the promotion of the welfare of the community at large.[14]

But no plan was worked out for bringing such unions into being, and when matters of detail came under discussion, considerable diversity of opinion became evident. Many farmers' delegates, for example, deprecated extreme attacks on squatters, while their support for protection—the key issue which was supposed to bind the new alliance together—was generally limited to 'fair trade' for agriculture, i.e., lifting duties on items like tea and replacing them with an import tax on grain.[15] A conference of the New South Wales Farmers' Union held later in the month officially endorsed this stand: while passing strong resolutions in favour of agricultural protection, delegates agreed in condemning 'the wholesale protection advocated by that trinity of idiots, Heydon, Luscombe and O'Sullivan'.[16] Strictures of this kind were a sharp reminder to the enthusiasts of the Land and Industrial Alliance that, however promising the response to their initial call for a 'Political Conference', it would be unrealistic to dream of creating at once a potent, extremist and monolithic protectionist movement. As deliberations at the conference itself suggested, it was more practical to envisage vaguely defined 'protection' as the link for a looser federation of groups and interests likely to respond to the idea that social and tariff reform were connected—for a set of alliances which might, in B. E. Mansfield's apt phrase, produce a 'populist' movement.[17]

The economic omens for such a movement were propitious. Between 1883 and 1885, when wool prices were falling and interest rates rising, drought accentuated the effects of economic difficulties.[18] A massive railway construction programme, begun by the Stuart Government in 1884 and resting on £13 million of borrowed capital, absorbed some redundant labour, but in Sydney unemployment, particularly among skilled artisans, became increasingly serious, and by 1886 meetings of men demanding work were common in the city.[19] Industry generally was stagnant: it was said that reduced orders for plant, equipment and repair work—especially in the shipping, pastoral and sugar industries—were to blame.[20] In 1885 a number of afflicted firms drew together in a new Chamber of Manufactures to explore possible remedies by concerted action.[21] But a year later an Iron Trades Employers' delegation examined sixty Sydney factories and gloomily reported that none was employing more than one-tenth its capacity staff.[22] Complaints grew against 'excessive' foreign and intercolonial competition, and among both employers and employees protectionist propaganda gained ground.

Many farmers, while adversely affected by drought, were also feeling the pinch of competition in these years. From districts where productive capacity had outstripped local demand they turned resentful eyes on Victorian and Tasmanian produce which undercut them in the Sydney market. Farmers' and selectors' organizations had campaigned in the late seventies to have internal railway rates reduced to levels that could compete with shipping costs from other colonies. But while the railways continued to be run at a loss, no parliament dared to 'pander' to a sectional interest, and rate reduction became a lost cause. In the Assembly, country members frequently warned that, as W. Clarke put it in 1881, 'the farming community are fast becoming protectionists because the government, after settling the people upon the lands, . . . will not allow the produce to be brought to market'.[23] Farmer interest in the protectionist activity of 1884–5 confirmed the prediction; and Clarke himself was by 1886 leader in the Assembly of a recognized 'Hay and Corn' party, said to be twenty-eight strong and known to meet regularly outside the chamber to organize tactics and speakers whenever the tariff was due to come up for discussion.[24]

Though the Political Conference of 1885 failed to devise a comprehensive system of 'political unions', individual protectionist bodies acted vigorously in the election campaign in October of that year. The Land and Industrial Alliance and the Protection and Political Reform League co-operated to sponsor lecture tours, print and distribute literature, form country branches, and provide approved candidates with moral and financial support.[25] The degree to which their work influenced the outcome of the election is, of course, impossible to tell precisely. But when the new Assembly met, the protectionist section of its membership had swollen from a mere handful to at least twenty.

Protectionist propaganda and organization inevitably stirred freetrade apologists in the latter half of 1885. B. R. Wise and E. Pulsford engaged in a vigorous press controversy with protectionist advocates, and steps were taken by doctrinaires and leading members of the mercantile community to found a Freetrade Association.[26] This body was formally constituted in August, an interim Council having framed and adopted a constitution. In a manifesto issued early in October, the Association declared its objects to be: 'To advocate freedom of trade; to oppose, by all constitutional means, any attempt to levy taxes through the Custom House for the benefit of one part of the community at the expense of the bulk of the population; to refute the sophistries and expose the frequent misrepresentations of the protectionists'. It was emphasized that the Association was 'in no way connected with any political party', for 'most of the grievances of which protectionists complain are independent either of protection or freetrade'. The organizers at this stage saw the body as a purely propagandist one: it was to have a library 'of economic and statistical literature' and 'collect and distribute information upon the freetrade question and the condition of the various branches of our national industries'.[27] Constituted to 'promote, not the interests of a class, but the welfare of the whole community', it was not yet prepared to undertake full-scale electoral organization. As the advocates of an amorphous cause of resistance, lacking sectional appeal and not obviously related to the pressing problems that protectionists were attacking, freetraders could perhaps not hope for more at this stage. But they had at least succeeded in creating a rallying centre for those of like mind should the protectionist threat become serious.

But as it happened, a special significance was soon given to movements outside parliament by the state of 'parties' within. For 1886—the year of the twelfth parliament—witnessed a breakdown in the faction system: a deadlock precipitated largely by the desiccating influence of those very issues—land, depression and taxation—which underlay the emergence of concern in the wider community about free trade and protection. Unparalleled scenes of disorder in the Assembly symbolized the frustration and uncertainty of politicians struggling with problems which interfered with old patterns of loyalty and could neither be sidestepped nor solved within the framework of the traditional faction politics. In the end, at least temporary success went to those who were adept enough to remould their politics to fit the new patterns emerging in the electorate. To this extent, the year 1886 marks a 'turning point' in the political history of New South Wales.

The government formed by Alexander Stuart in January 1883 survived the whole life of the eleventh parliament, to resign, ostensibly on account of Stuart's ill health, at the dissolution of parliament by the natural effluxion of time in October 1885. Universally respected as a man of high principle, Stuart had originally come into prominence in August 1882, when, at the beginning of the third session of the

tenth parliament, he had accepted election to the leadership of the
opposition in the Assembly.[28] Resistance to the powerful Parkes-
Robertson coalition had up to this point been negligible, since the
alliance in 1879 of the two old leaders had removed the material for
an organized opposition centring on an existing faction.[29] But a new
opposition group rapidly crystallized around Stuart.[30] It was composed
largely of malcontents disgusted by the arrogance of Parkes and
Robertson, and alienated by some of their policies. It gained moral
stature as it quickly assumed the leading role in a popular crusade
to recast the colony's land laws. On this issue, Stuart inflicted an
unexpected and crushing defeat on the government in November
1882, and returned to parliament after subsequent elections with a
generally accepted mandate to bring in new land legislation. Stuart's
own prestige, the hopes reposed in him by land reformers, and his
skilful management of legislative business combined to give the new
'Reform' cabinet an outward stability, and the new Stuart faction
an inner coherence. There was a little unsteadiness among members
during the first session of the parliament, but thereafter the lines
of division hardened, and over the five sessions which followed the
government was able to count on forty-two steady supporters.
Another ten members, though less consistently reliable, normally
voted with Stuart, and these men, added to the thirty-one independents, offered a fund of potential support from which the government
might hope to draw. In a House where the opposition was reduced
to a nucleus of twelve Parkes-Robertson followers, this was a particularly favourable balance of forces.

The new Land Bill was not introduced until October 1883 and its
consideration was the major legislative work of the next year. Stuart's
supporters and many independent members were undoubtedly kept
together until the end of 1884 by the danger of losing this Bill. Subsequently a lively expectation of favours to come held the loyalty of
many when the government began disbursing a record vote of £13
million of loan moneys for railway extensions, while Dalley's dispatch
of a contingent to the Soudan early in 1885 aroused a wave of patriot-
ism which brought a temporary renewal of favour. To offset these
advantages, the government was constantly harassed by pressure
groups and unsettled by growing financial difficulties, both of which
had brought by its last days a serious decline in prestige. Well-knit
squatter and selector groups had struggled violently for minor gains
during the land debates, and there was substance in the opposition's
charge that to preserve its Bill the government had dealt over-leniently

with the squatters.[31] Importunate protectionists jockeyed repeatedly
for concessions, and Stuart often found it necessary to reassure the
House about his own freetrade principles.

But his greatest difficulties arose from the combined effect on the
public finances of land reform and drought. In fulfilling an election
promise to suspend auction sales of land, the government at once
lost over £500,000 in revenue. Though at first sanguine about balancing the budget, the Treasurer (Dibbs) betrayed increasing uneasiness, and, obliged in January 1884 to admit that revenue for the
previous year had fallen below expectations by £343,000, he brought
down proposals for a property tax and some remodelling of the
tariff.[32] A caucus of forty-eight government supporters immediately
denounced the new taxes, and amid opposition jeers at his 'pliability',
Dibbs angrily 'lowered [his] sails to the tempest' and substituted
retrenchment for the new imposts.[33] Dibbs and Stuart had both
pointed to the crucial financial issue of the day: that land reform,
especially in a period of depression, must inevitably involve financial
reform. That so strong a government could not convince its own
followers of this elementary fact was an ominous hint of the dis-
ruptive potential of the burgeoning taxation issue. In subsequent
months Dibbs periodically suggested that all was well financially,[34]
but the government abruptly secured a dissolution on 7 October 1885
without making a precise financial statement, or even seeking supply
to cover the election period. The reasons for this action are obscure.
Parkes and his followers were at the time mounting a frenzied attack
on the government—and especially on its Minister for Works,
Wright[35]—for alleged corruption and improper practices, and the
danger may have been enough to suggest that an appeal to the country
was urgent. But it is more likely that at the fag-end of a long parliament, and with declining strength in the House, the government
was reluctant to reveal the extent of the colony's financial plight.

With parliament prorogued, Stuart resigned because of ill health,
and the Governor called on Dibbs to reconstruct the cabinet. Three
of the strongest and most popular ex-ministers, Stuart, Dalley and
Farnell, had resigned; Dibbs took the Premiership and Treasurership,
and Sir Patrick Jennings, hitherto Vice-President of the Executive
Council, became Colonial Secretary. Genial clubman and squatter,
Jennings brought to the ministry some prestige to compensate for
the loss of Stuart, but it was nevertheless a much weaker team than
its predecessor.

When the twelfth parliament met it was an open secret that serious

financial difficulties would soon be revealed: the Governor's speech
was suspiciously silent on this matter. Uncertainty hung over the debate on the address in reply, as the faction leaders jockeyed anxiously
for support in a House unsettled by the atmosphere of crisis and the
advent of forty-eight new members. A large meeting of independent
members had discussed beforehand the possibility of adopting a
united course of action towards the government, and of perhaps
forming a 'third party'.[36] Neither move came to fruition, but both
betokened serious disillusion with the existing leadership on both
sides of the House. In the upshot, the government survived a hostile
amendment by two votes,[37] and Dibbs proceeded to deliver his
financial statement. A shocked House learnt that the deficit for 1885
had climbed to £1,052,614. The Treasurer proposed economy and
the issue of three-year treasury bills to bridge the gap. Before the
angry debate which followed had proceeded far, on 16 December
1885, the government resigned on the ground that it could not
assume an adequate working majority in the House.[38]

Robertson, who had led the opposition for three years, reluctantly
accepted the Governor's commission to form a new administration.
Parkes, former colleague in office and distant associate in opposition,
gave Robertson his blessing but refused to join the projected ministry.
His specious explanation was that he was utterly unable to accept
Robertson's expected nominee for the Treasurership, J. F. Burns.[39]
Robertson, aged and weary, and acting, as he put it, not from a desire
for office but from a sense of duty, bitterly resented Parkes' 'treachery'
—'he helped me to put the former government out, and then left
me high and dry'—and saw ambition rather than responsibility to
the country as the mainspring of Parkes' course.[40] It was, indeed,
to be shown soon enough that Parkes held the key to Robertson's
success or failure.

Robertson's government, sworn in on 22 December 1885, had
collapsed by late February 1886. The Treasurer, Burns, estimated
the deficit for 1885–6 at £1,703,918, and proposed a tax of ½d. in the £
on real property to replenish the revenue. The government fell before
a motion of censure moved by J. P. Garvan. Robertson accused Garvan
of collusion with Parkes, though Garvan probably acted as the *ad hoc*
leader of a 'new party' of independents.[41] But Parkes and six followers
voted with the opposition in a division won by eight votes: had he
honoured his initial promise to support Robertson, the latter would
have stayed in office.

In resigning, Robertson advised the Governor to dissolve the
House. He estimated that in the existing state of parties no stable

administration could be formed: he put his own supporters at fifty-seven, those of Jennings (i.e., the regular opposition, with the Stuart-Dibbs-Jennings faction at its core) at forty-seven. The 'floating' Parkes and Garvan groups he thought numbered seven and six respectively; four members remained who were apparently un-attached.[42] This calculation was over-simple (among other defects, it underestimated—as subsequent events showed—the degree of many members' independence), but it illustrated well enough the confusion into which the allegiances of the previous parliament had been thrown by the crisis. The point was made even more evident when the Governor refused a dissolution and summoned Jennings. The Premier-elect negotiated an agreement with Robertson to form a coalition cabinet with portfolios allotted in equal numbers to the two factions. The composite government was about to be announced to the House when Robertson reluctantly withdrew on the insistence of one follower who had been denied the attorney-generalship.[43] But the apparent hopelessness of basing a stable administration on one existing faction had almost forced an alliance analogous to that of Parkes and Robertson in 1879.

Jennings formed a cabinet from the remnants of the old Stuart-Dibbs group, and presented his re-elected ministers to the Assembly on 24 March 1886. The ambitious Parkes at once probed the govern-ment's strength with two censure motions, to the disgust of Robertson, who asserted that the interests of the country demanded that Jennings be given fair play. Robertson and his followers voted with the govern-ment, both motions were defeated with handsome majorities, and Jennings settled confidently into office. This unexpected reformula-tion of the lines of division suggested, among other things, that Robertson's earlier calculations underestimated the number of in-dependent men who might be amenable to an appeal to their patriot-ism: it was also a tribute to the trust that Robertson's own followers reposed in their chief, even when being led into support of former enemies.

Jennings announced a four-point programme to restore the finances: he would retrench, increase stamp duties, establish land and income taxes, and amend the tariff to impose new specific duties and a 5 per cent *ad valorem* duty. Censure moves on this general programme were repulsed, and resolutions in favour of new stamp duties and the direct taxes passed the Assembly with little debate and only moderate resistance. Parkes and the opposition shrewdly chose to make their most determined stand on the tariff issue. Protectionist organizations out of doors had by now made this the explosive question of the day:

within the Assembly a hard core of about twenty protectionists were hailing Jennings' proposals as the 'thin end of the wedge'. Welcome in one sense, the warm support of this group was an embarrassment to the government in another. Jennings patiently repeated that a 5 per cent *ad valorem* duty, temporarily imposed (for 3 years only) did not mean protection. But given the emotion of partisans on both sides, rational argument was a poor counter to the opposition taunt that ministers had become renegade freetraders, the tools of a dedicated protectionist minority.[44]

When Parkes began to 'scatter his fireworks', as Dibbs put it, with the cunning demand that freetraders be given 'a fair field on which to contend against the advocates of protection',[45] Jennings found himself being nudged into a dilemma. Whatever his private convictions, he dared not drop the tariff proposals, if only because to lose the support of even a large minority of protectionists would lead to defeat in the House. On the other hand, the protection-free-trade issue threatened to act as a solvent both on established loyalties and on the 'patriotic' sufferance of independents and opponents. The reactions of two influential members in fact made this danger apparent the moment the tariff proposals reached the House. G. H. Reid, a clear Dibbs-Stuart man and a particularly acid critic of Parkes, delivered the first of a series of powerful speeches which were to make him the recognized intellectual champion of free trade in parliament, and to carry him progressively into opposition.[46] And Robertson denounced the request that 'we . . . slaughter the trade of the port', identified 'the party now in power' as that which had 'brought the country into its present difficulties by handing over the land to a few people who do not pay sufficient for it',[47] and seemed to be shifting from toleration of the ministry towards the revival of old faction antagonisms. Age and ill health finally forced Robertson to leave political life in June 1886, without formally leading his followers to the opposition benches. But after his resignation, the larger section of his followers joined Parkes, thus completing a *rapprochement* implicit in Robertson's reactions to the government tariff proposals.[48]

After preliminary skirmishes in the Committee of Ways and Means during May, the real battle over the tariff was joined in June. The second reading debate on Jennings' Customs Duties Bill lasted over a fortnight. As the Bill came to the committee stage Parkes abortively moved censure on the ground that the protectionists, twenty strong, were holding the balance of power and dictating the policy of the country.[49] Tempers already frayed in these early proceedings broke during the long committee debate in July and August, and amid recurring scenes of wild disorder in the House, the government equipped the ante-rooms with bedding for its supporters and resisted a determined opposition filibuster by forcing continuous sittings. Parkes' attempt to rally a potent opposition around the freetrade cry failed, and the Bill went through. His thirst for office was perhaps a little too obvious for his 'principles' to disturb the genuine trust in Jennings felt by many tepid freetraders. But Parkes' fulminations and those of protectionist fanatics, together with the violent emotions they had laid bare, nevertheless made it obvious to members that the tariff was clearly to be the great coming political question.

As 1886 wore on, the government steadily lost all chance of demonstrating quickly that recovery could be won by integrated measures in which considerations of free trade and protection were irrelevant. Its income and land tax measures were held up in the Legislative Council, and in the Assembly it suffered defeat on some clauses of its Income Tax Bill.[50] Parkes attacked relentlessly, giving the government little rest and keeping the House in almost continuous uproar. By October none of the promised measures had become law, and to win some of them a stern struggle with the Upper House clearly lay ahead. Jennings wearily announced that the deficit for 1866 would exceed £2 million, and asked for supply. Another censure move by Parkes miscarried, and the government, after forcing its estimates through in a series of all-night sittings, prorogued parliament on 25 October. Two months later, his majority still apparently intact, Jennings resigned, ostensibly in consequence of a serious cabinet quarrel with Dibbs.

Lord Carrington sent for Parkes, who in characteristic tone assured His Excellency that 'I was not desirous of undertaking heavy official labours, but that it was not my duty to withhold my services if they were required'.[51] Commissioned to form a new administration, he chose colleagues chiefly from his old faction nucleus (Foster, Sutherland, Clarke, Abigail and Roberts), but included one representative of the 'new and well-tried members of this parliament' (Inglis) and two old Robertsonians (Burns and Garrett). In recognition of 'the growing friendliness of the Read [*sic*] section of the House' he also offered a portfolio to G. H. Reid who—undoubtedly to Parkes' relief— declined.[52] The cabinet, in other words, was constructed in the traditional manner, with an eye to placating all friendly or potentially friendly faction groups and not primarily as a collection of freetrade champions.[53]

Parkes had accepted office on condition that the Governor grant a dissolution to allow him to take his minority government at once to the country. In a ministerial statement he outlined his policy: retrenchment (with a change in the system of railway management and a civil service enquiry); a land tax, but no income tax; a local government bill; measures (unspecified) to increase land revenue; repeal of the Customs Duties Act. Amid cheers from the protectionists he declared:

> We will appeal to the whole of the electors of the country to give their votes under this motto: 'He who is not with us is against us'; we will appeal to them to set their faces against all the chicanery of the so-called independent candidates, who seek to steal into Parliament under a cover which simply hides their selfseeking or worse purposes. Let those who believe in the retrograde policy of protection say so, fight for it, and we shall respect them . . . there will be no mincing about the issue to the country. It will be for the government of against it; for freetrade or for protection.[54]

A few realistic members objected sceptically to this oversimplified reformulation of political divisions, but their voices were hardly heard. And outside parliament, new electoral bodies stood ready to force the faction politicians to conform to the new mould they had themselves half created in their muddled search for a way out of a year of crisis.

In September 1886, undoubtedly stimulated by the tariff furore in parliament, protectionist organizers had moved to establish a new body, the National Protection Association. Trade unionists and officials of existing protectionist associations were prominent at the inaugural meeting. T. Rose, a well-known radical agitator, was elected chairman, and his opening declaration of the urgent need for protection in New South Wales was enthusiastically supported by J. V. Wiley, President of the Trades and Labour Council. J. Scott Ross, manufacturer and President of the Protection and Political Reform League, moved the most important resolution of the meeting: that existing protectionist organizations should send delegates to a conference to discuss the establishment of a Central Council to direct the whole protectionist movement. Rope manufacturer A. Forsyth joined with E. W. O'Sullivan in warmly supporting this suggestion, and it was unanimously adopted.[55]

The proposed conference, held less than two months later, fathered the colony's first effective protectionist party organization. It appointed a committee to devise a constitution for 'The Protection Union of New South Wales', a new body which would 'unite the advocates of protection and the various organizations formed for and now advocating the introduction of a protective policy for New South Wales into an active political organization', the object of which would be 'to disseminate information by lectures, essays, pamphlets, tracts and public meetings; to collect funds, to arrange, provide, and assist candidates for the various electorates, and initiate branches of the union throughout the Colony'. With the constitution duly drawn up, a preliminary committee of twenty-one was elected to initiate the new organization. By a system of personal, affiliated and branch membership (with regular subscriptions in each case) the Union was to be at once a body in its own right, having its own branches, and a federation of existing protectionist bodies, and as such, the organizing centre for the whole movement.[56]

A special 'demonstration committee' planned a spectacular display to launch the Union. On 13 November a procession of six bands, two thousand persons and a hundred floats paraded through Sydney to the Domain, where on four separate platforms speakers harangued the crowds and simultaneously proposed the resolution that 'the depressed condition of the colony justifies the immediate adopting of a discriminative protective tariff for the purpose of promoting agriculture, fostering industry and giving employment to the people'. Protectionist M.L.A's, manufacturers, and representatives of farmers' and trade unions took a prominent part in the demonstration. Speaking to the main resolution from one of the Domain platforms, the President of the Trades and Labour Council struck the keynote of the demonstration:

> This is a red-letter day in the history of New South Wales. Today there has been a grand wedding, the wedding of capital and labour ... The employers have worked hand in hand with those they employ to bring about this victory which we are met to celebrate, and to show to their countrymen the only means of securing abundant labour for the people.[57]

Having celebrated its formation, the Union chose a Protection Council to act as its permanent executive, secured offices in Sydney, and began the work of preparing literature and organizing lecture tours, prodded into vigorous action by the unsettled state of parliamentary affairs and the possibility of an early election. As soon as parliament was dissolved in January 1887, representatives of the Protection Council conferred with protectionists from the Assembly; a joint executive was quickly formed, and finance, literary and electoral committees were created to direct the approaching campaign in the protectionist interest.[58] The protectionist politicians came effortlessly

within the orbit of the Union. The debates on Dibbs' tariff had
moulded them into a well defined pressure group, whose most eager
members had often bid defiance to the old faction loyalties and demanded new principles of political division which would force proper
parliamentary consideration of what they took to be the real concerns
of the community. It was a simple and logical step for these men to
establish immediate liaison with the new extra-parliamentary bodies,
in whose construction they had in any case often played an important
part. And what resulted from this joint action may be fairly described
as the first full-scale 'party' organization in New South Wales: a
structure based on a federation of local bodies, allowing for group and
individual membership, and directed by a central executive composed
of parliamentary and extra-parliamentary elements.

For the freetraders, the legacy of the defunct parliament was more
confusing and the existing propaganda organization less suitable
for party purposes. No clear-cut freetrade pressure group had evolved
in the Assembly. Parkes had of course used the freetrade cry to rally
and perhaps augment his following and had denounced his opponents as traitors to the old freetrade order. But political realists could
hardly regard this as more than a predictable faction manoeuvre,
and there were many men who were prepared to agree with Dibbs
that to accept his mild tariff was compatible with freetrade principles
which they, in common with most New South Wales politicians,
had long held. Faction loyalties in practice cut across opinion on
the tariff proposals, and when the Freetrade Association made
ready for its electoral campaign, it lacked a distinct parliamentary
group with which to co-operate. Even Parkes, who as self-appointed
leader of the 'real' freetraders might have been expected to seize the
chance to construct a powerful freetrade machine, evinced a certain
coolness towards the Association. As a potential solvent of the faction
system in whose management he was so adept, and as an open organization of principle with extra-parliamentary support likely to
rob its leaders of absolute freedom of action, it was clearly a threat
to him.

On 28 January, as the election campaign got under way, the Council
of the Freetrade Association formally constituted itself into a 'central
committee for furthering the election of free trade candidates'.[59]
Parkes had been pressed to attend the meeting which made this
decision and give it his blessing,[60] but he was not present, and B. R.
Wise—not yet a parliamentarian—took the chair. The precedent
thus set was followed throughout the election campaign. Parkes and
his more prominent followers took no part in the deliberations of the

Council, and, though endorsed by the Association, offered it little encouragement beyond occasionally accepting invitations to address meetings it organized. The Association thus for the time being remained what it had been at the outset—a purely 'voluntary' and unofficial organization[61]: the ministry, under Parkes' direction, meanwhile operated in the traditional manner through its network of agents to promote freetrade candidates likely to provide it with factional support in the new House.[62] But despite this lack of co-operation from the ministry, the Freetrade Association displayed great vigour in response to the threat of protectionist organization.

While campaigning lasted, the Protection and Freetrade Councils met daily, and the Sydney press carried very detailed reports of their activities. It is clear from this evidence that both bodies undertook co-ordinated electoral work on a scale and with an openness hitherto unknown in the colony. Each promoted the formation of local associations, printed and distributed propaganda, tried to adjudicate between rival candidates when vote-splitting threatened, and organized meetings, lecture tours and canvassing. Regularly published advertisements besought interested parties in the constituencies to apply to the Councils for candidates when suitable local men were not offering, and announced lists of candidates formally approved of by the central bodies. Between mid-January and mid-February the *Sydney Morning Herald* and *Daily Telegraph* reported the daily activities of the central organizations in great detail. An abbreviated account of one day's work by the freetrade executive may be quoted to capture the flavour of these reports:

The Secretary of the Freetrade Association informs us that the office was almost besieged yesterday by applicants for parcels of pamphlets and leaflets for distribution all over the city, suburbs, and country districts, and he states that there is every appearance of the freetrade battle being fought with great enthusiasm. A large number of telegrams were received from country electorates. During the day it was arranged that Mr. Nicholas B. Downing should contest Northumberland . . . It is possible that Mr. W. S. Lloyd, of Islington, Newcastle, will be the second freetrade candidate. Mr. J. T. Lingen, barrister, will contest Braidwood. A meeting of the freetraders is to be held there tonight to arrange election matters on his behalf. The Bathurst branch Association telegraphed an invitation to Mr. Wise to contest that electorate, but being already fixed for South Sydney he, of course, could not accept. An eligible candidate is expected to be decided on probably during the day, and also one for West Macquarie. A telegram received from Emmaville (Glen Innes electorate) states that Mr. W. Fergusson has retired. The Association is in communication with a likely candidate for the seat . . . Four telegrams were received from the Carcoar electorate pressing for a second freetrade candidate.[63]

Though press evidence leaves no doubt of the vigour with which these activities were pursued or of the importance which contemporaries attached to them, it is impossible now to attempt an accurate assessment of their effectiveness, especially as the records of the organizations themselves do not appear to have survived. Neither side at any stage published estimates of the number of branch organizations they controlled. The omission suggests that in fact their success in promoting local associations may have been limited, though it was also undoubtedly good tactics for each body to keep its opponents guessing and hint whenever possible that its associational basis was of overwhelming strength. In November 1886, Wise had complained that 'whenever two or three persons meet together [to discuss protection] a telegram announces the formation of a "Protection Association", although in reality there has been no change in the opinion of the district and the members who compose the "Association" are neither numerous nor influential'.[64] There was no protectionist outcry against this charge, but Wise's vague contrasting description of the Freetrade Association—it now had, he said, 'branches in many and correspondents in almost all electoral districts of the colony'—was hardly more impressive. In the press releases reporting requests for candidates during the campaign itself, the central bodies—presumably whenever they could do so— mentioned branch organizations by name, but vague statements about 'freetraders' or 'protectionists', or particular 'constituencies' asking for men, were as frequent. While distinct local organizations clearly existed,[65] agents undoubtedly worked singly or within the ordinary local candidates' committees to promote the interests of the central organizations. Conversely, local candidates and their supporters, anxious to secure the advantage of 'official' freetrade or protectionist endorsement, often deferred to the respective Councils. At a freetrade banquet held on 14 March, Wise revealed that the central Council had spent only £700 on the election, and that most of that still had to be subscribed. Describing freetrade success in the election as primarily a 'moral' victory—achieved 'without money, without experience, and without organization'—he went on to urge the need for more vigorous agitation to found local associations: 'they had still to organize the country districts, and they ought not to rest until they had planted their arsenals in every part of the enemies' country.'[66] Statements of this kind suggest that the extent and the efficiency of organization employed in the election should not be exaggerated.

The 1887 election, indeed, presents the picture of an electoral system in process of transformation. New and openly organized political movements—in the protectionist case, based on a federation of special interests which had now for some time been clamorously active in electoral agitation—pushed their tentacles outward from Sydney in an attempt to shape the contest in all constituencies in terms of the principles for which they stood. But—like the old faction networks they were implicitly challenging—they encountered everywhere a variable complex of local power-groups and issues with which they had to come to terms. To this was added the strong pull of traditional faction loyalties, which complicated negotiations and kept in operation a second system of manipulation whose ends did not always coincide with those of the Freetrade and Protection Councils.

These circumstances explain the troubles frequently encountered by the Associations in achieving even so elementary a gain as the prevention of vote-splitting. More important, they emphasize the difficulty of interpreting the meaning of the election results. Victory went to the freetrade cause, and undoubtedly freetrade organization played a large part in this. But the ministry was also identified with free trade, not through the newly formed organizations, but through the person of Parkes. It would be pointless even to speculate whether votes for free trade or votes (on the old factional lines) for the ministry were the more important in giving Parkes the strength he enjoyed after the election. The point may be appreciated better by noting the possible effect in the election of just one extraneous issue. Many contemporaries thought that protectionism drew much of its strength in this period from Catholics to whom Parkes' name was anathema— that the so-called fiscal division had, in other words, a strong sectarian element mixed in with it.[67] And there can be no doubt that Parkes' electoral success in 1887 reflected in some measure a strong rallying of the Protestant vote which he had so long exploited. He had had, for example, explicit official support from the Local Option League, 'working in harmony with all the Churches and Lay Temperance organizations':[68] on the eve of the election the League's secretary, busy 'oiling' its machinery, had assured Parkes that it was important that 'all our lodges, 600 in number, should be prepared for the Free [trade] fight'.[69]

But whatever the other forces at work in the election, the new organizations must be judged of fundamental importance in forcing a reformulation of the lines of political division. Their propaganda

supported and extended the originally opportunistic cry of Parkes
and his followers that the tariff issue was *the* issue of the day, and by
obliging all candidates to declare a fiscal faith, they did much to
squeeze the old faction divisions into a new two-party mould. It was
predictable enough that ministerial candidates should almost to a
man be freetraders.[70] But it was more surprising to find that, with
the exception of three men (Dibbs, Want and Wilkinson), all those
elected as anti-ministerialists had declared themselves to be protectionists. Opposition members in the previous parliament had certainly
included numerous freetraders, and there can be no doubt that the
pressure of protectionist organization was of primary importance
in the 'conversion' that many of them underwent during the election
campaign. And, ground between the millstones of the freetrade and
protectionist machines, few candidates were strong enough to maintain a position of strict independence.

Of those elected, only four freetraders and six protectionists had
stood firmly as independents, and some of these men drifted into
fairly steady support of the appropriate party once parliamentary
proceedings began. The decreased effectiveness of 'independence'
was amusingly exemplified in the case of Dibbs, the late opposition
leader. At the election he firmly declared his loyalty to free trade,
as well as his undying antipathy to Parkes. When the House assembled,
Dibbs sat on the cross benches, and the leaderless protectionist
opposition elected J. P. Abbott in his stead.[71] But when, in July
1887, Abbott resigned this leadership, Dibbs underwent a 'conversion'
to protection,[72] thus making complete a metamorphosis of the
political situation so that the Parkes faction with accretions had
become the freetrade party and the Dibbs faction with accretions
the protectionist party.

The 'accretions' were in each case the new members elected in 1887.
Some of these men were extreme—often doctrinaire—exponents
of their respective tariff principles and many of them owed
their original advancement to the new party organizations. Committed more directly to principle than to the faction leaders, they
constituted in each of the two parliamentary constellations an incipient party 'conscience'. On the protection side, this was not altogether novel: the hard core of enthusiasts clustered round O'Sullivan
in the previous parliament had fulfilled an analogous role as an effective
pressure group among the anti-Parkes forces of the House, and
now provided an established rallying point for those of like mind.
Doctrinaire freetraders were, however, a novel element. New members like McMillan, Wise and Carruthers, associated with and in

many respects the special products of the Freetrade Association, stressed principle above all else and stood as the representatives of a 'new' freetrade movement whose existence had become manifest in the election.[73] Like the more enthusiastic protectionists they were eager to see public life revitalized: there was, for example, implicit criticism of the old faction leaders in McMillan's election manifesto, which declared that the political and economic ills of the colony could 'be traced to the low moral tone of our public life, the want of a sense of responsibility in the high function undertaken, the petty municipal Liliputian attempt at Statesmanship'.[74] And already men of this stamp were groping towards a political philosophy which would 'use the word "freetrade" in its broadest and most comprehensive sense'.[75] As one of them told the electors: 'A free-trade policy was more in sympathy with our institutions than any other they could imagine; it was more instinct with the ideas of a free people like ourselves—with liberal notions and liberal institutions, than any other policy.'[76] The presence behind Parkes of members whose thoughts ran in these directions suggested that in the new parliament his freedom to manoeuvre in spite of principle might well be modified.

Parkes and the freetraders won an unequivocal victory in the election itself, as the following tabulation of the results indicates.[77]

Declared ministerial supporters (all freetrade)

Steady and unsteady Parkes supporters re-elected from twelfth parliament	27
Independents from twelfth parliament re-elected as ministerial supporters	7
New freetrade members	39
Total	73

Declared protectionist oppositionists

Steady and unsteady Dibbs supporters re-elected from twelfth parliament	23
Independents from twelfth parliament re-elected as protectionist oppositionists	2
New protectionist members	7
Total	32

Declared independents
   Freetrade   ↄ
   Protectionist   ℓ

                                                                  —
Total   1℃

Other   ℓ

Parkes' appeal to the country on the tariff issue had certainly repaid
him well. The call to vindicate free trade—combined, undoubtedly
with the work of the Freetrade Association—had brought a flood of
new ministerial supporters into the House. The equivocal position
of the old Dibbs faction on the tariff issue may have assisted this
trend: certainly Dibbs supporters from the twelfth parliament suffered
disastrous defeat in the election.[78] As the new parliament convened
Parkes appeared to be in an impregnable position. If election promise
meant anything he could count on support from seventy-six of the
Assembly's 124 members. He faced an opposition reduced to thirty-
six.[79] The pool of independents and doubtful men was only twelve—
too few to affect the balance of power. For the first time since the
inauguration of responsible government a ministry held office with the
majority support of a consolidated phalanx of declared followers
and depended neither on a coalition of factions nor on the goodwill
of independent members tenuously held on the fringes of a single
faction. It was a reorientation of political divisions along party lines,
as many members themselves—with considerable satisfaction—
declared it to be.[80]

In the new parliament the defeat (by sixty-four votes to nineteen)
of an opposition motion of censure confirmed the verdict of the
election and set a pattern for the next two years. Minor defections
and losses at by-elections scarcely affected Parkes' majority, and he
left office finally in January 1889 not because the opposition had
won control of the House but because he chose virtually to abdicate
in the full flush of power. Stability had in the meantime brought a
notable legislative record. The ministry carried important amendments to the bankruptcy and criminal laws, imposed stringent restrictions on Chinese immigration, and secured major administrative
reforms by its Public Works and Government Railways Acts.

The budget had been 'balanced' by late 1888. The ministry had the
good fortune to take office as better seasons and general economic
recovery were bringing increases in all forms of revenue.[81] It effected
mild civil service retrenchment, acted administratively to secure a

dramatic increase in receipts from land rents and sales,[82] and put by
the accumulated deficit in a separate account to be accommodated
by an issue of Treasury Bills.[83] Tariff reform was implemented equi-
vocally enough to avoid losses in customs revenue.[84] Thanks to this
astute combination of financial expedients, new taxation seemed to be
unnecessary.

In financial debates early in 1887 some ministerial supporters sharply
criticized the moderateness of tariff reform and the absence of immediate proposals for direct taxation.[85]   They were temporarily
mollified by government arguments that the tariff could only be
'safely' reduced in stages, and that a local government bill and proper
investigation of 'the property of the country'—both on the ministerial
programme—were necessary preliminaries before a satisfactory
scheme of direct taxation could be formulated.[86] But by November
1888 there were clear signs of restlessness again, as some freetraders
began reluctantly 'to doubt the intention of the government to carry
out the measures to which they pledged themselves'.[87] McMillan
in particular emerged as a 'candid critic', in effect the voice of the
party 'conscience', disturbed at the new importance of land revenue,
worried that no efforts were being made to liquidate the accumulated
deficit, and disillusioned by the ministry's reluctance to grasp the
nettle of direct taxation. 'I want to know', he asked, 'what will history
say of us in the future if with a majority of two thirds in this Parliament . . . we fail to inaugurate a system of finance, before the con-
tingencies of future elections, which will make the freetrade cause
in the country secure?'[88]

Against the background of such discontent, Parkes committed
political suicide on 9 January 1889 by contemptuously refusing to
reply in the House to charges laid by J. H. Want against the integrity
of Fehon, one of the government's first appointees to the new Railway
Commission.[89] Though in some ways justifiable, Parkes' arrogant
attitude on this occasion shocked even his own supporters, eight of
whom voted with the opposition in a thin House to defeat the government on a snap adjournment division. Parkes subsequently admitted
that he had 'courted defeat', which he greeted 'with a feeling of
welcome'.[90] He was over-wearied by the burden of office. Despite
a handsome and pliant majority in the House, he had suffered determined obstruction from a handful of men in opposition who had
copied his own filibustering techniques and who had remained
irrepressible even under new standing orders which had in May
1887 equipped the government with wide powers to apply the gag.
Disorderly, extended sittings had put Parkes and his colleagues 'from

the first in a state of weariness, over-tension of mind, with sleeples
nights and harassed days'.[91] Moreover, ill fortune had dogged th
ministry itself. Cabinet had not always worked harmoniously, and i
had in addition suffered fortuitously from three resignations, two o
them in particularly painful circumstances.[92]

After all these unhappy experiences, Parkes was in no mood t
accept criticism from his own supporters. In a parting homily, h
told them that 'where party prevails as the motive power' of parlia
mentary government, it was the function of the ordinary party membe
to support his leaders unquestioningly as the interpreters and ex
ecutors of policy:

> It amounts to this: that trusting to party to govern the country
> you trust [your leaders] on their known views of political policy
> on their known public character; and you must trust them in th
> intricacies of Administration, or the affairs of the country wil
> soon come to error.[93]

J. H. Want, the author of the government's downfall, declined th
Governor's commission, which passed to Dibbs. When the Premier
elect had formed his government, Burns, the retiring Treasurer
moved the customary supply bill, on behalf of the new administration
to cover the eriod of ministerial elections. This motion was th
signal for a dramatic display of freetrade solidarity. McMillan took th
unprecedented course of proposing as an amendment that the Gover
nor be forwarded an address listing a series of 'inconveniences and
dangers' the colony would suffer unless a new ministry had th
confidence of parliament, and assuring him that there was 'no reasor
to believe' that he would 'experience any serious difficulty in obtaining
such a ministry from among the freetrade members of the House'
In supporting this amendment, McMillan argued that the vote which
had overturned the government had been a vote against the person
of the Premier, and not against the policy of his party. 'The position
which the freetrade party occupies tonight,' he said, 'is that of a
compact and integral party . . . we have got the freetrade phalanx
here yet', still with a sound majority, and 'the question is this: I
the cause of Free Trade . . . which we believe sacred to the majority
of the people of this country, to be demolished, or put in jeopardy
by an accident?'[94]

The amendment was triumphantly carried, despite nettled denun
ciation from Parkes, and a bitter tirade by one of his old factior
supporters who accused 'a number of political fledglings' ('the Wise
Seaver-McMillan-Smith party') of plotting to 'thrust aside . . . th
venerable and hon. gentleman by whose breath they have scrambled

into this House'.[95] In the division, Parkes and those of his ministers who were present voted against the amendment. They were joined by two of their ertswhile supporters. The rest stood behind McMillan in a vote which in effect gave notice that principle, and not attachment to a leader, was the real cement of the freetrade party.[96] No faction in the old sense now survived at Parkes' back: the question for the future was whether he would be offered—and would accept—leadership again of a party that had declared its independence of him.

A dissolution of parliament—now made inevitable by McMillan's *de facto* censure of Dibbs—stirred the respective parties into immediate electoral activity. On 18 January, the protectionists met, appointed secretaries and a Central Elections Committee, secured offices for daily meetings, and established contact with their extra-parliamentary organizations.[97] A week earlier, the Freetrade Association had warned its Parliamentary Elections Committee to prepare for an early election.[98] When the dissolution came, the parliamentary freetrade party met under McMillan's chairmanship, formed a 'strong executive or working committee of nine' to direct the elections, secured rooms, and resolved to frame a platform and employ a paid secretary.[99] Meanwhile the Freetrade Association began regular meetings twice a day and made arrangements 'to work in complete harmony' with the parliamentary party.[1] Again Parkes played no active part in organizational work, though in a letter which in effect recognized the existence of the parliamentary executive committee, he told freetraders: 'one thing we must learn from our opponents—to stand together. The quality next to honesty and valour in any heroic struggle is fidelity.'[2]

Two well organized and consolidated party machines thus faced each other in the election of 1889. Each was fortified by a new sense of solidarity and equipped to profit from the experience of 1887. The same work of placing candidates, canvassing, printing literature and organizing lecture tours was carried out, though with an efficiency and an aggressiveness which brought to mind—even among contemporaries—the analogy of the Birmingham Caucus.[3] The freetraders won the election, but with the barest of majorities. They could claim seventy-one seats: thirty-nine in country electorates, thirty-two in Sydney and suburbs. The protectionists won sixty-six seats: sixty-one in country constituencies.

The election over, freetraders had to face the question of leadership. Parkes, sulking uncertainly on the sidelines, played out an elaborate game of verbal hide-and-seek with McMillan, and finally asked that the party be informed of his unwillingness to 'accept the post of Leader in the Parliament', adding:

The ministerial majority in the late Parliament disclosed aspects of political conduct which I do not care to meet again in ministerial office. The friends of the ministry were the first to find fault with ministerial proceedings, the foremost in attacking ministerial measures, and ever and anon the readiest to encourage the attacks of others. No lie could be invented too black to be listened to by professed friends.[4]

Such ungracious remarks were an insult to a body of men who had in fact loyally supported Parkes until he himself deserted them. But Parkes' words did indicate that—as he had already pointedly told Mc-Millan—he was well aware of the misgivings with which 'candid friends' had followed him.[5] He chose now to retire voluntarily, with protestations of injured innocence and a pious reference to his former services to the colony:

There are times when men are called upon to sacrifice everything for their country, but this will hardly be called such a time. Besides, I have sacrificed all the best part of my life already.[6]

But Parkes' political skill and prestige were still too great to be lightly cast aside, and no alternative chief was offering. Accordingly, a meeting of the opposition held under McMillan late in February elected the absent Parkes as leader. Notwithstanding the peevish attitude he had assumed in the preliminaries, Parkes now found it 'difficult to decline this handsome testimony of the confidence of a great party'.[7] But, as the circumstances of his recall displayed, Parkes came back on the party's and not his own terms.

The point was emphasized when, after conducting immediate censure proceedings which overturned the Dibbs government in the new House, Parkes was commissioned to form an administration. Interviews took place between himself, McMillan 'and other leading members of the Freetrade party', and it at once became an open secret that none of Parkes' former ministers, with the possible exception of Brunker, was likely to be offered a portfolio.[8] As the *Sydney Morning Herald* put it: 'should Sir Henry take his old colleagues into office again, it is regarded as almost certain that the Government would not receive the support of the majority of the freetrade party'.[9] The prediction was correct: in the new ministry Brunker alone of Parkes' old faction colleagues survived. He was in fact the only member of the previous team associated closely with the 'new' freetraders of 1887. And these were the men—McMillan, Bruce Smith, Carruthers and O'Connor—who formed the hard core of the new ministry. Looking back some years later, Parkes described the government aptly enough:

A number of comparatively young men of much promise had taken their places on the Free-trade side of the House. They had shown zeal, ability and political firmness in the elections, and, some of them, in the previous Parliament. They could not be, and they ought not to be, overlooked in allotting men to portfolios. In the government which I succeeded in forming, half the ministers were entirely new to official life ... [But] In talent, energy and character the new Government was equal to any that had gone before it.[10]

It was perhaps pleasant in retrospect to claim credit for an adventurous experiment. But at the time of its formation the new government was a reflection not of Parkes' good judgment, but of the temper and solidarity of a party which had by now deprived him of his old freedom to manoeuvre.

Parkes had in fact constructed his government of 1889 in the shadow of a dramatic reorganization of freetrade party structure and ideology. A week before ministers' names were announced, a 'largely attended meeting of members of the freetrade party—freetrade members of the Assembly, freetrade members of the last Parliament, and defeated freetrade candidates at the general election'—had decided to form a 'Liberal Political Association' to serve as a new centre for rallying freetrade support in the colony.[11] In one leap the freetraders had reached and passed the stage the protectionists had attained when the Protection Union was formed three years before.

Parkes' name was associated neither with this initial move nor with the series of meetings which followed later in the month and which resulted in the reorganization and renaming of the freetrade party. By early April a new platform had been framed and adopted: free trade remained the central plank, but it was supported and extended by a series of ancillary objectives 'upon which the progress and prosperity of the colony depend'.[12] Direct taxation—to ensure a measure of social justice and to make tariff policy independent of revenue needs—headed a list of agreed aims which ranged from stimulating the growth of local government to promoting water conservation. As the party's new name—'Liberal'—testified, this programme was an attempt at once to claim, and to refurbish, the colony's old liberal tradition in changed circumstances.

Near defeat in the recent election—and particularly the conviction that 'freetraders lost in the country districts ... because they were not so well organized as a party as the protectionists were'[13]—had acted as a catalyst for these changes. The same stimulus had produced a burst of activity in the old Freetrade Association which established nearly fifty new branches in the first fortnight after the election.[14] Then, drawn both by common objectives and by overlapping personnel towards the new Liberal Political Association, the Freetrade Association agreed to formal amalgamation. The Council of the older body merged into the Organizing Committee of the new, to form the controlling group of a 'Freetrade and Liberal Association of New South Wales'. This new Association adopted the constitution and rules of the Freetrade Association, with the addition of the platform formulated by the Liberal Political Association.[15] What resulted was a unified party structure, with a permanent executive (representing a continuing body uniting parliamentary party and constituency associations) and party rules which required all members to pledge themselves to the platform.[16]

Protectionists showed some concern at being outdistanced by free-trade reorganization,[17] but rested content for the time being with their past successes. In their case a simple relationship had existed from the beginning between parliamentary party and extra-parliamentary organizations, the former having been the direct creation of the latter on the basis of a clear-cut sectional movement of protest against the political *status quo*. The freetraders on the other hand had passed through a more agonizing process before they could erect an effective party structure. They had had to feel their way through to new policies of broader appeal and based on traditional articles of faith, and they had both benefited and suffered from the inevitability of accepting Parkes—still the master faction tactician of the day—as their leader. But whatever the steps by which the respective parties had emerged, they had clearly brought revolutionary changes to the politics of New South Wales by mid-1889. Though overtones of the old faction system survived, that system no longer provided the mainspring for the operation of the colony's political institutions. New men, new issues, and new organizations had undermined its viability, broken through the sanctions which the old 'liberal' ethos had erected against sectional political activity, and insensibly prepared the ground for the painless acceptance in 1891 of the Labor Party.

Conclusion

THE MAIN FEATURE of political life in New South Wales from the end of the fifties to the middle of the eighties was the struggle of rival leaders for power in a non-party context. Superficially personal, this struggle was in fact carried on between small groups of men who formed nuclei or cores around which the leaders built larger parliamentary groups, the FACTIONS, which in turn provided the basis for parliamentary majorities. The leaders had to win majorities to win office, but such majorities were often slim and always impermanent. The faction cores, on the other hand, normally lasted for a decade or more and their persistence largely explains the order and stability of the faction system.

No one factor explains the cohesion of the factions, their cores or the majorities built around them. Members might be won over by appeals to their political sentiments, by meeting their requests for various kinds of administrative action in their electorates (often on behalf of interests they represented), or by finding them or their political friends jobs in the civil service. Some men followed a leader steadily in the hope of winning office and power; others because of personal friendship and admiration for his political acumen. Professions of principle had their uses for faction leaders provided they were general enough to be ambiguous, but they could not be used as bases for distinct and lasting programmes without destroying the flexibility which was characteristic of the system.

Programmes and platforms were at a discount for another reason too. 'Good government', meaning efficient administration and rapid development of the colony's material resources, was the ideal of almost all the parliamentarians of the time. The proper work of government was conceived to be not reform, but the profitable employment of revenue and the efficient management of an extensive system of public services. As long as ministries managed this work competently and did not have to face major economic crises, no one paid much attention to the occasional reformers and idealists who questioned the fundamental assumptions of established policies. On no

149

occasion in fact were the faction chiefs challenged by any new leader armed with a creed and a following built upon widespread electoral dissatisfaction.

The struggle for power in the Assembly inevitably extended to the constituencies. Principles and programmes were of even less interest to the voters than to the average 'practical' member of parliament and the faction leaders were forced to devise electoral methods to match the techniques they used in the House. In the electorates they acted covertly, seeking through widespread 'wirepulling' to exploit a variety of local conflicts to promote the election of members likely to support them in parliament. Faction conflict did not extend to the administration itself or to the Upper House. Although office gave faction leaders access to resources which they used to advantage in the struggle for power, there was never any hint of a spoils system in the colony. The Upper House occasionally felt the backwash of faction politics in the Lower, either through new appointments or because ministries unwilling for faction reasons to refuse a measure unpalatable to them in the Assembly took advantage of the likelihood that it would be stopped in the Council. But faction leaders were in effect relieved of the necessity to seek influence in the Upper House by the success with which its powers had been curbed in 1861.

Electoral politics provided, as it were, a neutral background for events in the Assembly itself. The demands which originated in the constituencies or from interest groups were normally satisfied through channels provided by the factions. Knots of members occasionally formed in the House to protest on behalf of some interest which they thought had been neglected, but until the eighties no pressure groups had any permanence or threatened serious modification of the faction system. People spoke not of 'the electorate' but of 'the electorates'; the voters' function was to elect representatives, not to choose between alternative governments and policies. The faction leaders did not have the power to overcome the isolation and localism of most electorates, or to allay their suspicions of central government and Macquarie Street politicians. The leaders could not force local men to define their views in terms of candidates and policies determined upon in Sydney, and even when a pledged supporter was elected the leaders had no strong hold over him. If he won benefits for his constituents they regarded him, rather than the ministry which he supported, as their benefactor.

As soon as three or more factions were established in the Assembly, coalition became one of the two standard manoeuvres by which office

and a majority might be won. The other was to win the adherence
of segments of the Assembly's membership temporarily unattached
to a faction leader. In either case the leader anxious to secure a working
majority normally had in addition to win the sympathy of independents. The result was that responsible government, in making ministries
depend on majorities, forced the factions into what can appropriately
be called bipartism. This was in fact recognized at the time, as the
contemptuous references to the battle of the 'ins' and 'outs' suggest.

These regular methods of political warfare, in both the electorates
and the legislature, are evidence that the faction system had a logic
or order of its own. This order made it possible for faction leaders
to anticipate opponents' moves and to calculate their chances of
success in a struggle for office or, once in office, to foresee the dangers
that might face them. Furthermore, the stability of the system itself
must be emphasized. In the seventies it survived two crises and the
loss of particular leaders and factions. On these occasions, new faction
combinations arose with sufficient power to deny old leaders an
overwhelming predominance in parliament and they adopted—not
by imitation but from political necessity—the same techniques of
action and exhibited the same general characteristics as the old.

Contemporary writers who deplored the faction politics of New
South Wales all passed silently over the fact that a major change of
the system of government had been accomplished in the fifties with
only slight disturbances to the life of the colony. They failed to distinguish between the faction and the nonfaction ministries and did
not admit that the former had made the new institutions work. Once
the new constitution had been brought into operation, major changes
were made in the electoral system and the new elected Lower House
had become the more important of the two chambers. The chief
executive offices had passed from the hands of permanent officials to
politicians chosen almost exclusively from the Lower House; a variety
of changes had been made in the administrative apparatus of the
colony and the position of the Governor had been transformed. The
government had become a more complex structure of interdependent
institutions but it functioned with a minimum of friction and, despite
criticism of it, particularly for inefficiency, its operations provoked
no movement for fundamental reform. Parliamentary government
in the broadest sense had clearly been established in the fifties and
sixties and by the end of the eighties was strong enough to withstand
approaching economic and political crises.

The cabinet stood at the centre of the institutional complex, clear
evidence that responsible government was a viable form of govern-

ment despite the absence of political parties. Although it did not abide by all the rules of its counterpart in Britain, it possessed comparable unity in action in its relations with the administrative departments, the Assembly and the Governor. On matters peripheral to the main currents of political conflict, where the Governor's discretion was still intact, cabinet could advise, but because its power was incomplete both its responsibility and its collective action were imperfect.

The faction system was slowly undermined from the mid-seventies onwards as economic development and diversification, accompanied by a steady growth in population, at once reduced the effects of the colony's geographical fragmentation and differentiated the community more sharply into groups with identifiable and sometimes competing interests. The formation of bodies like the Free Selectors Associations and the Working Men's Defence Association were early symptoms of these changes. But their gropings towards direct political representation were initially frustrated both by the continuing viability of the faction system itself and by prosperity, which helped to cloak incipient social tensions and reduce the opportunities for leaders to generalize limited sectional grievances into effective political movements. For the time being, they could operate merely as pressure groups—more effective indeed than their predecessors—but of a kind that could still be absorbed readily enough into the faction system.

It took a sudden break in the boom during the mid-eighties to precipitate a crisis which laid bare the extent of accumulated social and economic changes. Now the traditional liberal ethos had a hollow ring in the face of distress and the urgent dissatisfaction of men moved by economic grievances to denounce the old politicians and to demand new policies to meet sectional needs. These demands were soon being expressed most forcefully through a diversity of political organizations which managed to federate around the rallying cry of protection. The rapid evolution of this new movement symbolized the inadequacy, in changed circumstances, not only of the old liberal attitudes, but also of the leisurely old methods of channelling pressure from constituencies to parliament through a network of faction obligations.

Once it became feasible—as it did in the conditions of the mid-eighties—for extra-parliamentary organizations to secure broad enough support to cut through existing conventions about representation and to elect champions of their principles to parliament, the faction system was facing a fundamental challenge. Faction leaders could not manipulate and exploit the demands arising from a changed social and economic order when these were shaped into a coherent whole around some central principle and focussed on the legislature through outside organizations with wide electoral support. The coming of the parties of the late eighties was a sign that the factions had faltered.

But the factions did not disintegrate completely, nor was their increasing failure to control the parliamentary system something forced upon them entirely from without. Their more prominent leaders, instinctively opportunistic, at first promoted, and then sought to capitalize on, the very slogans which gave vitality to the extra-parliamentary organizations. There followed a period of transition, defined broadly by the elections of 1887 and 1889, when, with new parties and old factions inextricably mixed in parliament, the established leaders reluctantly came to terms with emerging political movements which they could use, but not control. This process was most obviously symbolized by Dibbs' 'conversion' to protection in 1887, and Parkes' assumption of power in 1889 at the invitation of the freetraders and in effect on their own terms.

But the very survival of the old faction leaders—albeit in a changed role—inevitably involved the survival also of residual faction loyalties and even of faction methods in the conduct of the parliamentary game. For all their formal solidarity, the parties of the late eighties thus remained to some extent an amalgam of the old and the new. This was at least one explanation of their subsequent lack of discipline and their failure to deal constructively and unitedly with disrupting issues—like the federation question and industrial disturbance—which arose soon after their formation.

But whatever their inbuilt parliamentary weaknesses, the parties had brought a revolution in the terms of political conflict in the colony. The Liberal Party of 1889 stands in many respects as a model for the type of party structure soon to be 'devised' by Labor. Its constituency associations, its central executive linking the parliamentary and extra-parliamentary elements, its platform, its pledge and—in effect—its elected leader made it the most advanced organization to emerge from the political disturbances of the eighties. The theoretical possibilities of this type of organization had been glimpsed as far back as the mid-fifties. But parliamentary leaders had discovered then that influence was as effective as organization and much easier to maintain—even in the closely settled metropolitan constituencies. Improved communications and changes in the size, character and location of the voting population were now reducing the efficacy of influence and providing opportunities for initiative through organization that had not existed before. The Liberal machine had been constructed in the shadow of two election campaigns during which its forerunner and its protectionist opponents had proved the effectiveness of openly organized agitation and manipulation in the service of competing sets of political principles. Its coming signified that the parties forged from this experience had assumed a life of their own in the struggle for power.

Appendix I

MEETINGS OF FACTIONS IN THE LEGISLATIVE ASSEMBLY, 1856–1887

Meetings of other groups of members are not included although several of them have been reported. Dinners and picnics attended by members on a ministerial or opposition invitation are also excluded, but they too are evidence of the group life of the factions.

1. Liberal members in opposition: 7 May 1856. At D. Cooper's residence. Twenty-four members attended, a few of whom were later found to be ministerialists. *Empire*, 8 May 1856, Martin in *S.M.H.*, 23 May 1856, Cowper in *S.M.H.*, 27 May 1856.

2. Liberal members in opposition: 'frequent conferences' before September 1856. Martin in *S.M.H.*, 8 September 1856.

3. Liberal members in opposition: about 21 August 1856, just before taking office. Met in committee room of Assembly. 'The object of the meeting is to enable those members who are supposed to entertain similar views in reference to Crown Lands, the Electoral districts and the financial policy of the Government to determine what course it may be advisable to pursue in reference to them during the present session of Parliament'. Cowper to Parkes, circular, 19 August 1856, P.C., A876, p.402; Hay in *S.M.H.*, 30 April 1857.

4. Liberal members in opposition: probably 23 August 1856. Discussed whether Cowper should attempt to form a ministry after the Governor had sent for him. Some doubtful, but not Robertson. Robertson in *Maitland Mercury*, 30 April 1857.

5. Liberal members, supporting Cowper: probably 25 August 1856. Discussion after Cowper had failed to get a barrister to take office as attorney-general in the ministry he was forming. A 'large majority' decided it was best not to abandon the attempt to form a ministry. Robertson in *Maitland Mercury*, 30 April 1857.

6. Liberal members supporting Cowper ministry: 25 September 1856. Discussed course to be pursued by ministry after defeat in House. All but 'one or two' (two-thirds according to Robertson)

agreed to support Cowper in attempt to defy motion of censure
and advised Cowper to seek a dissolution. He did and was refused.
S.M.H., 26 September 1856; Robertson in *Maitland Mercury,* 3
April 1857. Another meeting had apparently been held after the
ministers had been returned in ministerial elections but there
no record of its discussions. *S.M.H.,* 15 September 1856.

7. Liberal members in opposition: 7 March 1857. Fewer than ten
attended. Jones and Flood in unspecified disagreement with
others. Discussed parliamentary strategy. One member 'declared
against a dissolution until assured of the materials for another
and better ministry'. *S.M.H.,* 16 March 1857; [unidentified] to
Donaldson, 7 March [1857], Letters, Donaldson Ministry, items
338, 340; Cowper to Parkes, 31 March 1857, P.C., A876, p.478,
admits 'comparative disorganisation of our side'; and Cowper
to Parkes, 22 June 1857, ibid., p.440, indicates Jones was prob
ably the one to advise against a dissolution and that opposition
was ill-organized and without a coherent programme.

8. Liberal members in opposition: early in August 1857. Meeting
not reported; called to discuss policy and tactics. Leaders antici
pated early fall of Parker ministry, were pleased to observe liberal
side increased in numbers and more solid. Parker's Electoral Bill
the immediate topic under discussion. Cowper to Parkes, 22 June
1857, 30 July 1857, P.C., A876, pp.440, 421; Cowper to Arnold
27 July 1857, W. M. Arnold Correspondence, Aa47, n.p.; Cowper
to Jamison, 4 August 1857, Jamison Papers, vol. 3, Letters
to R. T. Jamison, D.38–3, p.27.

9. Cowper-Robertson faction in office: 29 October 1860. Held in
office of Colonial Secretary.   Twenty-eight usual supporters
attended, three sent letters of apology. Press not admitted. Called
by circular signed by Robertson, Premier and Colonial Secretary.
Ministry had been defeated in House on free selection clause of
Land Bill three days before. Unofficial report that a motion
carried, with four against, that ministry ask House for vote of
six months' supply and then seek dissolution. Names of those
attending and of those taking part reported. *S.M.H.,* 29 and 30
October 1860.

10. Opponents of Cowper-Robertson ministry: 1 November 1860.
Held at Metropolitan Hotel, called by circular to forty members.
Eighteen attended, names reported. Resolved to oppose granting
of six months' supply to Government (which forced it to advise
dissolution without supply for coming weeks). *S.M.H.,* 1 and
November 1860; *Empire,* 2 November 1860.

11. Martin faction, with others in opposition. Planned motion to defeat Cowper ministry and secured support for it. Allen in *S.M.H.,* 9 October 1863.

12. Martin faction in opposition: early in January 1866. Two meetings mentioned. Planning tactics to overthrow Cowper ministry, agreed by vote to take Parkes into coalition if ministry defeated and Martin called on to form new one. One dissentient left faction in protest. Walker, *Reminiscences,* p.70, *Recollections,* p.2; Martin to Parkes, 8 January 1866, P.C., A925, p.65; Parkes to Martin, 8 January 1866, P.C., A932, n.p.

13. Martin and Parkes factions in office: 11 December 1866. Meeting called by circular, no report of its being held. Circular reads: 'Mr. Parkes [Colonial Secretary] would be glad if you would attend a meeting of members of the Legislative Assembly who supported the Public Schools Bill to be held at this office on Wednesday morning at 11 o'clock to consider the measure as affected by the Legislative Council's amendments'. Letters to H. Halloran. Uncat. MSS., set 292.

14. Martin and Parkes factions supporting ministry: 22 October 1867. Called by circular. Held in Colonial Secretary's (Parkes') office. Twenty present but not ministers. Twelve others sent letters of apology. Deliberations not made public. Dr Lang in chair. Report that resolution carried pledging support for ministry, which had suffered defeat. Ministers apparently did not attend because, refusing to consider defeat as one calling for resignation, anxious not to run risk of having motion of confidence put in House. *S.M.H.,* 23 October 1867; Parkes in *S.M.H.,* 25 October 1867 and editorial.

15. Martin and Parkes factions in office: 14 January 1868. Twenty-seven at meeting, four absentees apologized and assured ministry of support. Two ministers absent. Nothing to be made public about meeting, but called to discuss ministry's shaky position and the state of public business. *S.M.H.,* 15 January 1868.

16. Cowper-Robertson faction in opposition: 15 January 1868. Twenty-five or twenty-six present, avowed opponents of ministry only; discussed tactics of opposition. Robertson in *S.M.H.,* 16 January 1868.

17. Martin and Parkes factions in office. 25 September 1868. Met in Colonial Secretary's office to discuss tactics in coming session, including the choice of member to be nominated for chairman of committees. Discussed Parkes' recent resignation from the ministry. But meeting inconclusive: several members absent and those

present reluctant to give opinions of ministry without knowing who was to take Parkes' place. *S.M.H.,* 24 and 26 September 1868, and J. Stewart in *S.M.H.,* 9 October 1868. Some of Martin's supporters met shortly after this to insist that ministry be reconstructed to remove Parkes' supporters Wilson and Byrnes but the ministry fell before this could come to a conclusion. Farnell and Wearne in *S.M.H.,* 21 December 1870.

18. Martin and Parkes factions in office: 15 October 1868. Twenty-one present. Met in committee room of Assembly, to discuss ministerial crisis and tactics to be followed. A resolution carried, but its substance is not known. Feeling apparently was that ministry could not carry on. Members present at meeting subsequently met the Premier, Martin. A cabinet held after that. Martin advised dissolution four days later, and it was refused. *S.M.H.,* 16 and 17 October 1868.

19. Cowper-Robertson faction in opposition: 21 October 1868. To discuss formation of a ministry in place of Martin's. *S.M.H.,* 22 October 1868.

20. Martin and Parkes factions in opposition. Possibly three meetings to discuss tactics in opposition and decide on motion of censure to be moved against Robertson ministry by Parkes. Walker, *Reminiscences,* p.76, refers to meeting of Martin's faction at Martin's home in October 1868 to discuss no confidence motion. De Salis to Parkes, 7 November 1868, P.C., A882, p.34, refers to a 'war council of November'. *S.M.H.,* 10 and 13 December 1868 describes meeting on 8 December 1868, at which twenty-six members present including all Martin's late colleagues to discuss motion of censure.

21. Martin faction in opposition, with some of Parkes' supporters: 11 June 1869. Overnight trip to Goulburn. Referred to as a 'meeting of Sir James Martin's parliamentary supporters'. Names given of eleven who attended. Discussed forthcoming journal, the *Lictor,* being put out in the interest of the faction. Walker's note to Piddington, 1 June 1869, and Brierly[to Walker], 3 June 1869, both in W. Walker Papers, Uncat. MSS., set 501.

22. Cowper-Robertson faction in office: 2 December 1870. Held in Colonial Secretary's office. Called by circular, signed C. Cowper. Thirty-one attended, including ministers. Names published. Letters from two unable to attend. Three and a half hour meeting, all present assured ministry of support, but 'the result of the conference is that on Tuesday an intimation will be made of the determination of Ministers to resign accompanied by an offer . . .

to renew the Stamp Duties Act for six months and to give one month's supplies for 1871' before resigning. Also discussed leadership after Cowper announced his acceptance of Agent-General's office in London. Robertson was perhaps chosen as leader. Cowper to Belmore, 2 December 1870, Letters to Belmore, A2542/3; *S.M.H.*, 2 and 3 December 1870, Robertson in *S.M.H.*, 25 January 1871.

23. Martin faction with some of Parkes faction in opposition: One or two meetings early in December 1870. Martin about to form ministry with the alternatives being canvassed of coalition with Parkes or Robertson. On these occasions, Martin admits, there were 'of course' meetings of members supporting the member forming a government. In fact no full meeting of all supporters held; 'several' members met with Martin and after disagreement on invitees to a meeting to discuss composition of ministry it was decided to seek opinions of members by circular instead. Twenty-five circulars sent out, twenty-four returned, recipients asked to mark, on list of members of Assembly, five men they thought should be in ministry under Martin. Martin advised them to choose only those men likely to be returned in ministerial elections and that he would be 'led' but not 'bound' by the result. Fifteen names marked in the lists: five won only one vote each. Piddington had most votes, then Farnell. Wilson, Byrnes, Wisdom and Robertson each received several votes. *S.M.H.*, 10 and 12 December 1870; Farnell, Wearne and Tunks in *S.M.H.*, 21 December 1870; Martin in *S.M.H.*, 25 January 1871. Discussed by Parkes in his *Fifty Years in the Making of Australian History*, pp.214–17.

24. Opposition to Martin-Robertson ministry: early in January 1872. Elected Forster as its leader to take advantage of ministerial crisis. Arranged motion of censure and secured support of thirty-one members for it. Windeyer to his wife, 26 January 1872, Windeyer Uncat. MSS., set 186, box 3; Butler to Parkes, n.d. [January 1872], Autograph Letters, Australian, A62, pp.100–3.

25. Martin's and Robertson's supporters: 29 January 1872. Held at Colonial Secretary's office. Called by Martin to discuss course ministry should take after defeat—whether to resign or advise dissolution. A cabinet held before the meeting to discuss the question, ministers being divided on it. Windeyer to his wife, 26, 27 January 1872, Windeyer Uncat. MSS., set 186, box 3; *S.M.H.*, 30 January 1872; Belmore to Kimberley, 29 January 1872, Copies of Correspondence of the Earl of Belmore, A2542/2, p.278.

26. Parkes' faction in opposition: 29 April 1872. Names of those present listed. Held prior to fall of Martin-Robertson ministry. Meeting appointed sub-committee to draft amendment to address-in-reply, then adopted draft and appointed Parkes to move it. (Ministry fell on the amendment.) Parkes Diary, 1872, p.2, entry for 30 April 1872, P.C., A1013; *S.M.H.*, 30 April 1872.

27. Martin faction in opposition: June 1872. Martin implies that some of opposition met and had pledged themselves to a nominee for the chairman of committees in opposition to the ministry's nominee. *S.M.H.*, 14 June 1872.

28. Parkes ministry's supporters: late in February 1874. Called by circular, about thirty attended, a few usual supporters absent. Unanimous in agreeing to ministry's proposals for public business in coming session. No formal resolution, but understanding reached to support government to get estimates passed, an amendment to the Electoral Act, a law consolidation and amendment bill, agreement on mail arrangements with San Francisco and other measures. *S.M.H.*, 28 February 1874.

29. Parkes faction in opposition: 10 January 1877. To consider appointing leader in place of Parkes, who resigned in December 1876. Meeting not properly convened, only fifteen or sixteen present, adjourned. *S.M.H.*, 12 January 1877 and for Parkes' resignation, *S.M.H.*, 28 December 1876. Second meeting held and adjourned, *S.M.H.*, 17 January 1877. Third meeting, 23 January 1877; decided to appoint leader. Unanimous in pledging support to whoever was chosen. Piddington and Fitzpatrick nominated, Piddington elected. *S.M.H.*, 24 January 1877.

30 and 31. Ministerial 'caucus' held: end of April 1877, no further details. Opposition caucus held 1 March 1877, decided to move motion of censure and chose Parkes to move it. *S.M.H.*, 2 March 1877, and Lyne, *Life of Sir Henry Parkes,* pp.346–7.

32. Opposition members, including Parkes faction: 28 November 1877, on eve of fall of Robertson ministry. Farnell, commissioned to form new ministry, denied that he had promised to take office with Parkes and asserted that he alone had drafted the amendment to the address-in-reply on which the ministry was defeated. *S.M.H.*, 12 December 1877.

33. Parkes faction and Robertson faction: 17 December 1878, after Farnell ministry had withdrawn resignations on instance of Governor, Robertson having meanwhile tried and failed to form ministry after Farnell's defeat. The Parkes and Robertson factions

agreed to fuse and to invite Parkes to take the leadership of the opposition, which he did. Parkes subsequently gave notice of motion of censure and Lyne contends that the two factions agreed on fusion on condition of equal representation in a new ministry under Parkes. *S.M.H.,* 18 December 1878; Lyne, op cit., p.376.

34. Opposition to Parkes and Robertson in office: April 1880. Referred to as 'caucus'. Drafted motion of censure subsequently moved by Fitzpatrick. Fitzpatrick accepted this manoeuvre even though he would have preferred to obstruct supply. *N.S.W. P.D.,* vol. II, 28 April 1880, pp.2062, 2079.

35. Opposition to Parkes and Robertson in office: mid-1882. Chose A. Stuart as leader after death of Fitzpatrick in December 1881. *S.M.H.,* 23 August 1882.

36. Stuart ministry's supporters (emerging Dibbs-Jennings faction): 13 February 1884. Forty-eight to fifty members present, but not ministers. Called by circular, held in library of Assembly, apologies from several absentees. Held to discuss tactics in face of motion of no-confidence by leader of opposition, Robertson. The question arose because the supporters themselves were critical of the ministry's finance proposals. Decided by resolution, with only one dissentient, to oppose Robertson's motion. Reports of those at the meeting do not wholly agree about the attitude of the meeting to the finance proposals of the Treasurer (Dibbs), although there is no doubt that they were disliked and that a clear indication was given by the meeting that they had to be modified. The meeting was unwilling to threaten that they would bring the ministry down if modifications were not made. *S.M.H.,* 14 February 1884; *N.S.W. P.D.,* vol. XI, McElhone (p.1777), Smith (p.1789), Garrett (p.2041), Heydon (pp.2080–1).

37. i. Robertson's supporters with Parkes' supporters in opposition: 4 November 1885, just after general election. Between twenty-five and thirty present, some named, several absent. Held at time when Dibbs ministry shaky. Reports of meeting disagree; matters said to have been discussed were: the leadership, Robertson taking over in place of Burns who had acted as leader during Robertson's illness; the strength of the opposition in the House; an opposition picnic; payment of 'some small accounts' from the late general election; a vote of censure on the ministry. Two unnamed members at the meeting were quoted in support of this account of it, while two letters, one from Robertson himself and one

from Abigail, were printed issuing general denials of the accuracy of the first report to appear in the press. *Daily Telegraph,* 5 and 6 November 1885.

ii. At the opposition picnic held on 16 November 1885 it was agreed unanimously that Barton be supported for the Speakership. *Daily Telegraph,* 17 November 1885.

iii. Independents met, 13 November 1885, to discuss whether to form a 'third party'. Thirteen attended. *Daily Telegraph,* 14 November 1885.

38. Dibbs-Jennings faction in opposition: 10 February 1886. Met in opposition room of Assembly. Twenty-three or twenty-five present, two absent. Names reported. Held shortly before fall of Robertson ministry. Called to consider political situation and to appoint permanent leader. Lyne refused leadership, Jennings elected. Decided to support Garvan's motion of no-confidence in the Robertson ministry. *S.M.H.,* 11 February 1886.

39. Dibbs-Jennings faction in office: July 1886. Between forty and fifty members present. Dibbs, Treasurer, in chair. Resolved 'that every legitimate latitude should be accorded to members who desired to discuss the provisions of [Dibbs' Customs Duties Bill], and that debate within reasonable limits should be encouraged . . . in the event of a minority endeavouring to coerce the majority by unconstitutional means or indulging in stonewall tactics, they should be resisted in every orderly manner, most of the members present expressing their willingness to remain in the Assembly chamber until the Bill was disposed of.' *S.M.H.,* 7 July 1886.

40. Protectionists in opposition to Parkes: 9 March 1887. Held in opposition room of Assembly. Abbott elected leader unanimously. No direct motion carried to define attitude opposition would adopt to the ministry and its policy, but general understanding that no extreme course to be adopted. Abbott reported to be determined to control opposition or resign leadership of it. Two freetraders, Dibbs and Want, not regarded as part of 'direct opposition'. *S.M.H.,* 9 and 10 March 1887.

Appendix II

LIBERAL PARTY, 1889. PLATFORM, RULES, ETC.

(P.C., A893, pp.15–19)

Private and Confidential.   6th March, 1889.

Messrs. McMillan, Brunker, Abigail, Lee, Carruthers and Garrett, the Sub-committee selected to prepare proposed Platform of the Liberal Party, met yesterday and beg to submit the following for the consideration of the Organising Committee.

1st. Fiscal Policy

1. Freedom of Trade.
2. Direct Taxation.
3. Retrenchment of Expenditure.
4. The administration of the Public Works Act and Railways Act in their integrity and the abolition of political patronage and preference in the Civil Service in order to secure economy of administration.

2nd. Land Policy.

1. Laws to provide bona fide settlers with the most practicable expeditious and liberal means of settlement.
2. The enactment of laws to regulate the occupation of Crown Lands for pastoral purposes upon a fair and liberal basis including special provisions to meet the conditions of the Great Western area of the Colony.

3rd. Mining Policy.

1. Laws to regulate mining on private property.
2. Encouragement to bona fide mining on Crown Lands and the enforcement of the conditions of leases.
3. Special Laws to regulate Coal Mining in order to remedy existing grievances.

4th. Agricultural Policy.

1. Comprehensive system of Water Conservation and Irrigation.
2. Improvement of internal communications to facilitate the carriage of produce to market.

3. Establishment of Agricultural Schools and Model Farms in order to afford special instruction on Agriculture.

5th. National Policy.

1. Establishment of Local and Divisional Government throughout the colony by means of a liberal and comprehensive Law.
2. Electoral reform providing for an Elective Upper House and for the reduction of the number of members of the Legislative Assembly to a reasonable limit.
3. The Federation of Australia.

6th. The Encouragement of local industries by any legitimate means not imposing a tax upon the many for the benefit of the few as by—

1. Water conservation etc., to assist farmers.
2. Cheap and steady communication for producers to and from markets.
3. Technical Education to improve the skill and knowledge of those engaged in special pursuits.
4. Liberal laws to enable mining and other industries to be carried on with more security and bona fides.

Private and Confidential.

DRAFT RULES for the management of the Liberal Party of New South Wales.

1. That a Liberal Association shall be formed—the object of which shall be to endeavour as far as possible to ensure good government in this Colony by the aid of liberal laws.
2. The means to attain this object shall be by such political organisations as shall encourage the growth of opinion towards that end in all the Constituencies of the Colony.
3. This Association shall consist of a Central Association with branches in each City and Town and in such places in the Colony as may be deemed necessary.
4. The Central Association shall be in Sydney and its officers shall be a President, two Vice-Presidents and a Council of twenty members who shall elect from amongst themselves a Secretary and a Treasurer.
5. The number of Members of the Central Association and of the Branches shall be unlimited and any Elector of the Colony signing the declaration of membership and pledging himself to the platform of the Association and paying the annual fee in

advance shall be eligible for admission as a Member and such fee shall be ten shillings for Members of the Central Association and five shillings for the Members of any Branch.

6. Branch Associations shall consist of not less than twenty Members and the officers of such Branch shall be a President, two Vice-Presidents and a Council of six with the like power as to the election of a Secretary and a Treasurer as is contained in Clause 4.

7. Meetings of the Central Association and of Branch Associations shall be held not less than once in every three months at such times and places as may be appointed by the respective Councils.

8. Half-yearly meetings of the Central Association shall be held in Sydney in the last weeks of the months of May and November in each year.

9. An Annual Meeting of each of the Branch Associations shall be held in the first week of the month of October in each year and a full report of all matters connected or dealt with by each Branch shall be transmitted to the Central Association within fourteen days thereafter.

10. The Central Association at its Semi-annual Meeting in November and each Branch Association at its Annual Meeting shall elect a Delegate or Delegates to the Conference hereinafter mentioned in the manner hereinafter set forth.

11. In the last week in the month of November in each year a Conference of such Delegates shall be held in Sydney and the Central Association and every Branch Association shall be entitled to send Delegates as follows—for every Association which shall have less than five hundred Members, two Delegates and for every Association which shall have more than five hundred Members, three Delegates.

12. Such Conference shall not be limited in its range of action or discussion but shall as closely as possible concentrate its attention on the best means of furthering the objects of the Association.

13. Such Conference shall on its last day of sitting elect five Members with a President and Vice-President who shall together form the Executive Council to whom the Central Association and each Branch Association may remit, for opinion or decision, any question or dispute which may arise.

14. The respective Councils of the Central Association and of each Branch Association shall have the power to make or to

adopt and from time to time to amend alter or review any Rules Regulations or Bye Laws as they deem necessary for their good government provided the same shall not be inconsistent with the objects of the Association.

(Signed) R. W. Thompson
Albert J. Gould
Frank J. Smith

Abbreviations

Notes

INTRODUCTION

[1] L. Overacker, *The Australian Party System*, p.30.

[2] H. V. Evatt, *Australian Labour Leader*, p.1.

[3] Donaldson's, 1856; Parker's, 1856–7; Forster's, 1859–60; Farnell's, 1877–8; Average life: $7\frac{1}{2}$ months.

[4] Cowper's, 1856; Parkes', 1877; Robertson's, 1877; Dibbs', 1885; Robertson's, 1885–6. Average life: less than 3 months.

[5] The only change in the first was that Cowper took over the premiership from Robertson. In the second Robertson retired temporarily from office and was replaced by Cowper who continued in office and as premier when Robertson returned to the ministry.

[6] The Parkes ministry, Jan. 1887 to Jan. 1889, to the Storey ministry, 1920–1, inclusive but excluding the Dibbs ministry, 1889 and the Waddell ministry, 1904.

[7] S. Encel, *Cabinet Government in Australia*, pp.110–11.

[8] There is, unfortunately, no adequate history of politics to which readers can be referred, though a detailed chronicle of governments, legislation and policy between 1856 and 1883 can be found in T. Richards, *An Epitome of the Official History of New South Wales*. See also 'Summary' in index.

[9] *S.M.H.*, 20 Jan. 1866.

[10] N. G. Butlin, *Investment in Australian Economic Development 1861–1900*, p.285.

[11] Henry George Grey (third earl), *Parliamentary Government Considered with Reference to a Reform of Parliament*, pp.204, 215; *Fraser's Magazine*, June 1858, quoted in C. M. H. Clark (ed.), *Select Documents in Australian History, 1851–1900*, p.539; *Journal of the Royal Statistical Society*, vol. 24, March 1861, pp.130–1, quoting the *Australian Gazette*, London, 9 Feb. 1861; W. Westgarth, *Australia*, pp.79–80; J. Martineau, *Letters from Australia*, p.144; A. Trollope, *Australia and New Zealand*, Division II, New South Wales, p.151; Henry George Grey (third earl), 'Earl Grey on Victorian Politics', *Victorian Review*, vol. 1, no. VI, 1 Apr. 1880, p.861; W. Forster, 'Personal Government', *Melbourne Review*, vol. VII, no. 26, Apr. 1882, pp.169–79; J. A. Froude, *Oceana*, pp.136, 195; C. Dilke, *Problems of Greater Britain*, pp.170–1; H. de R. Walker, *Australasian Democracy*, pp.264–5. And some editorials from the press: *S.M.H.*, 21 Dec. 1863, 20 Jan., 19 Feb. 1866, 19 Oct. 1877; *Bulletin*, 14 Nov. 1885.

[12] J. A. Froude, *Oceana*, p.195: 'Even at home parties have lost their outlines . . . they are degenerating into factions', and *Economist*, 13 June 1857, editorial, for similar comment.

[13] E. Burke, *Works*, vol. 1, pp.375–6.

[14] Ibid.

[15] S. H. Beer, 'The Representation of Interests in British Government', *American Political Science Review*, vol. LI, no. 3, Sept. 1957, p.613.

[16] E.g. Westgarth, op. cit., pp.79–80; Trollope, op. cit., pp.510–11; W. H. L. Ranken, *The Dominion of Australia*, pp.191, 296; *S.M.H.*, 21 Jan. 1874, 12 Dec. 1878.

[17] Noted by J. D. B. Miller, 'Party Discipline in Australia' (1), *Political Science* (Wellington, N.Z.), vol. 5, no. 1, March 1953, pp.6–7.

[18] R. N. Ebbels (ed. L. G. Churchward), *The Australian Labor Movement, 1850–1907*, p.29; L. F. Crisp, *The Parliamentary Government of the Commonwealth of Australia*, pp.103, 125; L. F. Crisp, *The Australian Federal Labour Party, 1901–1951*, p.10; P. Loveday, 'A Note on Nineteenth Century Party Organisation in New South Wales', *H.S.*, vol. 9, no. 36, May 1961, p.424.

[19] W. Forster, 'Personal Government', loc. cit.

[20] L. F. Crisp, *Parliamentary Government,* p.106. Also A. Brady, *Democracy in the Dominions,* pp.204–7.

[21] J. A. McCallum, 'How Fares Parliamentary Government in the Federal System' in G. Sawer *et. al., Federalism in Australia,* pp.111–12; A. B. Keith, *Responsible Government in the Dominions,* vol. 1, p.262; W. K. Hancock, 'The Commonwealth, 1900–1914' in *Cambridge History of the British Empire,* vol. 7, pt 1, p.493; W. K. Hancock, *Australia,* pp.174–5.

[22] Cf. E. Jenks, *The Government of Victoria,* pp.377–84, for the view that the development of cabinet depended on parties in England, that cabinet existed in Victoria, but because there were no parties, it was likely to be transformed or fade out of existence.

1   1856

[1] *S.M.H.,* 23 and 24 May 1856.

[2] Quoted by W. J. V. Windeyer, 'Responsible Government—Highlights, Sidelights and Reflections', *J. & P. R.A.H.S.,* vol. 42, part 6, 1957, p.287.

[3] 17 Vict. No. xli of 1853, being schedule 1 to 18 & 19 Vict. c.54.

[4] 22 May 1856.

[5] Quoted by Windeyer, op. cit., p.304.

[6] The Imperial Act, 18 & 19 Vict. c.54, clause 4, included the provision that any clause of the Constitution Act could be amended by simple majorities in both Houses, subject to limitations of the 'two-thirds' clauses of the Act as long as they remained unrepealed. These clauses provided that any bill to alter the Electoral Act of 1851 must be passed by a two-thirds majority of the Lower House, and that any bill to alter the construction of the Upper House must be passed by two-thirds majorities in both Houses. 17 Vict., no. xli, clauses 15, 36. Amendment of other parts of the constitution by simple majorities was apparently taken for granted and not expressly provided for in it. The Imperial Act remedied this defect.

[7] Report from the select committee on changes in the administration under the new Constitution Act of 1853, 7 Dec. 1855, *V.&P. N.S.W. L.C.,* vol. 1, 1855, p.625.

[8] Macarthur in E. K. Silvester (ed.), *The Speeches in the Legislative Council of New South Wales on the Second Reading of the Bill for Framing a New Constitution for the Colony* (Sydney, 1853), p.133.

[9] T. H. Irving, 'The Idea of Responsible Government in New South Wales before 1856', *H.S.,* vol. 11, no. 42, Apr. 1964, pp.199–205.

[10] 31 May 1856.

[11] R. Therry, *Reminiscences of Thirty Years' Residence in New South Wales and Victoria,* pp.67–8, and for a comment at the time from the conservative point of view, J. M. Antill to Macarthur, 20 March 1856. Macarthur Papers, vol. 27, A2923, p.466.

[12] Wentworth in Silvester, op. cit., pp.36–7.

[13] Rusden to Macarthur, 4 Dec. 1853, Macarthur Papers, vol. 27, A2923, p.187.

[14] J. N. Dickinson, *A Letter to . . . the Speaker of the Legislative Council on the Formation of a Second Chamber.*

[15] *Progress report of the select committee on the present state of the Colony* (Sydney, 1866), pp.9–15.

[16] *S.M.H.,* 9 Apr. 1856.

[17] *S.M.H.,* 12 Apr. 1856.

[18] *S.M.H.,* 3 Apr. 1856.

[19] T. Morton Richards to Berry, 22 Sept. 1855, Berry Papers, Uncat. MSS. set 315, vol. 15, n.p.; J. Jervis, 'A. Berry, The Laird of Shoalhaven', *J.&P. R.A.H.S.,* vol. 27, part 1, 1941, pp.18–87.

[20] Antill to Macarthur, 30 Dec. 1857, Macarthur Papers, vol. 28, A2924, p.167, italics in original.

[21] Chisholm to Macarthur, 20 Mar. 1861, Macarthur Papers, vol. 28, A2924, p.551.

[22] A. W. Martin and P. Wardle, *Members of the Legislative Assembly of New South Wales, 1856–1901,* p.19; *S.M.H.,* 7 Apr. 1856.

[23] Martin & Wardle, op. cit., p.19; *S.M.H.*, 1 Apr. 1856, 22 Apr. 1856; Barker to Macarthur, 20 Feb. 1856, Macarthur Papers, vol. 27, A2923, p.431.

[24] Martin & Wardle, op. cit., p.144; *S.M.H.*, 7 Apr. 1856, 15 Apr. 1856; Manning to Macarthur, 3 Apr. 1856, Macarthur Papers, vol. 27, A2923, p.480.

[25] Martin and Wardle, op. cit., p.96; *S.M.H.*, 9 Apr. 1856.

[26] A.C.V. Melbourne, *Early Constitutional Development in Australia*, pp.422–3.

[27] Quoted in R. Bedford, *Think of Stephen*, p.184.

[28] Silvester, op. cit., p.113.

[29] Ibid., pp.132, 142.

[30] Ibid., p.177.

[31] The Act, 14 Vict. no. 48, required a property qualification of electors either in the form of owning freehold to the value of £100, or being an occupier of premises worth £10 p.a., or of being a holder of a stock pasture licence. Electorates were classified as urban, country and pastoral to provide for the representation of mercantile, agricultural and pastoral interests. Under the official designation the three interests had 11, 17 and 8 members respectively representing them.

[32] Silvester, op. cit., p.108.

[33] Ibid., p.223.

[34] Ibid., pp.141, 204.

[35] Ibid., pp.176, 182.

[36] Ibid., pp.39–50.

[37] Ibid., pp.110, 144, 159, 176, 205.

[38] Nicholson to Macarthur, 21 Apr. 1853 and 28 Oct. 1855, Macarthur Papers, vol. 27, A2923, pp.150, 374.

[39] *S.M.H.*, 24 Jan. 1860, 5 Mar. 1860, 5 Sept. 1861; T. A. Murray to Macarthur, 27 Apr. 1859, Macarthur Papers, vol. 28, A2924, p.271.

[40] The conservatives' dilemma is precisely illustrated by the attitude of Macarthur and Manning to Donaldson and Parker whom they supported on the 'express understanding' that no change would be made in the constitution beyond repeal of the two-thirds clauses. The understanding was necessary because Manning and Macarthur 'differed fundamentally' from Donaldson and Darvall, Manning warning that 'we must be on our guard' against them. When Parker, hamstrung in his efforts to hold a steady majority in 1857, introduced an electoral bill, Macarthur decided that the understanding had been broken and voted against the ministry even though this ensured that it fell. Manning to Macarthur, 12 June 1856, Macarthur Papers, vol. 27, A2923, p.542; *S.M.H.*, 10 and 12 June 1856, for the views of Donaldson and Darvall which aroused their suspicions; Macarthur to Oxley, 20 Oct. 1856 and Macarthur to Martin, 2 Aug. 1858, Macarthur Papers, vol. 24, A2920, pp.139, 254.

[41] See G. W. Rusden, *History of Australia,* vol. 3, pp.25–43, for this argument.

[42] Nicholson to Macarthur, 18 Jan. 1860 [*sic* 1861], Macarthur Papers, vol. 28, A2924, p.529; also E. Deas Thomson to Macarthur, 21 Apr. 1862, Macarthur Papers, vol. 29, A2925, p.76; Chisholm to Macarthur, 20 Mar. 1861, 21 May 1861, Macarthur Papers, vol. 28, A2924, pp.551, 576; Denison to Newcastle, 18 Jan. 1861, CO201/517.

[43] Cf. J. M. Ward, *Earl Grey and the Australian Colonies, 1846–1857*, p.202.

[44] For details of these classifications, see P. Loveday, Parliamentary Government in New South Wales 1856–1870 (Ph.D. thesis, Sydney, 1962), pp.28–30.

[45] *V. & P. N.S.W. L.C.*, 1853, vol. 2, pp.707, 733a, 745, for three petitions which make this point.

[46] Liberals believed their agitation had played a far greater part in getting it discontinued than it did. See Ward, op. cit., p.214.

[47] *S.M.H.*, 22–30 Mar. 1849.

[48] R. J. Lacey, The Political Role of the Sydney Middle Class, 1846–1853 (B.A. thesis, University of Sydney, 1959), pp.110–12.

[49] Cowper to Parkes, 22 Dec. 1854, 9 May 1855, P.C., A876, pp.378, 314.

[50] M. Roe, Society and Thought in Eastern Australia, 1835–1851 (Ph.D. thesis, Australian National University, 1960), pp.256-93, (since published as *Quest for Authority in Eastern Australia, 1835–1851*).

⁵¹ *Objects and Rules and Laws of the Constitutional Association and Address of the Provisional Council* (Sydney, 1848).
⁵² *S.M.H.,* 1 Apr. 1851.
⁵³ J. D. Lang, *The Coming Event;* cf. Ward, op. cit., pp.222–3.
⁵⁴ Parkes to Lang, 17 Apr. 1850, Lang Papers, vol. 22, A2242, p.1.
⁵⁵ J. T. Thomson to Lang, 6 Feb. 1855, Lang Papers, vol. 7, A2227, p.5.
⁵⁶ Of the fifty-two active members in the three Associations whose occupations have been identified, seventeen were mercantile-professional (surgeon, merchant, clergy, lawyer, investor, journalist), thirty-three were small traders or artisans, two were landowners.
⁵⁷ Parkes, editor-proprietor of the *Empire* newspaper, was accepted as a member of the Sydney Chamber of Commerce in 1854. *Report of the Sydney Chamber of Commerce* for the half year ending 31 Dec. 1854, Sydney, n.d., p.8; *Empire,* 12 Dec. 1853 for Parkes' attack on Lang's *Freedom and Independence for the Golden Lands of Australia;* Deniehy to Lang, 6 June 1854, Lang Papers, vol. 7, A2227, p.60, for Deniehy's attack on Parkes for lacking radical sympathies.
⁵⁸ *People's Advocate,* 29 Apr. 1854.
⁵⁹ Deniehy to Parkes, 10 Nov. 1855, Deniehy's Letters to Parkes, A709.
⁶⁰ 13 Aug. 1853.
⁶¹ The Anti-Transportation Association had ten members of the Council at its head, the Constitution Committee had seven.
⁶² P. Loveday, '"Democracy" in New South Wales', *J. & P. R.A.H.S.,* vol. 42, part 4, 1956, p.198.
⁶³ Ibid., pp.196–8; Deniehy to Parkes, 16 Dec. 1854, 10 Nov. 1855, Deniehy's Letters to Parkes, A709; Deniehy to Parkes, 30 Jan. 1855, 28 Sept. 1855, Autograph Letters to Sir Henry Parkes, A71, pp.37, 33.
⁶⁴ Darvall in *S.M.H.,* 18 Oct. 1854.
⁶⁵ Darvall and Cowper, in Silvester, op. cit., pp.59–60, 120.
⁶⁶ *Empire,* 23 Apr. 1856 (italics in original).
⁶⁷ E.g., Byrnes to Maj.-Gen. E. Macarthur, 29 Nov. 1856, Macarthur Papers, vol. 21, A2917, p.244.
⁶⁸ W. T. Denison, *Varieties of Viceregal Life,* vol. 1, pp.326–33, 342, 364, 475–97.
⁶⁹ Denison, op. cit., pp.342, 346.
⁷⁰ *Empire,* 8 May 1856; *S.M.H.,* 23 and 26 May 1856.
⁷¹ W. Forster, 'Personal Government', *Melbourne Review,* vol. 7, no. 26, Apr. 1882, pp. 176–9, for the view that this had been a genuine two-party division.
⁷² For details of figures used subsequently in this paragraph, see Loveday, Parliamentary Government in New South Wales, 1856–1870, p.126.

2   THE FACTION SYSTEM

¹ *Empire,* 8 May 1856 for the meeting; Macarthur in E.K. Silvester (ed.), *Speeches . . . on . . . a New Constitution* (Sydney, 1853), p.133; *S.M.H.,* 12 May 1856.
² Cowper and Forster in *Empire,* 13 Oct. 1856.
³ *S.M.H.,* 2 Jan. 1858, 18 Oct., 12 Nov. 1859, 24 Jan., 5 Mar. 1860, 5 Sept. 1861.
⁴ *S.M.H.,* 9 Oct. 1856; Darvall to Donaldson, 26 Aug. 1856, Letters, Donaldson Ministry, A731, p.135.
⁵ For pastoralists' unrest see G. S. Lang to Donaldson, 29 Aug. 1857, Letters Donaldson Ministry, A731, p.440, and for Macarthur's opposition to the ministry's Electoral Bill, Macarthur to Martin, 2 Aug. 1858, Macarthur Papers, vol. 24, A2920, p.254.
⁶ Robertson, *Maitland Mercury,* 30 Apr. 1857.
⁷ Robertson, *S.M.H.,* 26 May 1859.
⁸ For details of these calculations, see Loveday, Parliamentary Government in New South Wales, 1856–1870, pp.141–2.
⁹ *S.M.H.,* 29 Dec. 1857.
¹⁰ Cowper to Martin, 6 Nov. 1858, in *S.M.H.,* 17 Nov. 1858 and speeches.
¹¹ It was at first enlarged to eighty members, but the separation of Moreton Bay at the end of 1859 reduced it to seventy-two.

[12] The opposition, on Murray's motion, had its candidate elected chairman of committees, and on Parkes' motion condemned the ministry for continuing high duties on tea and sugar passed in 1854.

[13] *Empire,* 31 Oct., 30 Nov. 1859; Forster to Parkes, 5 May 1859, P.C., A922, p.18; *S.M.H.,* 7 Sept., 12 Oct. 1859.

[14] *S.M.H.,* 22 and 23 Mar. 1860.

[15] *S.M.H.,* 30 Nov., 2, 15, 23 and 24 Dec. 1859; 26 Jan., 7 Feb. 1860.

[16] Denison to Cooper, 1 Mar. 1860, Denison to Jones, 6 Mar. 1860, Government House Papers, Miscellaneous Correspondence, 1855–61, 4/1665, pp.499, 503.

[17] D. W. A. Baker, 'The Origins of Robertson's Land Acts', *H.S.,* vol. 8, no. 30, May 1958, pp.166–82; and C. J. King, *An Outline of Closer Settlement in New South Wales,* pp.50–60, 70–88.

[18] See Loveday, op. cit., pp.142, 159.

[19] See Loveday, 'The Legislative Council in New South Wales, 1856–1870', *H.S.,* vol. 11, no. 44, Apr. 1965.

[20] Young to Newcastle, 21 May 1861, 19 July 1861, CO201/518; Young to Newcastle, 23 Sept. 1861, CO201/519.

[21] Cowper to Young, 14 Sept. 1861, Cowper Correspondence, vol. 1, A676; *S.M.H.,* 3 Sept. 1861.

[22] Piddington to Parkes, 20 Aug. 1861, P.C., A926, p.382; Murray to Parkes, 18 Sept 1861, P.C., A925, p.276.

[23] Cowper to Young, 14 Sept. 1861, Cowper Correspondence, vol. 1, A676.

[24] Windeyer to Parkes, 21 Jan. 1861, P.C., A930, p.207.

[25] A. Campbell to Parkes, 25 Mar. 1861, Autograph Letters of Notable Australians, A70, p.300; Campbell to [Parkes], n.d., [1861], P.C., A880, p.35; *S.M.H.,* 12, 14 and 19 June 1861.

[26] Windeyer to Parkes, 20 Oct. 1861, P.C., A913, p.404.

[27] Hoskins was given a post as superintendent of minor roads at £350 p.a. Windeyer to Parkes, 20 Oct. 1861, P.C., A913, p.404, for evidence of Hoskins' seeking a post, *S.M.H.,* 19 Feb. 1863, *Blue Book* 1863, under 'Hoskins'.

[28] *S.M.H.,* 3 Sept. 1861.

[29] *S.M.H.,* 1 Mar., 7 May 1859; *V.&P. N.S.W. L.A.,* sess. 1861, vol. 1, p.781; *Empire,* 11 Feb. 1862.

[30] *S.M.H.,* 24 Oct. 1861; C. D. Rowley, 'Clarence River Separatism in 1860. A problem in Communications', *H.S.,* vol. 1, no. 4, Oct. 1941, p.225.

[31] Murray to Parkes, 18 Sept. 1861, P.C., A925, p.276; Windeyer to Parkes, 19 Dec. 1861, P.C., A930, p.210; *S.M.H.,* 24 Oct. 1861; *V. & P. N.S.W. L.A.,* sess. 1861, vol. 2, p.1215, sess. 1862, vol. 5, p.1041.

[32] Donaldson: *S.M.H.,* 9 Oct. 1856, and Darvall to Donaldson, 26 Aug. 1856, Letters, Donaldson Ministry, A731, p.135. Parker: Lang to Donaldson, 29 Aug. 1857, Letters, Donaldson Ministry, A731, p.440; *S.M.H.,* 3 Sept. 1857. Forster: *S.M.H.,* 13 Aug. 1859, 21 Aug. 1860; *Southern Cross,* 31 Dec. 1859; Forster to Parkes, 15 May [1859], P.C., A922, p.62.

[33] *S.M.H.,* 19 Nov. 1857.

[34] Garland, *S.M.H.,* 22 May 1857.

[35] Macarthur to H. Oxley, 20 Oct. 1856, Macarthur Papers, vol. 24, A2920, p.139.

[36] *S.M.H.,* 2 Nov. 1860; *Empire,* 2 Nov. 1860.

[37] Circular of the Association, Macarthur Papers, vol. 39, A2935, p.91.

[38] Morris to Parkes, 23 Nov. 1860, P.C., A895, p.259.

[39] *Empire,* 3, 5 and 6 Dec. 1860, for references to it.

[40] *Empire,* 14, 20 Oct., 19 Dec. 1863; *S.M.H.,* 3 Aug., 26 Nov., 5 Dec. 1863; *Albury Advertiser,* 15 Aug. 1863; *V. & P. N.S.W. L.A.,* sess. 1865–6, vol. 1, pp.666–70.

[41] *S.M.H.,* 12, 13 Oct. 1863; *Empire,* 13 Oct. 1863.

[42] See R. B. Walker, 'The Later History of the Church and School Lands', *J. & P. R.A.H.S.,* vol. 47, part 4, Aug. 1961, p.234.

[43] *S.M.H.,* 5, 12 and 16 Dec. 1863, 3 Mar. 1864; *Empire,* 26 Jan. to 21 Mar. 1864.

[44] Parkes to his wife, 17 Jan. 1866, Parkes Family Papers, A1044.

[45] Parkes' notes of interview with Cowper, 15 Sept. 1865, P.C., A920, p.319; Cowper to Parkes, 14 Sept. 1865, P.C., A920, p.318; fragment of a memo by Parkes, n.d. [1865], P.C., A932, and Parkes' notes of interview with Robertson and related letters, n.d. [June 1865], ibid.

[46] The original calculations of faction strengths from division analysis are set out in appendices to the two theses, P. Loveday, The Development of Parliamentary Government in New South Wales, 1856–70 (Sydney, 1962) and A. W. Martin, Political Groupings in New South Wales, 1872–89 (A.N.U., 1955). The material has been completely reworked, cross-checked and added to for the construction of the present tables. Detailed calculation sheets are in the possession of the authors.

The number of seats in the House for the respective parliaments were as follows (number of seats in brackets): parliaments 1–2 (54), 3 (80), 4–9 (72), 10 (108), 11 (111), 12 (121). The Constitution Act established an Assembly of 54, which was increased to 80 by the Electoral Act of 1858. When Queensland was separated, this number was reduced to 72. Redistribution of electorates in 1880 increased membership to 108, establishing a basic set of 72 constituencies, which increased their representation in accordance with a sliding scale as population grew.

[47] W. Walker, Reminiscences of a Fifty Years' Residence at Windsor, p.69.

[48] Ibid.

[49] Ibid., p.74.

[50] Ibid., p.73.

[51] Ibid., p.16.

[52] Ibid., pp.57–8.

[53] Ibid., pp.59–60. Walker was no longer a member of parliament by then.

[54] S. Scholey to Parkes, 26 Mar. 1877, P.C., A909, p.179.

[55] See e.g., affectionate reminiscences of E. W. O'Sullivan, in From Colony to Commonwealth, manuscript memoirs, M.L., B595, pp.173–81, 183–5.

[56] Lloyd to Parkes, 24 Oct. 1877, P.C., A891, p.413.

[57] Innes to Parkes, 10 Aug. 1881, P.C., A889, p.208.

[58] Parkes to Windeyer, n.d. [Jan. 1866], Windeyer Uncat. MSS., set 186, item 2; Windeyer to Parkes, 15 Jan. 1866, ibid.; Gleadall to Windeyer, 15 Jan. 1866, ibid.; S.M.H., 16, 17, 18 Jan. 1866; Gleadall to Windeyer, 17 Jan. 1866, Windeyer Uncat. MSS., set 186, item 2; Windeyer to Parkes, 18 Jan. 1866, ibid., item 4; Parkes to Windeyer, 24 Jan. 1866, ibid., item 2.

[59] S.M.H., 14 Oct. 1868.

[60] Redgate owned the Kempsey steam flour mills. Redgate to Parkes, 4 Aug., 5 Sept. 1863; P.C., A887, pp.311, 315, for evidence of his help to Parkes in elections.

[61] Windeyer to Parkes, 22 Sept. 1868, P.C., A913, p.380.

[62] Parkes to Windeyer, 26 Sept. 1868, Windeyer Uncat. MSS., set 186, item 2, for his reply.

[63] These details are from S.M.H., 2 Dec. 1870, 25 Jan. 1871, and Cowper to Belmore, 2 Dec. 1870, Letters to the Earl of Belmore, A2542/3, p.237.

[64] Dight, Hill, M.C. Stephen.

[65] Dodds. He continued to support Robertson in 1871.

[66] Baker, Fraser.

[67] Cowper and Robertson, associated since 1856–7; S. C. Brown, Driver, Neale and Phelps (steady supporters for 6 years); Alexander, Morrice, Sutherland and Samuel (steady supporters for 7–7½ years); R. H. M. Forster (steady supporter in 1863–4, then lost seat); Eckford, Egan and Garrett (steady supporters for 11½ years); Cummings and Hart (steady supporters for 7½ years but unsteady supporters in 1859–60).

[68] Bawden, Brookes, Butler, Dillon, Fitzpatrick, Moses, Spring and Dean (elected in Dec. 1869-Jan. 1870); Kelly, Bell and Church (with a brief period in the fifth parliament, giving them 2½ years service each or less); and Leary (who had been an independent in the fourth parliament). Kelly had been an unsteady supporter in the fifth.

[69] The details gathered in the census of 1881 were destroyed by fire before being printed and it is therefore impossible to characterize the electorates reliably in the later seventies, especially as the occupational structure of the electorates was becoming more complex. Note that the data from which Tables 3 and 4 have been compiled are chiefly

to be found in Loveday, Parliamentary Government in New South Wales, 1856–1870, Appendix xi, pp.519–33. In Table 4 the general classification of electorate types is by occupation and is based on census figures. Since censuses were taken in 1861 and 1871, the general classification may be made for parliaments 4 and 6, but not for parliament 5.

[70] Meetings were held from 1856 onwards—a list of them is provided in Appendix 1.

[71] S.M.H., 2 Mar. 1877, although this term was not regularly applied to them.

[72] Farnell, S.M.H., 21 Dec. 1870, pp.2–3; Martin, S.M.H., 25 Jan. 1871, pp.2–3.

[73] Fitzpatrick was the other nominee for the leadership. Parkes' letter of resignation was a circular to all opposition members suggesting that they consider the matter. Letter, 22 Dec. 1876, P.C., A915, p.547, and in S.M.H., 28 Dec. 1876, p.4, where Herald editorial argues Parkes reproached the opposition for its want of loyalty and its irregular support of him. S.M.H., 12, 17 and 24 Jan. 1877, for the meetings, and see C. E. Lyne, Life of Sir Henry Parkes, pp.345–6. Other similar cases: S.M.H., 23 Aug. 1882, p.5: opposition is like a flock of sheep without a shepherd since Fitzpatrick's death; is pleased to see that it had chosen Stuart as its leader. S.M.H., 11 Feb. 1886: meeting chooses Jennings as 'permanent leader', twenty-three present at meeting.

[74] Windeyer to his wife, 26 Jan. 1872, Windeyer Uncat. MSS., set 186, box 3.

[75] Its dependence on him was shown in March 1877: see S.M.H., 2 Mar. 1877 (editorial).

[76] Parkes' Diary, entry for 30 Apr. 1872, P.C., A1013.

[77] E.g., meeting of Parkes ministry's supporters, S.M.H., 28 Feb. 1874. 'The meeting was unanimous in concurring in the course that the Government proposed to take . . . the state of public business was discussed and an understanding arrived at . . . to support the Government in getting the estimates, the Electoral Act Amendment Bill . . . and some other measures passed as early as practicable.' Meeting of Dibbs-Jennings' supporters, S.M.H., 7 July 1886, p.9. Between forty and fifty present, and after considerable discussion the meeting 'resolved that every legitimate latitude should be accorded to members who desired to discuss the provisions of the [Customs Duties] bill [in the House] . . . in the event of a minority endeavouring to coerce the majority . . . or indulging in stonewall tactics they should be resisted in every orderly manner.' Dibbs, the Treasurer, was in the chair.

[78] See e.g., Cowper's meeting of 2 Dec. 1870, pp. 50–1, and the Martin-Robertson ministry's meeting on 29 Jan. 1872, when supporters had been advised that it was a question whether to resign or dissolve. S.M.H., 30 Jan. 1872, p.4., and Windeyer to his wife, 26 Jan. 1872, Windeyer Uncat. MSS., set 186, box 3.

[79] S.M.H., 3 Sept. 1861, p.5., for the meeting.

[80] S.M.H., 21 Dec. 1870, pp.2–3.

[81] S.M.H., 15 Dec. 1870, p.2, 21 Dec. 1870, pp.2–3. 26 circulars were sent out, 24 returned. 15 members received votes, 5 of them 1 vote only. Piddington had most votes, then Farnell. Wilson, Byrnes and Robertson each received several votes. Farnell attacked Martin for ignoring the result of the vote, by taking Robertson into coalition. The vote suggests that Martin found support among his followers for the coalition and the debate in the House suggested that Martin did not approach Robertson until he knew the outcome of the vote, and that it was only then that Farnell decided Martin had betrayed him.

[82] N.S.W. P.D., vol. xi, p.1789 (Smith), 13 Feb. 1884, pp.2080–1 (Heydon), 28 Feb. 1884, also pp.1777 and 2040–1.

[83] Parkes to Windeyer, 11 Mar. 1860, P.C., A1050.

[84] Wisdom, 24 Aug. 1882, N.S.W. P.D., vol. vii, p.106.

[85] Members anxious to see parliament deal expeditiously with the great backlog of administrative tasks which often faced it were always contemptuous of the more 'irresponsible' members who for 'party' or personal reasons adopted 'stonewalling' tactics in the House or raised petty issues which opened long and inconclusive debates on motions for adjournment.

[86] See e.g., Heydon, N.S.W. P.D., vol. vii, 24 Aug. 1882, p.115. W. Forster, 'Personal Government', Melbourne Review, vol. 7, no. 26, Apr. 1882, p.169.

[87] 'Thoughts on the Present Discontents', The Works of Edmund Burke, vol. 1, p.378.

[88] J. Martineau, *Letters from Australia*, p.144. Cf. the *S.M.H*'s analysis of the strength of Parkes' Ministry in 1873 (editorial, 6 Oct. 1873): 'A very large amount of patronage has fallen to the share of the present ministry ... There are great promises made for the liberation of Commerce ... The measures ripe for completion when the parliament opened have given them the appearance of constructive power ... A full treasury has enabled them to indulge many expectations which render members complaisant.'

[89] *S.M.H.*, 7 Dec. 1874. See also *S.M.H.*, 19 Oct. 1877 for direct quotation of Burke and definition of faction from his remarks.

[90] 13 Dec. 1883, *N.S.W. P.D.*, vol. xi, p.1084.

[91] 12 Dec. 1883, *N.S.W. P.D.*, vol. x, p.1016–17.

[92] Pigott (Canterbury), criticizing Cooke (Forbes), 29 Sept. 1882, *N.S.W. P.D.*, vol. vii, p.549.

[93] *Empire*, 27 Jan. 1864.

[94] *Goulburn Herald and Chronicle*, 27 Oct. 1877.

[95] Parkes, 9 Mar. 1881, *N.S.W. P.D.*, vol. iv, p.842–3.

[96] *S.M.H.*, 7, 8 Dec. 1874.

[97] E.g., Abbott's speech, 1882, on Robertson's skilful rallying of personal supporters to save Garrett from expulsion from the Assembly on a charge of corruption arising out of the Millburn Creek Copper Mining Company scandal. 24 Aug. 1882, *N.S.W. P.D.*, p.118.

[98] E.g., when Parkes attracted Abbott from the opposition to the office of Minister for Mines, *S.M.H.*, 28 Aug. 1874, and when Parkes and Robertson took Foster into their ministry as Minister for Justice in 1881 after he had been in opposition, Foster to Parkes, 14 Oct. 1881, P.C., A883, p.398, and speeches in the House, 14 Oct. 1881, *N.S.W. P.D.*, vol. vi, pp.1594, 1603.

[99] E.g., Abbott, 24 Aug. 1882, *N.S.W. P.D.*, vol. vii, p.117; Melville, ibid., p.169 Heydon, 22 July 1884, ibid., vol. xiv, p.4464.

[1] Parkes, *Fifty Years in the Making of Australian History*, pp.214–17.

3 THE FORMATION AND DEFEAT OF MINISTRIES

[1] Parkes, exaggerating Burdekin's deficiencies for the office, claimed that it was a mockery of responsible government to appoint a man to the post when three years in parliament had failed to develop in him any mastery of public questions and had left him as it found him, barren and feeble in mind and character. Burdekin's chief deficiencies appear to have been his youth—he was twenty-nine—and the irrelevance to the treasury of his profession as a barrister. The Governor, Sir John Young commented that 'the motion was aimed rather at the Government than at him—He is a young man of good character and fair abilities and the chief objections alleged against him were his youth and inexperience'. Young to Cardwell, 19 Jan. 1866, Government House Papers, Despatches 1864–6, A1266/7, p.8.

[2] Parkes to Martin, 8 Jan. 1866, P.C., A932; Martin to Parkes, 8 Jan. 1866, P.C., A925, p.65.

[3] W. Walker, *Recollections of Sir Henry Parkes*, p.2.

[4] Young to Cowper, 11 Jan. 1866, Cowper Correspondence, A677.

[5] Parkes to Martin, 14 Jan. 1866, P.C., A932; Parkes to Plunkett, 15 Jan. 1866, ibid.; Plunkett to Macarthur, 22 Jan. 1866, Macarthur Papers, vol. 30, p.226.

[6] Parkes to Martin, 14 Jan. 1866, P.C., A932.

[7] Parkes to his wife, 17 Jan. 1866, P.C., A1044.

[8] *S.M.H.*, 20 Jan. 1866.

[9] Cowper to Turville, 19 Dec. 1864, Cowper Correspondence, vol. 2, A677.

[10] Parkes to Windeyer, n.d. [Jan. 1866], Windeyer Uncat. MSS., set 186, item 2. See pp. 48–9.

[11] Windeyer took the seat rather than injure Parkes. But two years later he was still aggrieved: 'To this day I think that you who pulled the strings in that election took an unwarrantable liberty with my name.' Windeyer to Parkes, 22 Sept. 1868, P.C., A913, p.380.

¹² *S.M.H.,* 20 Jan., 19 and 21 Feb. 1866; Parkes, *Fifty Years in the Making of Australian History,* p.162.

¹³ *S.M.H.,* 20 Jan., 19 Feb. 1866.

¹⁴ Marks to Parkes, 26 Jan. 1866, P.C., A896, p.318.

¹⁵ Lyne, *Life of Sir Henry Parkes,* p.194; Buchanan in *S.M.H.,* 25 Jan. 1871.

¹⁶ The votes of Wilson in division lists do not distinguish him from supporters of Martin before this time, but there is little doubt that he was in fact a supporter of Parkes.

¹⁷ Report of the Commission appointed to enquire into the condition of the Customs Department, *V. & P. N.S.W. L.A.,* sess. 1867–8, vol. 2, p.307.

¹⁸ Young to Buckingham, 24 July 1867, Governors' Despatches, A1266/8, p.85.

¹⁹ Young to Cardwell, 23 July 1866, ibid., A1266/7, p.66.

²⁰ It amalgamated the two existing national and denominational school systems and placed them under the control of a Council of Education. It was a compromise measure, making the concession to denominationalists that denominational schools with their own teachers could be set up under special cirsumstances, and that the clergyman of any church might visit the schools to instruct children in his communion for an hour a day, and to the secularists that instruction should be secular for four hours daily.

²¹ *S.M.H.,* 1 Nov. 1867.

²² Young to Buckingham, 22 and 23 Oct. 1867, Governors' Despatches, A1266/8, pp. 150–1; *S.M.H.,* 22 and 23 Oct. 1867.

²³ Belmore to Rogers, 28 Jan. 1869, Correspondence Relating to the Dissolution of Parliament in N.S.W. in 1868 and 1872, A2542. Belmore's italics.

²⁴ J. L. Montefiore to Parkes, n.d. [late 1867], P.C., A895, p.75, and 29 Nov. 1867, P.C., A895, p.72. For a different estimate of Eagar's ability see P. N. Lamb, 'Geoffrey Eagar and the Colonial Treasury of New South Wales', *Australian Economic Papers,* vol. 1, no. 1, Sept. 1962, pp.24–41.

²⁵ Parkes to his wife, 25 Jan. 1866, P.C., A1044.

²⁶ Parkes to Martin, 7 Apr. 1866, P.C., A932. Parkes threatened to resign when Martin and Eagar effected an arrangement, without consulting him, by which the police (nominally under Parkes' control) were to assist customs officers in carrying out their duties.

²⁷ Eagar to Parkes, 2 Sept. 1867, P.C., A921, p.737; Parkes to Eagar, 2 Sept. 1867, P.C., A915, p.91.

²⁸ *S.M.H.,* 22 Sept., 9 Oct. 1868; Parkes to Marks, 19 Sept. 1868, P.C., A932.

²⁹ Parkes to Martin, 19 Feb. 1868, P.C., A932.

³⁰ Motions attacking the Treasurer on 7 and 13 Nov. 1867, 16 and 23 Mar., 15 Apr. 1868.

³¹ Belmore to Rogers, 28 Jan. 1869, Correspondence relating to the Dissolution of Parliament in N.S.W. in 1868 and 1872, A2542.

³² Parkes to Duncan, 27 July 1868, P.C., A931. Most of the correspondence in the case is available in Correspondence relating to the removal of W. A. Duncan, *V. & P. N.S.W. L.A.,* sess. 1868–9, vol. 2, pp.75–106. Other papers are: Duncan to Parkes, 14 July 1868, P.C., A990; Parkes to Duncan, 20 July 1868, P.C., A931; Eagar to Parkes, 21 and 24 July 1868, P.C., A921, pp.735, 738; Duncan to Parkes, 27 July 1868, P.C., A921, p.416; Martin to Parkes, 2 Aug. 1868, P.C., A925, p.85; Belmore to Parkes, 26 Aug. 1868, P.C., A969 and 1 Sept. 1868, P.C., A919, p.514; Parkes to Belmore, 26 Aug. 1868 (2 letters), Belmore Letters, A2542/4, pp.591–2; Parkes to Eagar, 27 Aug. 1868, P.C., A931; Parkes to Belmore, 11 Sept. 1868, Belmore Letters, A2542/4, p.599; Duncan to Parkes, n.d., P.C., A921, p.440; Belmore to Parkes, 11 Sept. 1868, P.C., A919, p.518; Belmore to Martin, 20 Oct. 1868, Correspondence Relating to the Dissolution of Parliament in N.S.W. in 1868 and 1872, A2542; Belmore to Buckingham, 29 Jan. 1869, Governors' Despatches, A1266/9, p.15; Parkes to Lang, 26 Nov. 1868, Lang Papers, A2242, p.32a; Martin to Parkes, 17 Sept. 1868, P.C., A925, pp.92, 95; *S.M.H.,* 14 Oct. 1868; Parkes to Windeyer, 19 Sept. 1868, Windeyer Uncat. MSS., set 186, item 4; Windeyer to Parkes, 22 Sept. 1868, P.C., A913, p.380; Lang to Parkes, 3 Dec. 1868, P.C., A924, p.200.

³³ Fragment of a letter by Parkes, apparently a first draft of this letter, P.C., A932.

³⁴ Parkes to Martin, n.d. [13 Sept. 1868], P.C., A932.

[35] Farnell and Wearne, S.M.H., 21 Dec. 1870.
[36] S.M.H., 26 Aug. 1868.
[37] S.M.H., 12 Aug. 1868.
[38] Parkes to Lang, 11 Feb. 1869, Lang Papers, vol. 22, A2242, p.51.
[39] The report and minutes of evidence are available in S.M.H., between 4 and 15 Feb. 1869. See also V. & P. N.S.W. L.A., 1868–9, vol. 1, pp.715–81, passim. (Draft Report of Committee, with Evidence.)
[40] See E. L. French (ed.), Melbourne Studies in Education, 1960–1961, facing p.37 for a cartoon of 1889 illustrating the point.
[41] Robertson to Cowper, 10 Oct. 1865, Cowper Correspondence, vol. 2, A677; S.M.H., 14 Jan. 1870; Belmore to Granville, 2 Dec. 1869, Copies of Correspondence of the Earl of Belmore, A2542/2, p.207.
[42] S.M.H., 20 and 21 Apr. 1870.
[43] S.M.H., 3 Dec. 1870; Cowper to Belmore, 2 Dec. 1870, Belmore Letters, p.237, A2542/3.
[44] S.M.H., 12 Aug. 1870. Cowper discussed a reconstruction with his colleagues during the year, and the proposal fell down when Robertson disagreed; Samuel to Cowper, 25 July 1870, Cowper Correspondence, A678.
[45] S.M.H., 10, 12, 15 and 21 Dec. 1870, 25 Jan. 1871; Parkes, Fifty Years in the Making of Australian History, pp.214–18. Piddington got most votes, then Farnell. Wilson, Byrnes, Wisdom and Robertson got several votes each, and five others, out of fifteen with votes, had only one each. Twenty-four of the twenty-six members given circulars returned them.
[46] Windeyer to Parkes, 22 Sept. 1868, P.C., A913, p.380.
[47] Especially Farnell, who had received considerable support in the voting for the ministry, and had been vaguely promised office by Martin. See also Parkes to Martin, 21 Dec. 1870, P.C., A932, Martin to Parkes, 22 Dec. 1870, P.C., A925, p.101.
[48] There were ten others whose allegiance is unknown for want of data.
[49] Martin had eleven supporters.
[50] Wisdom to Parkes, 10 Sept. 1871, P.C., A914, p.213. Lloyd to Parkes, 27 Sept. 1871, P.C., A924, p.414.
[51] Windeyer to his wife, 26 Jan. 1872. Windeyer Uncat. MSS., set 186, box 3. Butler to Parkes, n.d. [Jan. 1872], Autograph Letters, Australian, A62, p.100. Butler predicted the motion would play into 'our' hands if it was carried. The convention was that the mover of a motion on which a ministry was defeated would normally be commissioned to form a new ministry.
[52] Windeyer to his wife, 26 Jan. 1872, loc. cit.
[53] Ibid., and S.M.H., 30 Jan. 1872.
[54] Windeyer to his wife, 26 and 27 Jan. 1872, loc. cit. The immediate advantage lay in the fixing of the dates of elections, which, being staggered, could be arranged to give as few defeated opponents as possible a second chance, and to enable defeated ministerial candidates to find relatively safe seats. The more remote advantage lay in the fact that a leader in office could make more plausible promises for allocation of appropriations than a leader in opposition.
[55] Belmore to Kimberley, 29 Jan. 1872. Copies of Correspondence of the Earl of Belmore, A2542/2, pp.278–9, and Belmore to Kimberley, 12 Feb. 1872, Governors' Despatches, A1266/12, p.21.
[56] S.M.H., 9 Feb., 11 and 12 Mar. 1872.
[57] This, with the letters it commented on, is in General Elections, January–March 1872 (a collection of newspaper clippings and MSS. notes), M.L.
[58] Parkes to M. Parkes, 27 Jan. 1871, P.C., A1044.
[59] Windeyer to his wife, 26 Jan. 1872, Windeyer Uncat. MSS., set 186, box 3.
[60] Parkes to Lang, 29 July 1871, Lang Papers, A2242, p.58. The approach to Wearne is reported in this letter.
[61] G. A. Lloyd to Parkes, 15 Aug. 1871, P.C., A924, p.411. See also J. L. Montefiore to Parkes, 18 Oct. 1871, P.C., A895, p.120. It is possible that Parkes had thought of a 'new party' at the end of 1869 and had been forced by his own impending bankruptcy

to delay it. An advertisement, inserted without acknowledgment of its authority, appeared in *S.M.H.,* 18 Nov. 1869, calling for 'New Blood in Parliament' and offering a list of suitable men, among whom were Wearne, Montefiore, Lloyd and other friends of Parkes.

See, e.g., Duffy to Parkes, 14 Dec. 1870, P.C., A921, pp.34–5; Butler to Parkes, 5 Sept. [1871], P.C., A872, p.288. Butler to Parkes, 23 Dec. [1870], Sir Henry Parkes Private Affairs, 1887, vol. 1, Letters, Dixson Library, Sydney.

Lyne, *Life of Sir Henry Parkes,* p.305; Butler to Parkes, n.d., P.C., A919, p.651; Parkes to Windeyer, 1 Dec. 1858 (letter in the possession of the Hon. Sir Victor Windeyer, who kindly made it available to us).

Butler to Parkes, 5 Sept. [1871], loc. cit.

Ibid.

C. J. Byrnes, *Goulburn Herald,* 6 Mar. 1872.

See Martin, 'Henry Parkes and Electoral Manipulation', *H.S.,* vol. 8, no. 31, Nov. 1958, pp.269–72.

Diary, 1872, Parkes Papers.

Parkes to Wearne, 11 May 1872, P.C., A932.

Parkes made similar observations about the task of forming a ministry in 1877. After listing a number of 'ministrables', he explained, to Lloyd: 'There are others who ought not to be overlooked, the Suttors for example. To select from these with a view to greatest fitness, the greatest amount of support in Parliament, and the greatest chance of internal agreement and at the same time with a fair recognition of claims— is of itself a task that staggers me . . .' Parkes to Lloyd, 16 Mar. 1877, P.C., A915, p.573.

Diary, p.25.

Forster to Parkes, 5 May 1859, P.C., A922, p.18; 15 May [1859], ibid., p.62; 25 May 1859, ibid., p.24; 23 June 1859, ibid., p.27.

Diary, p.26.

Parkes to Wearne, 11 May 1872. The division list analysis shows Farnell in opposition to Robertson in the third parliament and as a follower of Parkes from the fifth parliament onwards.

Australian Israelite, 25 Oct. 1872.

Lyne, *Life of Sir Henry Parkes,* p.303.

Lloyd's mercantile experience was wide and successful; Piddington was a successful bookseller; Sutherland a builder and contractor with investments in insurance, and other companies; Samuel a mining director with mercantile investments and pastoral experience.

Butler to Parkes, n.d. [1872], Autograph Letters, Australian, A62, p.97.

S.M.H., 19 Mar. 1872.

Parkes to Wearne, 11 May 1872, P.C., A932 (italics in original).

Parkes to Lang, 17 May 1872, Lang Papers, A2242, p.65.

S.M.H., 15 Mar. 1870. Wearne was also a Mason. The other affiliations are as given in A. W. Martin and P. Wardle, *Members of the Legislative Assembly of New South Wales, 1856–1901.*

S.M.H., 3 Dec. 1869.

Butler to Parkes, n.d. [but before 10 May 1872], P.C., A872, p.193.

Parkes to Butler, 27 Jan. 1872, P.C., A915, p.220.

Goulburn Herald & Chronicle, 27 Oct. 1877. Parkes, thinking of retiring from politics in 1877, said that if he withdrew, Robertson and Farnell would gain friends 'from my nominal supporters'. Parkes to Windeyer, 21 Dec. 1877, Windeyer Family Papers, *D159.

See Farnell's statements, *S.M.H.,* 12 and 28 Dec. 1877.

Lyne, op. cit., pp.376, 378 and *S.M.H.,* 18 Dec. 1878, for a report of the 'fusion' of the two factions at a meeting of both.

4 THE ELECTORATES AND FACTION POLITICS

See, e.g. Cowper to Parkes, 27 Aug. 1856, P.C., A876, p.407.

Lang Papers, vol. 6, A2226, p.529.

[3] See Loveday, 'Patronage and Politics in N.S.W., 1856–1870', *Public Administration* (Sydney), vol. xviii, no. 4, Dec. 1959, pp.351–2.

[4] E.g., *S.M.H.,* 7 Oct. 1856.

[5] Parkes to Cowper, 17 Oct. 1856, Cowper Correspondence, vol. 2, A677.

[6] Progress Report from the Select Committee on the Civil Service, *V. & P. N.S.W. L.A.,* sess. 1872, vol. 1, p.653, Q.1259, 1306–9.

[7] Martin, 'Henry Parkes and Electoral Manipulation', *H.S.,* vol. 8, no. 31, Nov. 1958, p.268.

[8] W. A. Brodribb, *Recollections of an Australian Squatter,* p.173.

[9] *S.M.H.,* 16 Nov. 1863.

[10] *S.M.H.,* 4 and 5 Apr. 1856; *Empire,* 9 May 1856; Chisholm to Parkes, 28 Apr. 1856, P.C., A879, p.94.

[11] *S.M.H.,* 2 Aug. 1859.

[12] *S.M.H.,* 27 June 1859.

[13] 4 and 7 Nov. 1863.

[14] 14 and 28 Nov. 1863.

[15] *S.M.H.,* 14 Dec. 1859.

[16] *S.M.H.,* 20 Jan. 1865.

[17] Bell to Parkes, 17 Nov. 1869, P.C., A883, p.137.

[18] *Empire,* 26 Jan. 1864.

[19] Bell to Parkes, 20 Feb. 1868, P.C., A873, p.333.

[20] Bell to Parkes, 12 July 1866, 20 Aug. 1868, 30 July 1872, P.C., A873, pp.291, 308–17.

[21] Bell to Parkes, 17 Nov. 1869, P.C., A883, p.137 (italics in original).

[22] Martin, 'Henry Parkes and Electoral Manipulation', loc. cit., p.268.

[23] For this side of Brunker's activities see Brunker to Parkes, 1 and 17 Aug. 1863, Autograph Letters of Notable Australians, A69, pp.61, 63; 3 Aug. 1863, P.C., A873, p.186; Portus to Parkes, 3 Aug. 1863, P.C., A900, p.351.

[24] Brunker to Parkes, 1 and 30 Oct., 5 and 12 Nov. 1866, P.C., A873, pp.199, 146, 201, 196; Scholey to Parkes, 2 Oct. 1866, P.C., A928, p.697.

[25] See Loveday, 'Patronage and Politics in N.S.W. 1856–1870', pp.350–1.

[26] E.g., *S.M.H.,* 7 Nov. 1863; *Tamworth Examiner,* 21 and 28 Nov. 1863.

[27] For this attitude, e.g., *Braidwood News,* 20 Jan. 1864; McKellar to Selwyn, 2 Dec. 1864, Selwyn Papers, A736, p.319.

[28] For such an example, Forster to Parkes, 25 May 1859, P.C., A922, p.24.

[29] The figures for 1856 exclude three electorates in territory later included in Queensland: Moreton, Wide Bay, Burnett and Maranoa (213 electors); Stanley County (782); Stanley Boroughs (1244). *V. & P. N.S.W. L.A.,* sess. 1866, vol. 1, p.700 (for 1856); ibid., sess. 1861–2, vol. 1, p.791, (for 1861–2); ibid., sess. 1871–2, vol. 1, p.547 (for 1871–2); ibid., sess. 1881, vol. 4, p.1177 (for 1881–2); ibid., sess. 1885–6, vol. 2, p.229 (for 1885–6); ibid., sess. 1890, vol. 1, pp.805–7 (for 1889–90).

[30] For its hope of a central organization in Sydney, with branches throughout the country, sending delegates to governing convention, see *Sydney Evening Mail,* 18, 23, 25 and 31 Mar. 1859: it enrolled members at a fee of 1s. each (*S.M.H.,* 24 Dec. 1857).

[31] D. W. A. Baker, 'The Origins of Robertson's Land Acts', *H.S.,* vol. 8, no. 30, May 1958, pp.175–6.

[32] For proposed branch organization see *S.M.H.,* 30 Apr. 1859, 24 Oct. 1861, 9 Dec. 1863.

[33] *Empire,* 3 and 25 Feb., 21 Mar. 1864. The Free Trade Association advertised urging electors to make sure that their names were registered on the electoral lists and stating that it could supply the necessary forms at its central office. It had a central organization that included country and correspondence sub-committees as well as sub-committees for meetings and publicity, parliamentary activities and finance. It advertised that it intended to select candidates for election to parliament, to promote the formation of country branches and to revise the electoral lists.

[34] Bathurst: *Bathurst Free Press,* 13 Feb. 1858.
Mudgee: *Mudgee Newspaper,* 16 Feb. 1858.
Wollongong: *Goulburn Herald,* 20 Feb. 1858.
Maitland: *Maitland Mercury,* 21 and 30 Jan., 4 Mar. 1858, *Northern Times,* 5 June 1858.

Goulburn: *Northern Times,* 6 Mar. 1858.

[5] With the notable exception of the Electoral Reform League. Cowper's association with this League was attacked as a 'conspiracy' on the part of ministers to coerce parliament. Donaldson, *S.M.H.,* 7 May 1858.

[6] *S.M.H.,* 3 and 12 Sept. 1868. Independent evidence of the existence of one branch, at Bathurst, is in Craig to Parkes, 3 Mar. 1869, P.C., A920, p.478.

[7] *S.M.H.,* 5 July 1869. This was probably the Delegate Assembly of the P.P.A. to which one Orange Lodge also sent two delegates on request. Minute Book, Schomberg Loyal Orange Lodge, No. 2, Sydney, 12 Oct. 1868, M.L. MSS. 749.

[8] Membership was defined by subscription. *S.M.H.,* 24 Oct. 1868, 3 July 1869.

[9] *S.M.H.,* 12 Sept. 1868. A frank statement of its interest in patronage and in municipal and parliamentary elections is to be found in *Manifesto, Rules and By-Laws of the New South Wales Protestant Political Association* (Sydney, 1872), M.L.

[0] E.g. Davies to a Yass agent, 2 Mar. 1872: 'Please get James Pemell, esq., nominated for Yass if you have no local candidate'. These confidential telegrams were delivered to the wrong person who exposed Davies' operations in the local newspaper, *Western Examiner,* 24 Feb. 1872. *General Election, 1872,* Newspaper Cuttings, etc., M.L.

[1] Minute Book, Schomberg Loyal Orange Lodge, No. 2, Sydney, 12 Oct. 1868. The Lodge itself took part in electoral activities.

[2] John Davies, its president, Stephen Goold, and Aldermen Bradford and Murphy.

[3] *Protestant Standard,* 3 and 24 July 1869, *S.M.H.,* 22 Nov. 1869, 1 Mar. 1870 for J. Stewart's connection with both organizations; *S.M.H.,* 4, 6, 9, 11 and 14 Dec. 1869 for Speer's connection with both organizations.

[4] E. W. O'Sullivan, From Colony to Commonwealth, MS., pp.67–8.

[5] *S.M.H.,* 11 Dec. 1869, *Empire,* 6 Dec. 1869, for comment on its activity.

[6] *S.M.H.,* 21 Nov. 1868.

[7] Bell to Parkes, 17 Nov. 1869, P.C., A883, p.137.

[8] The poverty of the Association is forcibly suggested by the poverty of the Schomberg Loyal Orange Lodge, No. 2, in Sydney, whose Minute Book shows it reluctantly voting small sums to help defray election expenses. On one occasion, after promising to pay half of an election bill totalling £120, it quarrelled about whether to pay £4 or £2 or to open a subscription list because the funds of the lodge amounted to only 30s. Minute for 14 Mar. 1870.

[9] Martin, Political Groupings in New South Wales 1872–1889 (Ph.D. thesis, A.N.U. Canberra, 1955), pp.125–6.

[50] *Golden Fleece,* special issue of the *Farmer and Settler,* 31 Aug. 1907, p.77.

[51] *S.M.H.,* 9 Aug. 1873.

[52] *V. & P. N.S.W. L.A.,* sess. 1875, vol. 3, p.347.

[53] *S.M.H.,* 30 Nov. 1875.

[54] *S.M.H.,* 2 Dec. 1875.

[55] *S.M.H.,* 16 Oct. 1877, with a list of branches and names of delegates.

[56] *S.M.H.,* 1 Nov. 1877, for this manifesto.

[57] *S.M.H.,* 13 Oct. 1877 and *Mudgee Independent,* 6 Oct. 1877, for one example.

[58] E.g., *S.M.H.,* 5 Nov. 1877, Inverell; 31 Oct. 1877, Yass. See also Martin, 'Electoral contests in Yass and Queanbeyan in the 'seventies and 'eighties', *J. & P. R.A.H.S.,* vol. 43, part 3, 1958, p.121.

[59] For such reckoning, even in the absence of any apparent organized selector pressure, see Davies in Argyle, *Goulburn Herald,* 31 Oct. 1877, and Bowman in Hawkesbury, *S.M.H.,* 25 Oct. 1877, Maunsell to Parkes, 13 Oct. 1877, P.C., A921, p.780.

[60] It eased payment terms for conditional purchasers by reducing interest to 4 per cent, and established a system of annual payments of 1s. an acre to pay off the purchases as an alternative to either paying them off within 3 years or paying interest indefinitely. C. J. King, *An Outline of Closer Settlement in N.S.W.,* pp.89–90. The Act was also designed to prevent dummying, which selectors complained of, but it was ineffective in this.

[61] It was proposed that
1. interest on conditional purchases be remitted;

    2. the value of required improvements be reduced from £1 to 10s. an acre;

    3. selectors be forced to reside five years on their land before it could be transferred (directed at dummying squatters);

    4. 'family selection' be introduced, viz. selection by fathers on behalf of their children of land contiguous to their own, the residence requirement to be waived in such cases;

    5. the upset price of land sold at auction to be raised to 25s. an acre;

    6. pastoral rents be increased;

    7. lessees be denied the right to purchase more than 1/48th of their runs by virtue of improvements, the last three being directed at the pastoralists.

[62] E.g. Fitzpatrick, *S.M.H.,* 29 Nov. 1878; Leary, *S.M.H.,* 5 Dec. 1878; Day and Shepherd, *S.M.H.,* 6 Dec. 1878.

[63] *S.M.H.,* 7 Nov. 1877.

[64] Wisdom's speech, *S.M.H.,* 5 Dec. 1878. Martin, 'Pastoralists in the Legislative Assembly of N.S.W., 1870–90', in A. Barnard (ed.), *The Simple Fleece,* pp.584–5.

[65] Trades and Labour Council of New South Wales, *Minutes of General Meetings 1871–1876,* A3828, minute for 13 Apr. 1876 and *passim.*

[66] N. B. Nairn, 'The Role of the Trades and Labour Council in N.S.W., 1871–1891', *H.S.,* vol. 7, no. 28, May 1957, pp.429–30.

[67] Trades and Labour Council of New South Wales, *Minutes, Executive Committee,* A3823, minutes from 29 July 1880 to 1 Sept. 1880.

[68] J. A. La Nauze, 'Merchants in Action', *Economic Record,* vol. xxxi, no. 60, 1955, p.77, and for one example, *S.M.H.,* 31 Jan. 1866.

[69] *S.M.H.,* 21 June 1861 and 31 Oct. 1877 for examples.

[70] *S.M.H.,* 9 Dec. 1874 for L.V.A.'s activity.

[71] Pastoralists organized a committee of some sort as early as 1870. *S.M.H.,* 26 Jan. 1870, 19 Feb. 1872. In 1878 the 'Freehold and Pastoral Association of New South Wales' circulated a confidential letter among pastoralists warning them of the need for continued action against a pending land bill and in an anticipated general election. It sought correspondents who would set up local electoral committees and guaranteed their expenses. Circular dated 28 Oct. 1878, read in parliament, *S.M.H.,* 6 Dec. 1878.

[72] Martin, 'Pastoralists in the Legislative Assembly of N.S.W., 1870–90', in A. Barnard, op. cit., esp. pp.577–80.

[73] *S.M.H.,* 15 Sept. 1877.

[74] *S.M.H.,* 17 Oct. 1877.

[75] *S.M.H.,* 15 Jan. 1878.

[76] In opposition to immigration and free trade and in support of electoral reform, *S.M.H.,* 17 and 22 Oct. 1877, 15 Jan. 1878.

[77] *S.M.H.,* 17 Oct. 1877.

[78] *S.M.H.,* 13 Dec. 1877.

[79] *S.M.H.,* 10 Sept., 16 Oct., 1 Nov. 1877, for the W.M.D.A.'s complaint that the F.S.A.s had betrayed the working class, a clear indication that the W.M.D.A. sought, not to help the F.S.A.s but to win their help.

[80] 26 Oct. 1877.

[81] *S.M.H.,* 13 Dec. 1877, 3 Jan. 1878.

[82] *Sydney Magazine,* 1878, pp.76–80, for its constitution and programme, and *S.M.H.,* 16 May 1878 for its adoption. Membership was defined by an entrance fee of 5s. and dues of 1s. a month.

[83] *S.M.H.,* 25 Jan. 1878 for its manifesto. See also *S.M.H.,* 20 and 25 July 1877 for report of P.R.L. supporting working men's candidate in Northumberland, and R. Gollan, 'Newcastle Miners and Colliery Proprietors, 1860–1880', *J. & P. R.A.H.S.,* vol. 45, part 2, 1959, p.57, for formation of a political league among Wallsend miners.

[84] B. Atkins, 'Antecedents of the N.S.W. Protection Party, 1881–1891 — The Protection and Political Reform League', *J. & P. R.A.H.S.,* vol. 44, part 4, 1958, pp.239–40.

[85] B. E. Mansfield, 'The Background to Radical Republicanism in N.S.W. in the 1880's, *H.S.,* vol. 5, no. 20, May 1953, p.338.

[86] Nairn, op. cit., pp.435–7, for similar pressure on the T. & L.C.; E. W. O'Sullivan,

From Colony to Commonwealth, pp.166–72; and for one example of the attempts to shape, The Land and Industrial Alliance of New South Wales, *Land Reform, Fair Trade and Payment of Members, Report of the Proceedings at the Conference . . . 30 July 1885* (Sydney, 1885). It was hoped that the conference would bring combined action and united policy from 'all industrial classes' and the central committee of the Alliance was to recommend candidates for elections where local branches could not provide them.

[87] Martin, 'Electoral Contests in Yass and Queanbeyan in the 'seventies and 'eighties', loc. cit., p.121.

5 THE CABINET

[1] Archives Office of N.S.W., Papers removed from the office of T. M. Slattery, Protho-notary of the Supreme Court and Curator of Intestate Estates, 1874–1881. Minute to document entitled Minute of the Minister of Justice for the consideration of Cabinet, on the subject 'As to the power of the Curator of Intestate Estates to appoint Agents and to charge 5 per cent commission . . .', sgd F.B.S., 8 Mar. 1880.

[2] The Governor General's Commission and Instructions (under the new constitution), 8 Sept. 1855, *V. & P. N.S.W. L.C.,* 1855, vol. 1, pp.635–41.

[3] W. T. Denison, *Varieties of Viceregal Life,* vol. 1, p.342 and *passim* for the following remarks.

[4] There were of course one or two exceptions to this: the Governor could not pass the responsibility for decisions to pardon criminal offenders to the ministry, and in later times the Governor had to take responsibility for the final decision whether to grant a dissolution, to appoint members of the Upper House and for his choice of premiers, but these matters are not relevant at this point.

[5] *S.M.H.,* 28 May 1856.

[6] Denison to Donaldson, 29 July 1856, Denison Papers, B205, no. 26.

[7] *Minutes,* Executive Council, vol. 17, Jan.-Aug. 1856, p.469.

[8] *S.M.H.,* 6, 8 and 9 Aug. 1856, for the debate.

[9] Thomson to Denison, 2 July 1856, *V. & P. N.S.W. L.A.,* sess. 1856-7, vol. 1, p.877.

[10] *Minutes,* Executive Council, 22 Sept. 1856, encl. in Denison to Labouchere, 25 Sept. 1856, CO201/495.

[11] Manning to Donaldson, 4 Aug. 1856, Letters Donaldson Ministry, A731, p.117.

[12] Denison to Donaldson, 5 Aug. [1856], Denison Papers, B205. This reply did not entirely meet Manning's objection, which was that a Governor could conceivably be forced by instructions to insist upon a course of action which was opposed by ministers, and in support of which he could not find another ministry with a majority in the legislature. The situation did not, however, arise in later years because the colonial office did not fetter the Governor to any politically significant extent.

[13] Denison to Cowper, 2 Nov. 1857, Cowper Correspondence, vol. 1, A676. See also Denison to Stanley, 26 May 1858, CO201/502, for a report to the same general effect.

[14] Denison complained three times at least:
Denison to Cowper, 2 Nov. 1857, Cowper Correspondence, vol. 1, A676.
Denison to Cowper, 2 July 1858, Government House Papers, Miscellaneous Corres-pondence, 1856–61, 4/1665,p.357.
Denison to Cowper, 10 May 1860, Cowper Correspondence, vol. 1, A676.
and Young once, Minutes, Executive Council, vol. 25, July 1861-July 1862, 4/1541, p.97.

[15] Denison to Cowper, 2 Nov. 1857, Cowper Correspondence, A676. We have been unable to find a copy of his minute to the ministry on the subject.

[16] Denison to Forster, 15 Feb. 1860, and Denison to Black, 15 Feb. 1860, Government House Papers, Miscellaneous Correspondence, 1856–61, 4/1665, pp.485, 487.

[17] The Postmaster-General did not have cabinet rank until 1866.

[18] Cowper in 1870, and Jennings in 1883 held the offices while in the Assembly. On two occasions a ministerial portfolio was held concurrently by the man who was Vice-President.

[19] A. Aspinall, *The Cabinet Council, 1783–1835,* p.214.

[20] Cf. G. Marshall and G. C. Moodie, *Some Problems of the Constitution,* ch. 4, esp. pp.78–83.

[21] Thomson to Denison, 2 July 1856, *V. & P. N.S.W. L.A.,* sess. 1856–7, vol. 1, p.877.

[22] S. Redgrave, *Murray's Official Handbook of Church and State;* revised ed., *The Official Handbook of Church & State.* Copies of both editions are in the Library of the New South Wales Parliament, Sydney. Thomson had drawn also on the information supplied by H. C. E. Childers about the system already established in Victoria. Childers to Thomson, 6 Mar. 1856, Thomson Papers, vol. 3, A1531/3, p.531.

[23] Denison to Donaldson, 29 July 1856, Denison Papers, B205, no. 26.

[24] E.g. Parkes to Halloran, (n.d.), and on 19 July 1866, instructing him to call cabinet meetings. H. Halloran, Letters to, Uncat. MSS., set 292.

[25] Other examples of minutes in departmental archives:

Extract from a cabinet minute, defining relations between the engineer-in-chief and the commissioner for railways, sgd James Martin, 24 Apr. 1867, quoted in Minute paper, Engineer in Chief to Minister for Public Works, 8 Feb. 1878. Archives office of N.S.W., N.S.W. Railway Commissioner, Papers of Railways and Tramways, 1878–1888, 4/118.

Minute, sgd 'H.P [arkes] 29 Feb. 1868', that cabinet sees no ground for legislative interference with the employment of New Hebrides natives as labourers in Queensland. Archives office of N.S.W., Colonial Secretary's Archives, Governor's Minutes, 1868, 4/1071.

Minute. 'Cabinet concurs H.P. 24.9.80', to a minute for cabinet by minister for justice, J. G. L. Innes, recommending removal from office of District Court Judge F. W. Meymott. Archives office of N.S.W., Papers re removal from office of District Court Judge F. W. Meymott, 1867–1883, Part II.

Minute sgd 'Henry Parkes for the Cabinet', 9 Mar. 1888, deciding that orders be offered for the construction of railway locomotives in the colony. Archives office of N.S.W., Colonial Secretary's Archives, Minutes 1888, 1/2736.

Copy of cabinet minute, 'Approved at Cabinet, (sgd) John Lackey' and issuing from Colonial Secretary's office, 30 Jan. 1889. Copied for the Attorney-General by under-secretary to the Treasurer, G. Eagar, 14 Feb. 1889. Barton Papers, Uncat. MSS., set 249.

[26] E.g. *Minute of Cabinet* on the Constitution of the Legislative Council, sgd H. Parkes, 8 Aug. 1872, prepared for transmission by the Governor to the Secretary of State. *V. & P. N.S.W. L.A.,* sess. 1872–3, vol. 1, p.529.

[27] Examples:

Cabinet minute recording the Cowper ministry's views on a petition for separation of the Riverina as a separate colony, sgd C. Cowper, 14 July 1865, and prepared for transmission by the Governor to the Secretary of State. *V. & P. N.S.W. L.A.,* sess. 1865–6, vol. 1, p.666.

Two cabinet minutes, recording decisions relating to the suspension of W. A. Duncan, Collector of Customs in 1868, sgd H.P., 27 and 28 July 1868. *V. & P. N.S.W. L.A.,* sess. 1868–9, vol. 2, pp.86, 88.

Minute 'Approved, H.P. for Cabinet 30 Dec. 73' to a minute for cabinet proposing that with the abolition of the newspaper postage, railways carry newspapers free of charge to proprietors and that the postal dept. reimburse the railways dept. *V. & P. N.S.W. L.A.,* sess. 1902, vol. 5, p.612.

Minute of cabinet, to defer consideration of a transfer of some lands dept. business to the mines dept. sgd 'J.S.F.[arnell] 4.1.1878', *V. & P. N.S.W. L.A.,* sess. 1877–8, vol. 2, p.1.

Minute, 'Cabinet Approves [sgd] H.P. 6.2.79', to a minute of [*sic* for] cabinet, sgd 'J.H.[oskins] 6.2.79' advising that a commission of enquiry into the lands and survey dept. be terminated. *V. & P. N.S.W. L.A.,* sess. 1878–9, vol. 4, p.210.

[28] E.g. on dissolutions:

Cowper to Denison, 26 Sept. 1856, encl. in Denison to Labouchere, 28 Oct. 1856, CO201/495 and in draft form in Cowper Correspondence, vol. 3, A678.

Cowper to Denison, 18 Dec. 1857, encl. in Denison to Labouchere, 26 Dec. 1857, CO201/499.

Martin to Belmore, 19 Oct. 1868, Correspondence Relating to the Dissolution of Parliament in New South Wales in 1868 and 1872, A2542/1.
and on two other matters:

Minute, 17 Mar. 1862, sgd Charles Cowper, advising the Governor, Sir John Young, not to leave the Colony on a visit to Norfolk Island. Cowper Correspondence, vol. 3, A678.

Undated draft, unsigned, of a minute in Cowper's handwriting, advising the Governor on the question whether certain prisoners' punishments should be mitigated. Cowper Correspondence, vol. 3, A678.

[29] W. I. Jennings, *Cabinet Government* (3rd ed.), p.267.

[30] E.g. Byrnes' speech, *S.M.H.,* 3 Jan. 1871.

[31] *S.M.H.,* 14 Dec. 1860. We are indebted to D. W. A. Baker of the A.N.U. for drawing this information to our attention.

[32] Parkes to Carrington, 9 July 1887, P.C., A916, p.93. At formation of Parkes' ministry, it was decided that payment of members would be an open question and that Parkes himself would take responsibility for advice tendered to the Governor on the question.

[33] *V. & P. N.S.W. L.A.,* sess. 1858, vol. 1, pp.537–8, 5–6 Nov. 1858, report of division in committee.

[34] Cowper to Martin, 6 Nov. 1858, quoted by Martin in the Assembly, *S.M.H.,* 17 Nov. 1858.

[35] *S.M.H.,* 17 Nov. 1858, for speeches dealing with this dispute.

[36] Cowper to Martin, n.d. [6 Nov. 1858], cf. Cowper to Martin, 10 Nov. 1858, both in *S.M.H.,* 17 Nov. 1858.

[37] *S.M.H.,* 17 Nov. 1858.

[38] Forster to Martin, 28 Jan. 1865, Archives office of N.S.W., Colonial Secretary's archives, Letters Received, 1869, Despatches 1, 1860–9, Sundry Papers, 4/679.

[39] Forster to Young, 23 Jan. 1865. *A Collection of Acts, Bills and Papers relating to the Constitution of the Legislative Council of N.S.W.,* p.689, and Martin to Forster, 26 Jan. 1865, loc. cit.

[40] Young to Cardwell, 16 Feb. 1865, Governors' Despatches, 1864–5, A1266/7, p.18.

[41] Martin to Parkes, 22 Dec. 1870, P.C., A925, p.101.

[42] *S.M.H.,* 29 Oct. 1877, Garrett's speech at Camden, and Garrett to Robertson, 9 Oct. 1877, in *S.M.H.,* 12 Oct. 1877. See also *S.M.H.* editorial, 13 Oct. 1877.

[43] Robertson to Garrett, 11 Oct. 1877, in *S.M.H.,* 12 Oct. 1877.

[44] Robertson to the Editor, *S.M.H.,* 30 Oct. 1877.

[45] Cowper was less anxious than Forster to separate the duties, and clearly bowed to public feeling in not giving L. H. Bayley, who replaced Martin, a seat in cabinet. A few months later, he decided to ignore public feeling and Bayley was taken into cabinet and Council.

[46] *S.M.H.,* 17 Sept. 1856.

[47] *S.M.H.,* 9 Sept. 1856.

[48] Manning to Young, 16 Aug. 1865, Manning Papers, Uncat. MSS., set 246, item 1. Young to Cowper, 27 May 1865, Cowper Correspondence, vol. 2, A677.

[49] Young to Cardwell, 21 Sept. 1865, Governors' Despatches, A1266/7, p.147.

[50] Young to Cowper, 23 Aug. 1865, Cowper Correspondence, vol. 2, A677; Plunkett to Macarthur, 2 Sept. 1865, Macarthur Papers, vol. 30, A2926, p.151.

[51] Manning to Forster, 18 Feb. 1860, Forster to Manning, 2 Mar. 1860, Manning Papers, Uncat. MSS., set 246, item 1; *S.M.H.,* 9 Dec. 1868.

[52] Denison to Manning, 8 Mar. 1860, Manning Papers, Uncat. MSS., set 246, item 1.

[53] Parkes to Carrington, 9 June 1887, P.C., A916, p.93.

[54] *V. & P. N.S.W. L.A.,* 2nd sess., 1887, vol. 1, 17 May, p.193, 2–3 June, p.232.

[55] Parkes, *S.M.H.,* 6 July 1887.

[56] Ibid.

[57] Parkes to Carrington, 9 June 1887, P.C., A916, p.93.

[58] *S.M.H.,* 13 July 1887.

⁵⁹ *S.M.H.,* 6 July 1887. Garrett remarks that both sides of the House were divided by the question as well as the ministry and the bill was carried by 42/26 at its second reading.

⁶⁰ Parkes to Clarke, 2 May 1887, Confidential, P.C., A931, and copies to nine other ministers. Two enclosures, being copies of W. E. Hearn, *The Government of England,* 2nd ed., pp.223–4 on cabinet and a speech (?) by Gladstone, were intended to accompany the letter. They are to be found in P.C., A955. See also Parkes to Carrington, 7, 12 April 1887, P.C., A876, pp.127, 118.

⁶¹ Jennings, op. cit., pp.277–89.

⁶² S. Encel, *Cabinet Government in Australia,* p.260.

⁶³ Jennings, op. cit., p.281; Aspinall, op. cit., p.214.

6 THE FIRST PARTIES

¹ J. A. Froude, *Oceana,* p.158.

² W. Forster, 'Personal Government', *Melbourne Review,* vol. 7, no. 26, Apr. 1882, pp.176–9.

³ *S.M.H.,* 14 Dec. 1872.

⁴ T. A. Coghlan, *The Wealth and Progress of New South Wales,* 1900–1, p.156; *S.M.H.,* 24 Oct. 1873 (editorial).

⁵ Coghlan, ibid., *New South Wales Statistical Register, 1885,* pp.184–5. As Parkes admitted, the new tariff was far from being 'simple and symmetrical' (Parkes to Sir H. Robinson, 16 Oct. 1873, P.C., A932).

⁶ D. Buchanan, 27 Jan. 1880, *N.S.W. P.D.,* vol. I, p.900.

⁷ B. Atkins, 'Antecedents of the New South Wales Protection Party, 1881–1891: The Protection and Political Reform League', *J. & P. R.A.H.S.,* vol. 44, part 4, 1958, p.241.

⁸ F. B. Suttor to Parkes, 13 May 1880, P.C., A928, p.451.

⁹ Atkins, op. cit., pp.239–41.

¹⁰ *Debater,* 8 July 1882.

¹¹ B. E. Mansfield, 'The Background to Radical Republicanism in New South Wales in the Eighteen Eighties', *H.S.,* vol. 5, no. 20, May 1953, pp.338–48.

¹² E. W. O'Sullivan, From Colony to Commonwealth, p.164.

¹³ Ibid., pp.159, 164–7.

¹⁴ *D.T.,* 4 Aug. 1885. The debates of the conference are reported in full in *D.T.,* 31 July to 5 Aug. 1885.

¹⁵ See debate of 2 Aug., especially speeches of Clemisha and Stinson, against protection as such *(D.T.,* 3 Aug. 1885).

¹⁶ *D.T.,* 20 Aug. 1885.

¹⁷ Professor B. E. Mansfield generously permitted the authors to read the MS. of his recently published work, *Australian Democrat: The Career of Edward William O'Sullivan, 1846–1910,* which throws much valuable light on the protectionist movement of the 1880s.

¹⁸ See, e.g. *S.M.H.,* 31 Dec. 1884; 31 Dec. 1885; N. G. Butlin, *Investment in Australian Economic Development, 1861–1900,* p.285.

¹⁹ T. A. Coghlan, *Labour and Industry in Australia,* vol. III, pp.1442–7.

²⁰ See, e.g. Kethel's speech, 6 July 1886, *N.S.W. P.D.,* vol. XXI, pp.3096–7.

²¹ *S.M.H., D.T.,* 31 July 1885, for preliminary meeting; 28 Aug. 1885 for adoption of rules and constitution.

²² Reported by O'Sullivan and Forsyth, 6 July 1886, *N.S.W. P.D.,* vol. XXI, pp.3084–5, 3087.

²³ 17 Feb. 1881, ibid., vol. IV., p.480. Clarke claimed that 'The farmers have to compete with the farmers of South Australia, who can send their wheat by water for 10/– a ton, while our farmers have to pay something like £1 a ton from my district [Orange], distant by rail 190 miles from Sydney'.

²⁴ *D.T.,* 2 and 10 Sept. 1886.

²⁵ See e.g. reports of their activities in *D.T.,* 3 July, 20, 25 and 28 Aug. 1885.

²⁶ *D.T.,* 18, 26 and 29 Aug. 1885.

²⁷ *D.T.,* 5 Oct. 1885.

²⁸ G. H. Reid's speech, 22 Aug. 1882, *N.S.W. P.D.,* vol. VII, p.31.

[29] J. S. Farnell repeatedly denied that his government of 1877–8 had been founded on a real 'third party', and subsequent events seem to confirm the claim. Division analysis for the first two sessions of tenth parliament reveals the opposition to Parkes and Robertson to have been most unstable, certainly not founded on a Farnell faction surviving from the previous government. The fact that a few ex-Farnellites were later to be found in the Stuart-Dibbs-Jennings faction suggests some connection between the so-called 'third party' and the new opposition faction organized around Stuart. This limited continuity in personnel was to be expected, but there were no other signs of continuity which makes it clear that Stuart in effect established a quite new faction.

[30] Division analysis for the third session of tenth parliament reveals consolidation of a nuclear opposition composed of ten members: Farnell, Stuart, Wright, Abbott, Jennings and Reid (all ministers in the subsequent Stuart government), Copeland, Slattery, Fitzpatrick and Lyne.

[31] See Martin, 'Pastoralists in the Legislative Assembly of New South Wales 1870–90', in A. Barnard (ed.), *The Simple Fleece,* pp.586–8.

[32] Financial Statements of 7 Feb. 1883, *N.S.W. P.D.,* vol. VIII, pp.300–13, and 24 Jan. 1884, ibid., vol. XI, pp.1446–64.

[33] Ibid., pp. 1909, 2040–1.

[34] Financial Statements of 17 Sept. 1884, ibid., vol. XV, pp.5274–80, and 19 Nov. 1884, ibid., vol. XV (2), pp.24–59.

[35] Wright was principal of the carrying firm of Wright, Heaton & Co. On 30 Sept. 1885, J. P. Garvan moved disapproval of Wright's holding the Works portfolio, considering the alleged business conducted by his firm with the Railways department. When Dibbs reconstructed the government, Wright was given the Mines department.

[36] *N.S.W. P.D.,* vol. XVIII, pp.37, 57, 229.

[37] The voting was 58 for the government, 56 against. As the division was announced, Robertson cried: 'Mr. A. G. Taylor and Mr. Dalton are away; that squares it!' (ibid., p.372).

[38] Ministerial statement, ibid., p.523.

[39] Ibid., p.726. Ironically enough, Parkes chose Burns as his Treasurer in 1887.

[40] Ibid., vol. XVIII, pp.720–4.

[41] See Moore's speech, 16 Feb. 1886, on the 'Cave of Adullam in this House'—the 'shepherdless flock' that had called Garvan to its leadership (ibid., p.805).

[42] Robertson's letter to Carrington, ibid., p.829.

[43] Ibid., vol. XVIII, pp.881–906.

[44] Ibid., vol. XX, p.2065.

[45] Ibid., pp.2065, 2071.

[46] Even Parkes came to recognize Reid in this role (see e.g. speech of 17 June 1886, ibid., p.2746). Division analysis for twelfth parliament shows a clear tendency for Reid to go into opposition toward the end of the parliament. Four other members followed Reid's voting pattern. And see 52 below.

[47] Ibid., vol. XX, pp.2072–3.

[48] Evidence of division analysis. After June 1886, five Robertsonians supported the government, one became an independent, twelve became steady and eight unsteady followers of Parkes.

[49] *N.S.W. P.D.,* vol. XXI, pp.3171–81, 3197.

[50] The income tax bill annoyed many protectionists, and it is clear that the government's weakness on this measure resulted largely from a withdrawal of protectionist support. This was one example of the instability of groupings behind Jennings.

[51] Parkes, Diary entry, 18 Jan. 1887. Letters to Sir S. Samuel, A55, p.29.

[52] Parkes to G. A. Lloyd, 19 Jan. 1887, ibid., p.55, *N.S.W. P.D.,* vol. XXIV, pp.38–9.

[53] As the opposition gleefully pointed out, Roberts, Sutherland and Clarke had previously advocated the imposition of certain duties. Parkes had insisted on Clarke's renouncing protection as a condition of entering the cabinet (Parkes, Diary entry, 17 Jan. 1887, ibid., p.48).

[54] 24 Jan. 1887, *N.S.W. P.D.,* vol. XXIV, p.115.

[55] *D.T.,* 18 Sept. 1886.

[56] *S.M.H., D.T.,* 12 Nov. 1886.

[57] *S.M.H.,* 15 Nov. 1886.

[58] *D.T.,* 10 and 27 Jan. 1887.

[59] Ibid., 29 Jan. 1887.

[60] G. N. Griffiths to Parkes, 27 Jan. 1887, P.C., A886, p.113.

[61] *D.T.,* editorial, 8 Nov. 1886.

[62] Evidence of this activity abounds in the Parkes Correspondence. See as examples E. Hunt to Parkes, 25 Jan. 1887, A887, p.174; R. C. Close to Parkes, 28 Jan. 1887, A879, p.45; G. Munro to Parkes, 31 Jan. 1887, A896, p.82; W. Clarke to Parkes, 3 Feb. 1887, A878, p.116; H. J. Foreman to Parkes, 4 Feb. 1887, A884, p.442.

[63] *D.T.,* 1 Feb. 1887.

[64] *D.T.,* 8 Nov. 1886.

[65] A survey of press reports (not exhaustive) indicates that there were formal branches of the freetrade association active in e.g. Marrickville, Hurstville, Kogarah, St Peters, Tempe, Armidale, Bathurst, Forbes, Bingara, Port Macquarie, Stroud, Wollongong.

[66] *D.T.,* 15 Mar. 1887.

[67] Celia Hamilton, 'Irish Catholics of New South Wales and the Labor Party, 1890–1910', *H.S.,* vol. 8, no. 31, Nov. 1958, pp.254–6.

Wise had warned in 1886 that 'our greatest danger lies in the attempt which is being made to fan the sectarian hatred of Sir Henry Parkes into a sectarian flame' *(D.T.,* 8 Nov. 1886).

[68] E. J. H. Knapp (Secretary, Central Committee, Local Option League) to Parkes, 24 May 1886, P.C., A891, p.38.

[69] Knapp to Parkes, 29 Jan. 1887, P.C., A924, p.44. Note also F. Tait to Parkes, 22 Jan. 1887: 'I am afraid the Protection Cry may injure us [i.e., the Parkes faction] a little but I have good hope that the Orangemen and the anti-drink party will sink every other cry and rally around "Parkes and honest government"' (P.C., A929, p.116). An amusing sidelight on the importance of sectarianism in the election is offered by Clarke's alarmed report to Parkes that 'The Protectionists in Orange have succeeded in bringing out a Protestant Protectionist and they are rousing the farmers to go in for Protection' (Clarke to Parkes, 1 Feb 1887, P.C., A878, p.114).

[70] The only ministerial protectionist was Dr Ross of Molong, who, 'on the strength of long and consistent support to the present Premier, and steadfast opposition to the late Government, . . . escaped a contest with a freetrade candidate, and was returned unopposed' *(S.M.H.,* 28 Feb. 1887).

[71] *N.S.W. P.D.,* vol. xxv, pp.41–2. See also Appendix i, meeting 40.

[72] Dibbs tried in the early stages of the first session to sidestep the tariff issue; he held, he said, 'that the voice of the country had declared for freetrade, . . . and that to discuss the question of freetrade and protection until there was another general election was a waste of time' (ibid., vol. xxvi, p.1220). By July he had formally renounced his free-trade views, since 'Protection is coming' (see e.g. enclosures in J. Inglis to Parkes, 29 July 1887, P.C., A889, p.296).

[73] Commenting, e.g. on the freetrade banquet of March 1887, the *Daily Telegraph* noted that those present reflected the 'vitality of the freetrade cause . . . Mr. Wise, as an ardent young Australian with a political ambition, and Mr. Pulsford, as a thoughtful citizen whose intellect works on happy terms with his conscience, are both typical of the strength of the freetrade party. It is not a merchant's but a people's movement to which such men have committed and devoted themselves' (15 Mar. 1887).

[74] *D.T.,* 2 Feb. 1887.

[75] Ibid.

[76] S. Burdekin, *S.M.H.,* 3 Feb. 1887. For a discussion of the attempts to elaborate the connection between freetrade and liberal theory at this time, see Martin, 'The Legislative Assembly of New South Wales, 1856–1900', *A.J.P.H.,* vol. ii, no. 1, Nov. 1956, pp.64–6.

[77] This table is constructed on the basis of a division analysis of the twelfth parliament, and *S.M.H.* classification of candidates' party allegiance (F.M., P.O., F.I., P.I.) published on 28 Feb. 1887, corrected by reference to *S.M.H.,* summaries, on the same day,

of members' election statements. 'Other' indicates men who changed their allegiance between the twelfth and thirteenth parliaments, or whose declared position at the election did not fit either the F.M. or P.O. pattern. These men were as follows: Dibbs supporter in twelfth parliament, standing as F.M.—2 (Fitzgerald, H. H. Brown); Parkes supporter in twelfth parliament, standing as P.O.—1 (Vaughan); Protection ministerialist—1 (Ross); Freetrade oppositionist—3 (Want, Wilkinson, Dibbs); insufficient evidence to classify—2 (Colls, McGregor).

The division analysis shows that Dibbs had at least 57 steady and unsteady supporters in twelfth parliament. Less than half (23) of these were returned to thirteenth parliament.

Government supporters: 73 freetrade ministerialists shown in table plus Brown, Ross, Fitzgerald. Opposition: 32 protection oppositionists shown in table plus Dibbs, Want, Vaughan, Wilkinson.

See especially speeches of McMillan and Abbott on address in reply, 9 Mar. 1887, *N.S.W. P.D.*, vol. xxv., pp.37, 41–4.

Burns, financial statement, 30 Mar. 1887, ibid., pp.493–506.

P. N. Lamb, Land Policy and Public Finance in New South Wales 1856–1900, unpublished paper read to Section G, A.N.Z.A.A.S. Conference, 1964, p.21. Lamb shows that arbitrary increases of rentals on Crown land brought a jump of revenue from leases of £720,000 between 1886 and 1887. Suburban and country lands were offered for sale to the full legal limit.

Burns, *N.S.W. P.D.*, vol. xxv, p.493.

The Customs Duties Act abolished duties on 135 articles, leaving 35 liable to duty, and increasing duties on spirits. The government estimated that revenue under the Act would amount to £2,213,100. In the previous year, before tariff reform, customs and excise duties had yielded £2,178,404. (Salomons, introducing second reading of the Bill in Upper House, 6 July 1887, ibid., vol. xxvii, p.2603).

April-May 1887. See e.g. McMillan, ibid., vol. xxv, pp.722–4, vol. xxvi, p.1434–5; Wilkinson, McElhone and Neild, ibid., vol. xxv, p.941, vol. xxvi, pp.1129, 1135.

Parkes, 11 May 1887, ibid., p.1438.

Seaver, 31 Nov. 1888, ibid., vol. xxxv, p.744.

As early as June 1887 McMillan had moved resolutions condemning the current policy of increasing by administrative action rents already assessed by local land boards (7 June, ibid., vol. xxvi, p.1863). His most thoroughgoing attack on the general financial policy of the government was made in debates on Burns' financial statement of October 1888 (ibid., vol. xxxv, pp.428–36). The words quoted are from this speech (ibid., p.435).

Fehon was alleged to be associated with Wright, Heaton & Co., and by implication involved in the wool frauds of 1880–8; Want had objected to Fehon's appointment and received on 11 December a promise from Parkes that the matter would be investigated (ibid., vol. xxxvi, pp.1065–70). The charges were pressed again in the House on 9 January (ibid., pp.1511–26). Parkes subsequently claimed that he had been satisfied, after personal enquiries, of Fehon's innocence.

Ibid., vol. xxxvi, pp.1539–43.

Ibid., p.1539.

For evidence of cabinet dissention, see Parkes to Sutherland, 1 May 1887, P.C., A916, p.103; Parkes to Clarke, 2 May, 19 Nov. 1887, P.C., A931; Parkes to Carrington, 16 Dec. 1887, A916, p.72 ('The Government has nothing to fear from outside, but it is suffering severely from want of cohesion and clear purpose within itself'). Major losses were suffered through the resignations of Foster (disgruntled at not having received a judgeship), Garrett (asked to resign by Parkes because of his ill health, probably due to alcoholism), and Wise (alarmed because his legal practice was suffering neglect due to his ministerial responsibilities).

N.S.W. P.D., vol. xxxvi, p.5041.

16 Jan. 1889, ibid., pp.1586–9.

[95] Neild, ibid., p.1626. The reference to the 'Wise-Seaver-McMillan-Smith' party wa
to the Parkes' government's most acid critics, who formed the core of the arden
freetrade group.

[96] The vote was 38/41, Parkes, Roberts, Burns and Sutherland were the only ex-ministe
present. They voted with the Dibbs group, supported only by McCourt and Ros
of their late followers.

[97] D.T., 19, 21 and 22 Jan. 1889.

[98] D.T., 12 Jan. 1889.

[99] D.T., 19 Jan. 1889.

[1] D.T., 21 Jan. 1889. Press reports suggest that the two bodies remained separate
though it is clear that co-operation was very close, and that the parliamentarians worke
effectively to 'strengthen the hands of the parent organization' (ibid., 22 Jan. 1889
Key politicians, like McMillan, were in any case active members of the Freetrad
Associations.

[2] D.T., 19 Jan. 1889.

[3] For an excellent discussion of the organization in this election and of contemporar
interpretations of its significance, see B. E. Mansfield, 'Party Organization in th
New South Wales Elections of February 1889', J. & P. R.A.H.S., vol. 41, Sept
1955, pp.61–77. For comments on the operation of the central organizations as virtua
Caucuses, see especially S.M.H., 26 Jan. 1889, and D.T., 11 Feb. 1889 (letter to editor
'The Black List').

[4] Parkes to McMillan, 21 Feb. 1889, P.C., A916, p.154. See also McMillan to Parkes
19 Feb. 1889, P.C., A894, p.184.

[5] McMillan to Parkes, 19 Feb. 1889, ibid.

[6] Parkes to McMillan, 21 Feb. 1889, ibid.

[7] Parkes, Fifty Years in the Making of Australian History, p.519.

[8] S.M.H., 7 Mar. 1889.

[9] Ibid.

[10] Parkes, Fifty Years, p.523.

[11] S.M.H., 2 Mar. 1889.

[12] S.M.H., 2 Apr. 1889. The crucial debate on the platform is reported in detail in thi
issue. The draft submitted by the subcommittee was accepted with negligible altera
tions. For draft platform and rules, see Appendix II.

[13] S. Smith, S.M.H., 26 Mar. 1889. Speech at St Peters.

[14] S.M.H., 16 Mar. 1889.

[15] S.M.H., 1 May 1889, for meetings which arranged amalgamation.

[16] See Appendix II, especially Rule 5. Immediate consolidation of the new party wa
reflected in the proceedings of the first annual conference, held in August 1889
Delegates represented seventy-nine branches (fifty-four in country areas). Four days
of deliberation were accompanied by enthusiastic public meetings in the evenings
and plans were hammered out for tightening and expanding party organization
improving finance and propaganda arrangements, and bringing new point and flex
ibility to the platform. It should also be noted that Parkes, though Premier and leade
of the parliamentary party, took no part in the conference. He spoke for the Association at a public meeting, but told his audience that he did not 'appear here tonigh
as a free agent'. Report of the Proceedings and Public Meetings of the First Annual Conference
of the Free Trade and Liberal Association of New South Wales, especially pp.23–32, 90–1
(We are indebted to Associate Professor H. Mayer, of Sydney, for drawing our attention
to this Report.)

[17] Typical speech of Rose, e.g. at Windsor: 'The freetrade party had decided that the
old plank of freetrade was too narrow, and were going to widen it and include othe
principles. Protectionists would have to follow suit. It was a bad policy to let thei
opponents have it all their own way' (S.M.H., 10 Apr. 1889).

Select Bibliography

I CONTEMPORARY SOURCES

OFFICIAL

Manuscript (Mitchell Library, Sydney)

Colonial Office Papers in the Public Record Office, London, microfilm copy. Original Correspondence of the Secretary of State, series CO201, vols 493 to 610 for the years 1856–89, being Despatches from the Governors of New South Wales; and series CO202, vols 65 and 66, being entry books of communications sent from the Colonial Office.

Correspondence relating to the Dissolution of Parliament in New South Wales in 1868 and 1872. Copies, donated by the Earl of Belmore.

Minutes of the Executive Council of New South Wales, 1856–70.

New South Wales Governor's Archives (also known as Government House Papers), Despatches from the Secretary of State, 1856–70; miscellaneous correspondence of Governors, 1856–81.

New South Wales, Governors' Despatches, to the Secretary of State; typed transcripts, 1852–85.

Printed

New South Wales. Journals of the Legislative Council, 1856–89.

New South Wales Parliamentary Debates, Series 1, 1879–89.

New South Wales. Votes and Proceedings of the Legislative Assembly, 1856–89.

New South Wales. Votes and Proceedings of the Legislative Council, 1851–5.

Public General Statutes of New South Wales, 1852–62, 1862–74, 1879–85.

Great Britain and Ireland, *Parliamentary Documents,* vol. 65. A collection of papers from the Colonial Office, relative to the alterations in the constitutions of the Australian colonies, printed by order of the House of Commons (Mitchell Library).

Rules and Regulations for Her Majesty's Colonial Service. London, 1856.

Redgrave, S., *Murray's Official Handbook of Church and State*. London, 1852, and revised ed., *The Official Handbook of Church and State*. London, 1855 (in Library of New South Wales Parliament).

New South Wales Parliament, *Expenditure on Public Moneys*. A collection, n.d., of papers printed by order of the Legislative Assembly, 20 October 1869—10 February 1870 (Mitchell Library).

A Collection of Acts, Bills and Papers relating to the Constitution of the Legislative Council of New South Wales. Sydney, 1879.

New South Wales Parliamentary Handbook. 2nd ed., Sydney, 1882.

New South Wales Parliamentary Record (various eds).

Census of New South Wales, 1851, 1856, 1861, 1871, 1881, 1891.

Statistical Register of New South Wales, 1851–90.

Coghlan, T. A., *The Wealth and Progress of New South Wales*. Sydney (various issues between 1886–7 and 1900–1).

NON-OFFICIAL

Manuscript (Mitchell Library except where stated otherwise)

Arnold, W. M., Correspondence.

Autograph Letters, Australian.

Belmore, Earl of, Letters to the Earl of Belmore from his Ministers and others, 1868–72, with some draft replies.

Belmore, Earl of, Private and Semi-official Letter Book, containing copies of Letters and Despatches written to and by Somerset Richard, Fourth Earl of Belmore, 1868–72, copied by his daughter.

Berry Papers (uncatalogued MSS.).

Chamber of Commerce Cash Book, commencing 1851 (in possession of Chamber of Commerce, Sydney).

Cowper Correspondence.

Cowper Papers.

Deniehy's Letters to Parkes, 1854–7.

Denison Papers.

Donaldson Ministry, Letters.

Jamison Papers.

Jevons, W. S., Remarks upon the Social Map of Sydney, 1858.

Lamb, P. N., Land Policy and Public Finance in New South Wales, 1856–1900. Unpublished Paper, Section G, A.N.Z.A.A.S., 1964.

Lang, Rev. J. D., Papers.

Macarthur Papers, of the first collection.

Manning Papers (uncatalogued MSS.).

Martin, James, Papers.

O'Sullivan, E. M., The Honorable Edward William O'Sullivan, 1846–1910. Typescript, 1927.

O'Sullivan, E. W., From Colony to Commonwealth; Half a Century's Reminiscences.
Parkes Papers, variously subdivided as Parkes Correspondence, Parkes Family Papers and Parkes Papers.
Parkes, Sir Henry. Autograph letters to.
Parkes, Sir Henry. Private Affairs, 1887. Letters (Dixson Library, Sydney).
Schomberg Loyal Orange Lodge No. 2, Sydney, Minute Book, 1866–72.
Selwyn Papers.
Stephen Papers (uncatalogued MSS.).
Thomson, Deas, Papers.
Trades and Labor Council of New South Wales, Minutes of General Meetings, 1871–6.
Walker, W., Papers.
Wentworth Papers.
Windeyer Family Papers (uncatalogued MSS.).
Windeyer, W. C., Letters to his Mother.

Newspapers and Newspaper Cuttings

Albury Advertiser
Australian Israelite
Bathurst Free Press
Braidwood News
Daily Telegraph, Sydney
Empire
Freemans Journal
Goulburn Herald
Lictor
Maitland Mercury
Mudgee Independent
Northern Times
Orangeman and Protestant Catholic
People's Advocate and New South Wales Vindicator
Protestant Standard
Southern Cross
Sydney Evening Mail
Sydney Morning Herald
Tamworth Examiner
General Election, New South Wales, February-March 1872 (cuttings and MS. notes, Mitchell Library)

Parkes-Robertson Coalition Ministry, 1878-79 (cuttings, Mitchell Library)
Death of Sir Henry Parkes (cuttings, Mitchell Library).

Pamphlets

Allen, W. B., *Lecture on Protection*. Sydney, n.d., *c*.1860.

Allen, W. B., *The Alarming State of New South Wales*. Sydney, 1860.

Bell, F. A., *Industry and Commerce Relieved*. Sydney, 1866.

Catholic Association for the Promotion of Religion and Education, *Second Annual Report*. Sydney, 1869.

Chambers, C. H., *Address to the People of New South Wales, in Opposition to and Refutation of the Grievances Petitions of the Legislative Council to Parliament and displaying the Impolicy of the Constitutional Bills proposed for their redress by a Committee of that Council*. Sydney, n.d., *c*.1853.

Chapman, H. S., *Parliamentary Government or Responsible Ministries for the Australian Colonies*. Hobart, 1854.

Constitutional Association, *Objects and Rules and Laws of the Constitutional Association and Address of the Provisional Council*. Sydney, 1848.

Dickinson, J. N., *A Letter to the Hon. the Speaker of the Legislative Council on the Formation of a Second Chamber in the Legislature of New South Wales*. Sydney, 1852.

Duncan, W. A., *A Plea for the New South Wales Constitution*. Sydney, 1856.

Lang, Rev. J. D., *An Anatomical Lecture on the New Constitution and the Bad Subjects to whom it owes its Paternity*. Sydney, 1854.

Lang, Rev. J. D., *Freedom and Independence for the Golden Lands of Australia*. London, 1852.

Lang, Rev. J. D., *The Coming Event*. 2 lectures. Sydney, 1850.

Lucas, J., *Protection versus Free Trade*. Sydney, 1858.

Norton, J., *The Condition of the Colony of New South Wales*. Sydney, 1860.

Norton, J., *The Constitution Question*. Sydney, 1853.

Report of the Proceedings and Public Meetings of the First Annual Conference of the Free Trade and Liberal Association of New South Wales. Sydney, 1889.

Smith, A. B., *Freetrade and Liberal Associations, their True Province*. Sydney, 1889.

Smith, A. B., *Liberty and Liberalism*. Melbourne, 1887.

Stephen. A., *Thoughts on the Constitution of a Second Legislative Chamber for New South Wales*. Sydney, 1853.

Thomson, E. Deas, *Corrected Report of Speeches . . . delivered in the Legislative Council on . . . a Bill for the Division of the Colony into Electoral Districts.* Sydney, 1851.
Wise, B. R., *Position of the Liberal Party.* Sydney, 1888.

Printed Recollections, Memoirs and Descriptive Works

Brodribb, W. A., *Recollections of an Australian Squatter.* Sydney, n.d., *c.*1883.
Creed, J. M., *My Recollections, 1842–1914.* London, 1916.
Denison, W. T., *Varieties of Vice-Regal Life.* 2 vols, London, 1870.
Dilke, C., *Problems of Greater Britain.* London, 1890.
Duffy, C. G., *My Life in two Hemispheres.* 2 vols, London, 1898.
Froude, J. A., *Oceana.* London, 1886.
Lang, Rev. J. D., *Brief Sketch of my Parliamentary Life and Times from 1 August 1843, till the late Dissolution of Parliament.* Sydney, 1870.
Martineau, J., *Letters from Australia.* London, 1869,
O'Sullivan, E. W., 'Reminiscences, Mainly Political', *Lone Hand,* vol. VII, 1 August 1910.
Parkes, H., *Fifty Years in the Making of Australian History.* London, 1892.
Ranken, W. H. L., *The Dominion of Australia.* London, 1874.
Ryan, J. T., *Reminiscences of Australia.* Sydney, n.d., *c.*1894.
Therry, R., *Reminiscences of a Thirty Years' Residence in New South Wales and Victoria.* London, 1863.
Trollope, A., *Australia and New Zealand.* Melbourne, 1873.
Walker, W., *Recollections of Sir Henry Parkes.* Windsor, 1896.
Walker, W., *Reminiscences of a Fifty Years' Residence at Windsor.* Sydney, 1890.

Directories

Ford's Sydney Commercial Directory. Sydney, 1851.
Greville's Official Post Office Directory of New South Wales. Sydney, various years.
Hall's Business, Professional and Pastoral Directory of New South Wales. Sydney, various years.
Moore's Almanac. Sydney, various years.
Sands' Sydney Directory. Sydney, various years.
Waugh and Cox's Directory of Sydney. Sydney, 1855.
Waugh's Australian Almanac. Sydney, 1860.

II SECONDARY SOURCES

Books and Articles

Aspinall, A., *The Cabinet Council, 1783–1835,* n.d. Reprinted from *Proceedings of the British Academy,* vol. xxxviii, 1952.

Atkins, B., 'Antecedents of the N.S.W. Protection Party, 1881–1891: The Protection and Political Reform League', *J. & P. R.A.H.S.,* vol. 44, pt 4, 1958.

Austin, A. G., *Australian Education, 1788–1900.* Melbourne, 1961.

Baker, D. W. A., 'The Origins of Robertson's Land Acts', *H.S.,* vol. 8, no. 30, May 1958.

Barker, E., *Essays on Government.* Oxford, 1951.

Bedford, R., *Think of Stephen.* Sydney, 1954.

Beer, S. H., 'The Representation of Interests in British Government', *American Political Science Review,* vol. li, no. 3, September 1957.

Brady, A., *Democracy in the Dominions.* Toronto, 1955.

Burke, E., 'Thoughts on the Present Discontents', *Works,* vol. 1, London, 1900.

Butlin, N. G., *Investment in Australian Economic Development, 1861–1900.* Cambridge, 1964.

Cambridge History of the British Empire. Vol. 7, pt 1, Cambridge, 1933.

Chisholm, A. H. (ed.), *Australian Encyclopaedia.* 10 vols, Sydney, 1958.

Clark, C. M. H., *Select Documents in Australian History, 1850–1900.* Sydney, 1955.

Clarke, D. P., 'The Colonial Office and the Constitutional Crisis in Victoria, 1865–1868', *H.S.,* vol. 5, no. 18, May 1952.

Coghlan, T. A., *Labour and Industry in Australia from the First Settlement in 1788 to the Establishment of the Commonwealth in 1901.* 4 vols, London, 1918.

Costin, W. C., and Watson, J. S., *The Law and Working of the Constitution.* 2 vols, London, 1952.

Crawford, R. M., *Australia.* London, 1952.

Crisp, L. F., *The Australian Federal Labour Party, 1901–1951.* London, 1955.

Crisp, L. F., *The Parliamentary Government of the Commonwealth of Australia.* London, 1957.

Duverger, M., *Political Parties.* London, 1954.

Ebbels, R. N. (ed. L. G. Churchward), *The Australian Labor Movement, 1850–1907.* Sydney, 1960.

Encel, S., *Cabinet Government in Australia.* Melbourne, 1962.

Evatt, H. V., *Australian Labour Leader*. Sydney, 1940.

Fitzhardinge, L. F., 'W. M. Hughes in New South Wales Politics', *J. & P. R.A.H.S.,* vol. 37, 1951.

Fitzpatrick, B., *The British Empire in Australia*. Melbourne, 1941.

Fogarty, R., *Catholic Education in Australia, 1806–1950*. 2 vols, Melbourne, 1957.

Forsey, E. A., *The Royal Power of Dissolution of Parliament in the British Commonwealth*. Toronto, 1943.

Forster, W., 'Personal Government', *Melbourne Review,* vol. 7, no. 26, April 1882.

Gollan, R., 'Nationalism and Politics in Australia before 1855', *A.J.P.H.,* vol. 1, no. 1, November 1955.

Gollan, R., 'Newcastle Miners and Colliery Proprietors, 1860–1880', *J. & P.R.A.H.S.,* vol. 45, pt 2, 1959.

Gollan, R., *Radical and Working Class Politics. A Study of Eastern Australia, 1850–1910*. Melbourne, 1960.

Green, F. C. (ed.), *Tasmania, A Century of Responsible Government, 1856–1956*. Hobart, 1956.

Grey, Henry George (third earl), 'Earl Grey on Victorian Politics', *Victorian Review,* vol. 1, no. 6, April 1880.

Grey, Henry George (third earl), *Parliamentary Government Considered with reference to a Reform of Parliament*. London, 1858.

Grey, Henry George (third earl), *The Colonial Policy of Lord John Russell's Administration*. 2nd ed., 2 vols, London, 1853.

Hamilton, Celia, 'Irish Catholics of New South Wales and the Labor Party, 1890–1910', *H.S.,* vol. 8, no. 31, November 1958.

Hancock, W. K., *Australia*. Sydney, 1945.

Hartz, L., *The Liberal Tradition in America*. New York, 1955.

Heydon, L. F., 'The Morris-Ranken Land Report', *Sydney University Review,* 1883.

Irving, T. H., 'The Idea of Responsible Government in New South Wales before 1856', *H.S.,* vol. 11, no. 42, April 1964.

Jenks, E., *The Government of Victoria*. London, 1891.

Jennings, W. I., *Cabinet Government*. 1st and 3rd eds, Cambridge, 1937, 1959.

Jervis, J., 'Alexander Berry, the Laird of Shoalhaven', *J. & P. R.A.H.S.,* vol. 27, pt 1, 1941.

Jervis, J., 'History of Politics and Politicians in Parramatta', Parramatta and District Historical Society, *Journal,* vol. 3, 1926.

Keith, A. B., *Responsible Government in the Dominions*. 2 vols, Oxford, 1928.

King, C. J., *An Outline of Closer Settlement in New South Wales*. Sydney, n.d., *c.*1958.

Lamb, P. N., 'Geoffrey Eagar and the Colonial Treasury of New South Wales', *Australian Economic Papers,* vol. 1, no. 1, September 1962.

La Nauze, J. A., 'Merchants in Action', *Economic Record,* vol. xxxi, no. 60, 1955.

La Nauze, J. A., '"That Fatal, That Mischievous Passage": Henry Parkes and Protection, 1859–60', *Australian Quarterly,* vol. 19, no. 2, June 1947.

Loveday, P., 'A Note on Nineteenth Century Party Organization in New South Wales', *H.S.,* vol. 9, no. 36, May 1961.

Loveday, P., '"Democracy" in New South Wales: The Constitution Committee of 1853', *J. & P. R.A.H.S.,* vol. 42, pt 4, October 1956.

Loveday, P., 'Patronage and Politics in New South Wales, 1856–1870', *Public Administration* (Sydney), vol. xviii, no. 4, December 1959.

Loveday, P., 'The Legislative Council in New South Wales, 1856–1870', *H.S.,* vol. 11, no. 44, April 1965.

Loveday, P., 'The Member and his Constituents in New South Wales in the Mid-Nineteenth Century', *A.J.P.H.,* vol. 5, no. 2, November 1959.

Lyne, C. E., *Life of Sir Henry Parkes*. Sydney, 1896.

Macmillan, D. S., *The Debtor's War*. Melbourne, 1960.

Maine, H. S., *Ancient Law*. 12th ed., London, 1885.

Mansfield, B. E., 'Party Organisation in the New South Wales Election of February 1889', *J. & P. R.A.H.S.,* vol. 44, September 1955.

Mansfield, B. E., 'The Background to Radical Republicanism in New South Wales in the Eighteen Eighties', *H.S.,* vol. 5, no. 20, May 1953.

Marshall, G., and Moodie, G. C., *Some Problems of the Constitution*. London, 1959.

Martin, A. W., 'Electoral Contests in Yass and Queanbeyan in the Seventies and Eighties', *J. & P. R.A.H.S.,* vol. 43, pt 3, 1958.

Martin, A. W., 'Henry Parkes and Electoral Manipulation, 1872–1882', *H.S.,* vol. 8, no. 31, November 1958.

Martin, A. W., 'Pastoralists in the Legislative Assembly of New South Wales, 1870–1890', in Barnard, A. (ed.), *The Simple Fleece*. Melbourne, 1962.

Martin, A. W., 'Sir Henry Parkes and Public Education in New South Wales', in French, E. L. (ed.), *Melbourne Studies in Education, 1960–1961*. Melbourne, 1962.

Martin, A. W., 'The Legislative Assembly of New South Wales, 1856–1900', *A.J.P.H.*, vol. 2, no. 1, November 1956.

Martin, A. W., 'William McMillan: A Merchant in Politics', *J. & P. R.A.H.S.*, vol. 40, 1954.

Martin, A. W., and Wardle, P., *Members of the Legislative Assembly of New South Wales, 1856–1900*. Canberra, 1959.

Mayer, H., 'Some Conceptions of the Australian Party System, 1910–1950', *H.S.*, vol. 7, no. 27, November 1956.

Melbourne, A. C. V., *Early Constitutional Development in Australia*. St Lucia, 1963.

Miller, J. D. B., 'David Syme and Elective Ministries', *H.S.*, vol. 6, no. 21, November 1953.

Miller, J. D. B., 'Party Discipline in Australia' (1), *Political Science* (Wellington), vol. 5, no. 1, March 1953.

Morrison, W. F., *Aldine Centennial History of New South Wales*. Sydney, 1888.

Nairn, N. B., 'The Role of the Trades and Labor Council in New South Wales, 1871–1891', *H.S.*, vol. 7, no. 8, May 1957.

Ostrogorski, M., *Democracy and the Organisation of Political Parties*. London, 1902.

Overacker, L., *The Australian Party System*. New Haven, 1952.

Parkes, H., *Speeches*. Melbourne, 1876.

Pares, R., *George the Third and the Politicians*. Oxford, 1953.

Ranney, A., *The Doctrine of Responsible Party Government*. Urbana, 1954. Illinois Studies in the Social Sciences, vol. xxxiv, no. 3.

Richards, T., *An Epitome of the Official History of New South Wales*. Sydney, 1883.

Roberts, S. H., *History of Australian Land Settlement, 1788–1920*. Melbourne, 1924.

Rowley, C. D., 'Clarence River Separatism in 1860, a Problem in Communications', *H.S.*, vol. 1, no. 4, October 1941.

Rusden, G. W., *History of Australia*. 3 vols, Melbourne, 1897.

Sawer, G. and others, *Federalism in Australia*. Melbourne, 1949.

Serle, P., *Dictionary of Australian Biography*. 2 vols, Sydney, 1949.

Smiles, S., *A Publisher and his Friends: Memoir and Correspondence of the late John Murray ... 1768–1843*. 2 vols, London (in Library of the New South Wales Parliament), 1891.

Stephenson, C. and Marcham, F. G., *Sources of English Constitutional History*. New York, 1937.

Stewart, W. A. (comp.), *Early History of the Loyal Orange Institution in New South Wales*. Sydney, 1926.

200   *SELECT BIBLIOGRAPHY*

Todd, A., *Parliamentary Government in the British Colonies*. London, 1880.

Truman, D. B., *The Congressional Party*. New York, 1959.

Vincent, J. R., 'The Electoral Sociology of Rochdale', *Economic History Review*, 2nd series, vol. XVI, no. 1, August 1963.

Walker, H. de R., *Australasian Democracy*. London, 1897.

Walker, R. B., 'The Later History of the Church and School Lands', *J. & P. R.A.H.S.*, vol. 47, pt 4, August 1961.

Ward, J. M., *Earl Grey and the Australian Colonies, 1846–1857*. Melbourne, 1958.

Westgarth, W., *Australia*. Edinburgh, 1861.

Wight, M., *The Development of the Legislative Council, 1606–1945*. London, 1945.

Windeyer, W. J. V., 'Responsible Government—Highlights, Sidelights and Reflections', *J. & P. R.A.H.S.*, vol. 42, pt 6, January 1957.

Unpublished Theses

Crowley, F. K., Aspects of the Constitutional Conflicts between the two Houses of the Victorian Legislature, 1864–1868. M.A., University of Melbourne, 1947.

Ingham, S. M., Some Aspects of Victorian Parliamentary Liberalism, 1850–1900. M.A., University of Melbourne, 1949.

Irving, T. H., Electoral Reform and the Liberal Movement in New South Wales. B.A., University of Sydney, 1959.

Kearns, P. B., The Land Question in New South Wales Politics, 1856–1861. B.A., University of Sydney, 1958.

Lacey, R. J., The Political Role of the Sydney Middle Class, 1846–1853. B.A., University of Sydney, 1959.

Loveday, P., Democracy in New South Wales in the 1850s. B.A., University of Sydney, 1955.

Loveday, P., The Development of Parliamentary Government in New South Wales, 1856–1870. Ph.D., University of Sydney, 1962.

Martin, A. W., Political Groupings in New South Wales, 1872–1889. Ph.D., Australian National University, 1955.

Parnaby, J. E., Economic and Political Development of Victoria, 1877–1881. Ph.D., University of Melbourne, 1951.

Roe, M., Society and Thought in Eastern Australia, 1831–1851. Ph.D., Australian National University, 1960 (since published as *Quest for Authority in Eastern Australia, 1835–1851*).

Suttor, T. L., The Catholic Church in the Australian Colonies, 1840–1865. Ph.D., Australian National University, 1960 (since published as *Hierarchy and Democracy in Australia, 1788–1870*).

Name Index

Abbott, (Sir) Joseph, 140, 162 (40), 176 n.98, 187 n.30
Abigail, F., 133, 163
Alexander, M., 174 n.67
Antill, J. M., 12

Barbour, R., 102
Barker, T., 13
Barton, (Sir) Edmund, 162 (37.ii)
Bell, F. A., 72, 94–5, 100
Belmore, Lord, 69, 70, 71, 76
Bennett, S., 61, 95
Berry, A., 12
Berry, Sir Graham, 123
Black, J., 98
Brenan, J. R., 12
Brodribb, W. A., 93
Brown, S. C., 86, 174 n.67
Brunker, J. N., 96, 147, 163
Buchanan, D., 123, 186 n.6
Burdekin, M., 65, 176 n.1
Burke, Edmund, 3–4, 9, 14, 59
Burns, J. F., 96, 130, 133, 144, 161 (37.i), 187 n.39
Butler, E., 65, 79, 81–2, 83
Butlin, N. G., 3
Byrnes, Sir James, 49, 55, 68, 72, 75, 159 (23)

Cameron, A., 103
Campbell, A., 95
Campbell, R., 19
Carrington, Lord, 133
Carruthers, Sir Joseph, 140, 146, 163
Cass, G. E., 59
Chisholm, J. K., 12
Chisholm, J. W., 93
Clarke, W., 126, 133, 186, n.23, 187, n.53
Cooper, Sir Daniel, 31, 155(1)
Cowper, Sir Charles: liberal leader 1853–6, 10, 19, 24–5, 28; temporary retirement 1859, 30; removes Parkes from politics 1861, 33; tries to remove Parkes 1865, 37; resigns office to take Agent-Generalship 1870, 50, 74; views on collective responsibility of cabinet 1858, 113
Cowper, C., Jun., 93–4
Cox, G. H., 12
Crisp, L. F., 5
Cummings, W., 174 n.67
Cunneen, J. A., 66

Dalley, W. B., 47, 77, 128, 129
Darley, Sir Frederick, 82
Darvall, Sir John, 24, 117
Davies, J., 100, 181 nn. 40, 42
Day, G., 102
Deniehy, D. H., 20, 22, 172, n.57
Denison, Sir William, 6, 7, 9, 10, 24, 31, 106–9
Desailly, G. P., 93
Dibbs, (Sir) George, 38, 55, 129–45 *passim,* 153, 162 (39, 40), 188 n.72
Dickinson, Sir John, 11, 13
Docker, J., 68, 72
Dodds, A., 96, 174 n.65
Donaldson, (Sir) Stuart, 24–5, 28, 34, 108–9, 110, 112, 171, n.40
Driver, R., 174 n.67
Duffy, Sir Charles Gavan, 79
Duncan, W. A., 69, 71–2, 114

Eagar, G., 36, 68–72, 114, 177 n.24
Eckford, J., 96, 174 n.67
Egan, D., 51, 174 n.67
Encel,.S., 2, 119
Evatt, H. V., 1

Farnell, J. S., 38, 81, 82, 86, 102, 110, 129, 159(23), 179 n.74, 187 nn.29, 30
Fitzgerald, R., 46
Fitzpatrick, M., 82, 160(29), 161(34, 35), 175 n.73, 187 n.30
Fletcher, J., 118
Flood, E., 156(7)
Forster, R. H. M., 174 n.67
Forster, W.: deserts liberals 1857, 29; joins Martin ministry 1863, 36; resigns from Martin ministry 1865,

General Index

NEW SOUTH WALES MINISTRIES 1856-

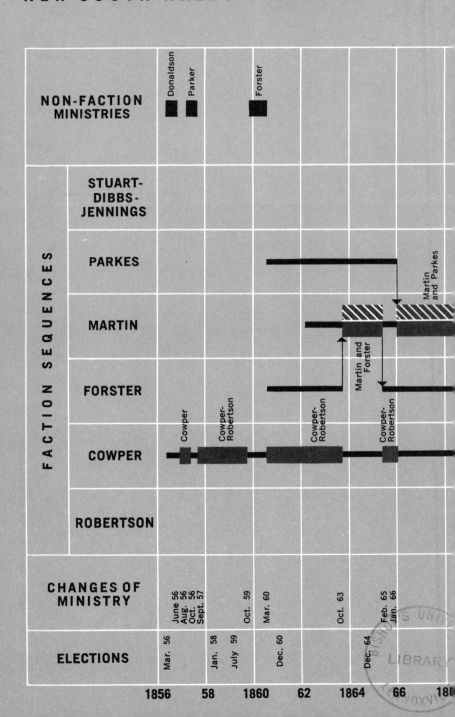

NON-FACTION MINISTRIES

Donaldson Parker Forster

FACTION SEQUENCES

STUART-DIBBS-JENNINGS

PARKES

MARTIN — Martin and Parkes

FORSTER — Martin and Forster

COWPER — Cowper / Cowper-Robertson / Cowper-Robertson / Cowper-Robertson

ROBERTSON

CHANGES OF MINISTRY — June 56 Aug. 56 Oct. 56 Sept. 57 / Oct. 59 / Mar. 60 / Oct. 63 / Feb. 65 Jan. 66

ELECTIONS — Mar. 56 / Jan. 58 July 59 / Dec. 60 / Dec. 64

1856   58   1860   62   1864   66   186